To Alli

I DIDN'T SIGN UP FOR THIS

Remember that all our
stories need to be
told.

Khadijah
2023

BOOK
POWER
PUBLISHING

I DIDN'T SIGN UP FOR THIS

My Redemptive Story of Memories, Mayhem, and Murder

Khadijah Shabazz

Book Power Publishing books may be purchased for educational, business, or sales promotional use

For information, please contact the author:
contact@kshabazz.com
www.kshabazz.com

First Edition

PRINTED IN THE UNITED STATES OF AMERICA

    Hardcover ISBN: 978-1-945873-76-8
    Paperback ISBN: 978-1-945873-77-5
    Digital Ebook ISBN: 978-1-945873-78-2

BOOK
POWER
PUBLISHING

In loving memory of my parents,
Donald Morton and Diane Williams
who taught me lessons that I now share with you

Glossary of Arabic Terms Used

Allah – The Arabic word for 'God'.

Allahu Akbar – God is the Greatest.

Alhamdulillah – All praise is due to Allah.

As salaam alaykum – Muslim greeting meaning God's peace be on you.

Bismillah – In the name of Allah.

Muslim – A person who believes in or practices Islam and submits to the will of Allah.

SubhanAllah – Glory be to Allah.

Subhana wa ta ala – Glorious and Exalted is He

A word from Mutah

Some people you meet and when you depart, they are quickly forgotten. While others you meet, stay with you for a lifetime. I met Auntie Khadijah through her husband, Brother Saud, over 15 years ago. Immediately, she felt like a long-lost family member. We bonded instantly, and she and her husband would go on to spend several Ramadans with me and my family before Brother Saud passed away.

Auntie Khadijah is one of the cornerstones of our community and she is an Auntie to most of us who know her. She spreads her love, assistance, encouraging words, and good soul food throughout the community, and her sincerity can be felt in everything she does.

Just like many greats in our communities who help uplift, educate, and support us, Khadijah has experienced a lot of events and circumstances that many would fold their hands and give up. But not only did Auntie Khadijah support, defend, and advocate for family members who were incarcerated, she has done so for so many others, and this work has made a big difference in the lives of many.

America, unfortunately, has the highest incarcerated population of any other country in the world. Some are incarcerated justly but many are unjustly imprisoned and left to fend for themselves or accept a life of bondage.

I grew up in the inner cities of Newark and Irvington, New Jersey. As a youngster, I encountered the law on many occasions and so did many of my friends and relatives. I have seen many who had no one to support them once they were in prison; no lawyer, relative, or friend, and I have seen the results of those left defenseless and voiceless. This is why I know Auntie Khadijah's story can help so many who are incarcerated or those who choose to support and advocate for others who are imprisoned.

It is common knowledge that a person who is incarcerated feels alienated and alone. But the often-overlooked story is the condition of family and friends; most of the time it's the mothers, wives, sisters, and aunts who decide to support those in the prison system. There is a lack of support and often many are shunned because of their decision. Khadijah's story can help all of those who struggle to be a support system for others. It lets them know, they are not alone and that they should never feel bad about their choices to support family and friends.

Her story explains the years she battled to support her incarcerated loved ones and her steps to empowerment and the skill sets she acquired to become an activist for positive change in her community.

Her story is definitely an American story that is often overlooked but needs to be told.

In these times, people like Sister Khadijah are rare, so I am happy that I was able to meet someone like her and we pray that Allah preserves and protects her.

Mutah 'Napoleon' Beale
Author of Life is Raw
Formerly of the Outlawz founded by Tupac

Foreword

It has always mattered to me that Toni Morrison wrote her books before dawn. She wrote in the hours before her children woke up, "before they said Mama," and before she ran to her 9-5. It matters as much to me, as the genius behind the writing, that she wrote some of the greatest pieces of literature inside these shared depths of Black motherhood. Toni Morrison didn't give us her 'best' hours, she gave us her most precious hours that didn't exist without her carving them out of the darkness for us.

The work of the following pages also did not happen on a sabbatical or on a well-funded writers' retreat. It did not happen in a room full of editors and writers, workshopping a sentence or storyboarding ideas. Black feminism teaches us that those who simultaneously experience the intersecting harms of racism, sexism, classism, and heteronormativity have a unique wisdom towards what we all must learn to become the best of ourselves as individuals and as a people.

Like Toni Morrison, Khadijah Shabazz (lovingly called Ms. Khadijah by many of us who know her well) also wrote when the babies were sleeping. Ms. Khadijah wrote after calls from loved ones inside prisons and jails, in the midst of fighting for justice upon losing a son to police violence, or while counseling a woman with an incarcerated loved one on how to get the support she deserves. It is these experiences that make this book a useful gift. Ms. Khadijah forged this work in the margins. Whether it is in personal losses of loved ones to incarceration, her experience of giving birth as a teen and of mothering countless others, or knowing what it's like to support three men in prison – Ms. Khadijah has for us, as we'd say in church, a word.

Like collecting branches, dried leaves, and hardwood to burn later, the experiences Ms. Khadijah shares with us here form the kindling for a fire that allows us to see what's been hidden in the shadows. *I Didn't Sign Up for This* brings to light the unseen impact that the last 40 years of mass incarceration policy has had on women. Over the time period of Ms. Khadijah's story, there was a 500% increase in the number of people incarcerated in the United States. Today the U.S. has the highest rate of incarceration of any country in the world. The results have been horrific. State-sanctioned brutality against Black communities, an embrace of punitive treatment over care, and a disregard for gender-based exploitation and harm has left 1 in 4 women and 1 in 2 Black women with a family member in prison. What have women with incarcerated loved ones had to bear during this age of mass incarceration? Ms. Khadijah knows.

I created Essie Justice Group exactly for and because of women like Ms. Khadijah. Our Healing to Advocacy program brings women who are enduring a loved one's incarceration alone into a loving and powerful membership body. I met Ms. Khadijah before Essie had enough resources to expand our programming from the Bay Area into Los Angeles. She found me and made her demand: "we need this here, too." And because Ms. Khadijah knows how to love a thing into existence, soon thereafter, we launched our Healing to Advocacy program for women with incarcerated loved ones in Los Angeles.

What I have learned is that Ms. Khadijah is really good at loving and caring for other people. She is a community resource center, shelter, food bank, violence prevention program, and trauma-healing ward in the body of a woman. Her love is so big, it comes at you like a playful dare – urging your heart to grow and your walls to fall. Like Harriet Tubman, Ms. Khadijah is a woman led by her faith, bringing freedom even to those who do not yet understand the extent to which they've been chained. Like Assata Shakur, Ms. Khadijah is courageous in these pages, taking the risk of telling a truth that those with power regularly find ways to suppress.

The story within Toni Morrison's triumphant book *Beloved* reminds us of what happens when you try to deny the past. She poignantly and heartbreakingly lays out the consequence of ignoring the "pleading child" – a metaphor for our hard histories demanding attention, recognition, and caretaking. On the theme of memory, the book you are about to read invites you into the remembering that Ms. Khadijah has done as a part of a healing journey. Ms. Khadijah's book reminds us of what happens when we give our past the space to live with us. It reminds us that we can be healed and powerful.

Gina Clayton-Johnson
Executive Director, Founder of Essie Justice Group
November 30, 2022

Trauma Drama

I was on a path from breaking my self-imposed isolation to becoming an activist. Trauma looks different on everybody. You can live your whole life and not recognize the role that trauma played in it. It can isolate you from living life to its fullest, and it can keep you from being the best version of yourself. That was me. I went from one trauma drama to the next, probably not too much different from your own life story. Oh, but the lessons I learned along the way, painful as they were, helped and taught me a lot. So, I am grateful for each and every one of them.

I bet you will find yourself in here somewhere. You don't think so? Well, let's just see.

I DIDN'T SIGN UP FOR THIS!

Chapter 1: Tunnel Vision

"It's dirt Saud!" I screamed, dropping the box the mailman gave me moments ago. "Oh my God, nooo." I stared at the dirt on my rug and slowly began to look at my husband, Saud. When our eyes met, we were both crying. The pain we felt was so deep it could not be contained. We sounded like wounded animals, and the pain would remain in our stomachs for a lifetime.

Are those tears?

It was 2016 and physically, I was sitting in Los Angeles, but my mind was transported back in time to the 80s in Pittsburgh, Pennsylvania.

Like I said, consciously, I knew I was in Los Angeles, about to graduate from a wonderful program with the Essie Justice Group, but while there, something happened. It was like a memory dam had been opened, and a flood of traumatic memories came rushing in, bringing with them a pain which was as raw and fresh as the day they happened.

My emotions were now uncontrollable.

The Essie Justice Group has a yearly cohort for women who have been impacted by a loved one's incarceration or even their own incarceration. The group meets for nine weeks, and at the end of the cohort, each woman graduates and joins the sisterhood.

I had just completed the cohort and sat there at my graduation, jumping backward and forward in time, plagued by some of the most painful memories of my life. I had locked away these memories and did not want to revisit them.

I could feel the tears streaming down my face, stinging my skin, and I briefly thought of how awful I might look. But then the memories sucked me back in. It was like watching my life on a television screen or having an out-of-body experience. It was like having tunnel vision, unable to see anything else.

Teddy.

Teddy was a friend of my husband, Saud. Once Teddy and I met, he quickly became like a brother. After he got into some trouble with the law and was sent to jail, I became his pen pal. I wrote him weekly and supported in every way I could. We would talk by phone about current events and things I wished I could be involved in.

When he got sick and was put in the infirmary in Allegheny county jail downtown Pittsburgh, Pennsylvania, we were allowed to visit him. My five-year-old daughter, Salina, and I went for a visit. To this day, we don't know why, but Salina fell ill and passed out. Doctors and nurses came running, and so did some of the guards, to see what had happened to Salina. We sat her up in a nearby wheelchair after we revived her, and could not find anything wrong with her. It gave us all a scare, especially Teddy.

"Get her out of here Sis. Get her outta here and don't bring her back, and don't you come either."

There, laying on his sick bed, in shackles, Teddy cut off his connections to the outside. He pushed us away with a stiff warning not to return. It must have been hard for him to do that. I know it was difficult for us. We left that day in tears, never to return.

I hadn't thought of these things for years, but my memories started to come back randomly, or what seems to be random. But sometimes, they come because my current experiences are closely related to the flashbacks.

***

I'm ironing in the living room. Saud is sitting on the couch reading the newspaper. We heard the mailman come up the steps to the porch.

"I'll get it," I said, seeing that Saud had no intention of moving.

"Good morning," I said to the mailman, "Whatcha got for me?"

"I have plenty," the mailman said. "You have a few boxes and a lot of letters. Catch y'all tomorrow," he called as he headed back down the steps.

"Thank you," I muttered as I went inside with all the bundles. There were a lot of boxes and letters that had Teddy's name on them.

"They must be moving him to prison," Saud said.

"Why do you say that?" I asked.

Saud looked at me over his glasses and said, "When you are transferred from jail to prison, they don't notify you or your family for safety reasons. They will send the family all of the inmates belongings, then when the prisoner gets to wherever they are sending them, you can resend their belongings."

"Oooh OK," I said.

Teddy often made me cards and gifts, so it wasn't unusual for me to get packages from him. I was excited to see what was in some of these boxes because I knew they held special gifts for me. There was one perfectly square box, no bigger than what a coffee mug could fit in. It was wrapped in a brown paper bag and tied with a string.

"Hey I got another gift," I said, in my singing voice. "You didn't get anything," I teased and laughed.

"This package says to be opened by me." As I continued to tease Saud I tried to loosen the string. It was too thick for me to pop open and the tape on the box was terrible too. I couldn't get it loose.

"Saud, can you please hand me a knife?" He looked at me again from over his glasses, indicating how annoyed he had become with me and my mail. I was interrupting his reading, nevertheless; he handed me his pocket knife. I sat the box on the ironing board and began to cut into the string.

After freeing the box from the string, I realized how much tape was on it and it was glued as well to the brown paper. By now my patience was gone, so I began to slice down the seams of the box, trying not to damage what was inside. I was able to make a small hole in the box so that maybe I could see what was inside. That's when I noticed that the knife came out of the package dirty. "What in the world?!" I said loudly to Saud.

"Khadijah! Khadijah!"

Hearing my name jolted me back to the graduation. "You're up next," I heard the interviewer shout out.

"Hey are you OK?" He asked.

I must have looked a fright because the interviewer's face showed hella concern. All I could do was flash my infamous fake smile and shake my head in the affirmative. At the time, I didn't understand what had just happened or where this memory came from, but it didn't stop there. That memory was the spark that lit a chain reaction of more memories buried deep within my psyche.

No one else noticed I was not OK.

My Essie sisters, Teresa, Mercedes, and Dianne, were stunning. Hewan, Lizz, Desire, Dianne's daughter, Arvene and Miss Anita had all done their interviews before I did.

I was so proud of them. I was proud of myself. And to think, I didn't even want to be a part of the Essie Group. A Muslim sister named Atra had invited me to participate. I'd known her for years, but I really didn't know her story. What I did know is that she had a son who was incarcerated, and she was aware that my husband used to be too.

Looking back on it, I know she recognized and understood the pain, struggle, and social isolation a person goes through when they decide to support and advocate for a loved one who is in the prison system. I had been suffering in silence. I'd recently lost a husband who had spent many years in prison. And yet, I never talked about it. There were people who knew, but I did not allow it to be the topic of any conversation. I had put myself in a self-imposed isolation. But Atra kept urging me to get out of the house.

"Yeah girl, come on. Get out of the house. What do you have to lose? Besides, they serve the best food at their meetings," Atra encouraged. I agreed, not having any real intention to participate in the program. I figured I could just sit there and pretend to listen and give a damn. By the time I got to Essie, I had loved and lost so much. I was tired. But the cohort was more than I expected and everything that I needed.

During our Essie cohort session, we started the process of healing from past traumas. After being armed with the right tools and resources, we were prepared to go out and fight the injustices of incarceration and the damage it caused us and our loved ones.

Essie provided a safe space for women to tell their stories without judgment. Over the nine weeks of healing, I befriended a sister named Esi. She was so regal and refined. Up until our graduation, I thought she was the Essie the group was named after! That goes to show you how little I paid attention in the beginning. Gina Clayton and Anita Willis were my cohort facilitators, I would later find out that Gina was the founder and executive director of Essie and that the organization was named after her great grandmother Essie. How had I missed that fact?!

Atra and I went through the program together and our friendship deepened. Now here we sat in St. Elmo's Village, ready to graduate. We were so excited. Everyone was taking pictures and videos. The organizers of the cohort picked the perfect place for the event. St. Elmo's Village is a cultural place in Mid City, Los Angeles between Venice and Washington, off of La Brea. It is made up of a group of houses on a street named St. Elmo.

Some of the houses on the street resemble a small African village. The sidewalks and driveways are brightly painted to make the houses look like African huts. There are no gates or fences in the backyard area. All of the yards are connected so that the area looks like a village. It's a very peaceful place. St Elmo's is also a place for people to express themselves through art, painting, writing, and poetry. My oldest daughter, Salina, was the first person to visit St. Elmo's. She attended after school and Saturday programs when she was still in elementary school.

Many years had passed since I lived in this area, and I had forgotten St. Elmo's and what it meant to me. But coming to the weekly Essie cohort meetings first brought back memories of my daughter Salina playing and drawing. Those were memories I loved, and they reconfirmed my attachment and love for this space. However, although the place was beautiful, and the camaraderie outstanding, it continued to trigger events from my past, some that were not as comfortable and happy as Salina drawing.

***

Saud and my eyes met as we watched the dirt from the box hit the floor. We knew what we were looking at, the dirt was Teddy's ashes, The jail had him cremated and never notified us of his death, even though he had some family I was listed as next of kin.

The death of someone you love is never easy. But it is almost unbearable when you have no idea how they died or any of the circumstances surrounding the death. For weeks after opening the box that contained Teddy's ashes, I tried to get an answer. I wanted to know what happened to Teddy. Here's all they said:

Office of the warden , Pittsburgh PA.

Your brother, Theodore Teddy, number BL2579, was the property of the State of Pennsylvania, and we had no legal obligation to inform you of his sickness or his death, and we consider the matter closed.

Consider the matter closed? Property of the State of Pennsylvania? I just kept reading these words over and over again, trying to make my mind fully comprehend these statements.

Weeks after that first letter, I found a letter from Allegany jail saying that Teddy had died of AIDS. He was one of the first people to die of AIDS in a State of Pennsylvania Correctional Facility. We never knew any of this. Teddy nor the jail had ever told us any of this. I was furious. They cremated him and never asked us anything, not anything at all about a proper service. They never called us so we could say goodbye. After months of trying to contact the warden to get answers to our questions I was met with silence. I was ignored for a very long time and to this date, over 30 years later, my questions still have not been answered.

I now understand my last visit with him. I understand why the medical staff had on so much protective gear and why Teddy was so afraid when Salina passed out. It explains the aggressive manner in which he told us to leave and never come back. So much was unknown about AIDS back then. People were really afraid and taking extra precautions to prevent infection. AIDS was the new plague in the late 70s and 80s, and the research on its transmission was just being examined. Teddy was a heroin addict who had found a way to get drugs inside of the jail. I had no idea he was an addict. But once I found out, I went on a warpath, determined to find out who gave him drugs and how did he get them? In jail, inmates only have physical contact with personnel and guards. Saud made me stop my crusade for reasons I did not understand till years later.

It bothered me so much that I couldn't help Teddy. Even now when I think of it, I sob. My brother died sick, in pain, and alone. Then they burned him up and threw him out like trash.

"Teddy, I am so sorry Teddy. Please forgive me, and may God forgive me too."

I don't remember what we did with Teddy's ashes or even how we got the ashes off of the floor. I think I am too afraid of where my thoughts may take me if I  think about it for too long. But to this day I have a problem leaving anyone in a jail or a hospital. Because of this, I think that's why my Essie graduation triggered my memories of Teddy. I could not help him, but Essie was giving me the chance and the tools to help others who experience injustices in the United States penal system. I don't want anyone to suffer like Teddy did, alone, isolated, no hugs, no kind words, and not even a kiss on the forehead.

All of this trauma drama happened when we were visiting friends in Pittsburgh. I had only been there for about a month and I remember thinking to myself at time that the best thing for me to do was focus on what was in front of me, and what was in front of me was another hot mess.

I had left my home of Cleveland without telling my parents. How was I going to tell them I wasn't coming back? How was I going to tell them that I had picked up and moved to Pittsburgh permanently with my baby girl, not knowing a soul in the city? And as if this information was not going to be shocking enough, how was I going to tell them that I had gotten married to a Muslim and that I had become Muslim myself?! Lawdy, how was I going to explain this?

So, let me give you a little background information on me so that y'all can keep up. I don't need you getting lost in all this, 'cause if I am tellin y'all all my business, Imma need you to pay attention ;)

Chapter 2: Soul Train and Afro Puffs (The Cleveland Years)

I grew up in Cleveland, Ohio, a child of the 60s. I remember when President Kennedy and Martin Luther King were killed; I was in grade school. I had never heard of Malcolm X though and it would be years before I knew who he was. But we all knew Cassius Clay, 'The Champ', our Black hero. We lived on the Eastside of Cleveland in a neighborhood known as Glenville. In our community we had the only Black hospital in the city. It was also the hospital where I was born, Forest City Hospital. The hospital was struggling to stay open, but it was a much-needed resource in our community. On August 9, 1972, Cassius Clay or Muhammad Ali agreed to fight an exposition fight in order to help keep the doors to the hospital open. He fought Terry Daniels and of course he won! This fight saved the hospital from closing at the time, but it eventually closed in 1978. The 70s held a lot of growing-up memories for me.

My family and I lived on 109th Street in an area of town called St. Clair. To be exact our address was 599 East 109th Street. It's funny what info sticks with you. My old childhood phone number was 216-681-5067. Our home was a three-bedroom, one-bath, single-family house with a big backyard. It also had an attic and a basement. My parents' room faced the front of the house and had a big window that looked out onto the street. From their window you could also see the adjoining street, Navarre Court, which was a small side street. My sisters and I shared a room that faced the backyard. We could almost see the next street, 110th. Right behind our house was the *Dairy Queen*. How many times did we climb that fence and run down that small hill to get some of that soft serve ice cream! It would be a long time before I would understand that all ice cream was not soft serve. On the other side of St. Clair stands, to this day, St. Aloysius Catholic Church. This church is well over 100 years old. It was a cornerstone of the community and sometimes we would go there for community parties.

My sisters and I attended O.W. Holmes Elementary School on 105th in St. Clair, FDR Jr. High on Parkwood, and I attended Glenville High. Yea Tarblooders! This is the same high school Steve Harvey attended. In fact, his family lived in our neighborhood on 112th Street, off of Superior. I am almost sure his family was part of my dad's mail route.

Daddy had several jobs and worked hard at all of them. He worked nights at Kroger Supermarket. But the one job that kept us in line was the job of being the mailman. Daddy worked out of the Station H Post Office which was right across the street from O.W. Holmes School. The post office is still there today; it's a historical landmark building now.

Daddy's mail route ran straight through our neighborhood. Everyone knew that my sisters and I were the mailman's girls, so we couldn't get away with much. Everyone would tell on us and send us home if they saw us doing something wrong. Even the street people were snitchin' on us. Yes, everybody knew Mr. Morton, the mailman, and his girls.

Most of the families on our block owned their own homes. Most fathers were the breadwinners, while most moms in the neighborhood stayed home. We never really got into any real trouble, nor did our friends. Although we felt a little sheltered, we were surrounded by people who loved and nurtured us. We had such a strong sense of community.

I had never been inside of an apartment building, even though we lived right next door to one. We lived in that same house until we grew up and moved out on our own. Now, we didn't look down on anyone, but we couldn't relate to some of our friends. We never wanted for anything. We didn't know what it was like to do without, and we could not relate to being hungry. Listening to some of our friends talk about mice, rats, and roaches, were conversations we couldn't relate to. We didn't know about social workers, food stamps, or welfare either.

My parents were from Atlantic City, New Jersey. As children, we would spend most of our summers visiting our grandparents there. I love to think about our road trips to A.C.. I can still smell the fragrance of the old boardwalk and the Atlantic Ocean. Now when I mention the boardwalk, I am referring to the old boardwalk before they messed it all up with the casinos. The Steel Pier was one of my favorite boardwalk places with its many rides and entertainment. We would watch the flying horse dive off the pier into the Atlantic Ocean. Yes, a real horse would jump from a platform above the ocean and he and his diver would jump off the diving board. It was amazing to see. Sometimes they would dress the horse up with costume wings. The boardwalk stopped this show around 1978 but it was a sight to see.

The Flying Horse on the Boardwalk, Atlantic City, New Jersey

At one time in our history, the boardwalk was segregated, dividing Black and white visitors. The southern end of the boardwalk, reserved for Black patrons, was called Chicken Bone Beach. My maternal grandfather was head of maintenance on the 'colored' folk's side. The boardwalk was full of carnival-like shops and activities. When I close my eyes and think about it, I can almost smell the aromas coming from the various businesses: the saltwater taffy shops, the crab barrows, and of course the sub sandwich! Atlantic City is the birthplace of the submarine sandwich, or at least I think so. If it's not, it should be. After eating one sub from Atlantic City, you would never again accept a subway or any other sub sandwich from anywhere in the country.

Daddy would always pack a few subs to bring home with us, packed on dry ice. In fact, any time he heard of someone going or coming back from Atlantic City, he would commission them to bring us some subs. We always hoped the sandwiches would make the trip back to Cleveland. You know how there is only one place in the world where you can get a real Philly cheesesteak...Philly? Well, the only place to get a real sub is Atlantic City.

When we traveled to Atlantic City during our summer vacations from school, we would spend one week at my mom's parents' home with Granny and Granddaddy, Harry and Helen Hicks, and my great-grandmother, Mattie Hicks, whom we fondly called Hicksey and lived with them also. They lived within walking distance of the boardwalk at 1307 Drexel Ave.

Granny owned a beauty shop. She was one of, if not the first, Black woman to own and operate her own shop. Grandaddy, as mentioned before, was head of maintenance on the then Black side of the boardwalk. They attended St. James Church on New York and Arctic Aves, where my Granny was secretary for over 50 years. My daddy's parents, James and Irene Morton, affectionately known as Nana and Grandpop, lived in Pleasantville at 804 Cedar Lane, a few miles outside of Atlantic City. Nana was a homemaker and Grandpop was a mailman too. Stepping into this world every summer gave me hope that I would not spend my entire life in Cleveland.

Looking out of the car windows and seeing how life changed from place to place, stopping at diners to eat, and seeing the tourist attractions along our drive made me long to see other places. I wanted to see the world! Although Atlantic City was really a small town, it offered me much more excitement than Cleveland life did. It was so much different from the hustle and bustle of Cleveland. I guess the saying, *the grass looks greener on the other side,* applied to me.

Back in Cleveland on 109th, there was a lot going on. Bill Mack, our neighbor from across the street, was running for some office. "Glenville loves Bill Mack" was his slogan. The Sharps were our next door neighbors along with the Armstrongs, Hamiltons, Kings, and the Goodmans. My best friend at the time was Miss Truffy, as we called her. Her real name was Trufinya

Wagner. She had 16 siblings so it goes without saying that her family had a large impact on the community. I could go on and on, as the memories of these wonderful neighbors remind me of myself, my origins. We knew all the shop owners and street people. Tom's Market was our community corner store. Mr. Tom and his family were good, nice people. St. Aloysius Church was on one side of that corner and the Jamaica Breeze Club on the other. I loved to listen to my parents as they told stories about growing up in A.C.. One year, our Aunt Olga, my mom's baby sister, came from A.C. to Cleveland to live with us. She was everybody's favorite Auntie. She was, and still is, a wonderful singer. I never understood why she didn't sing professionally. She sang better than most artists today.

I loved to hear Auntie talk about Al's Casino and the Cafe Society where she would perform, and sometimes she would appear at the Tijuana Club. All three were on 105th. The Tijuana Club was a bustling place where you could hear live entertainment like our Queen of Soul-Aretha Franklin, the Tempting Temptations, and the Four Tops. Whew, now I know I am officially old! I couldn't wait to go inside these clubs and get to see the Black greats in action. But I was still underage so I could only imagine what it was really like.

We were so close knit on 109th that my oldest sister married a young man from across the street, and our neighbor across the street married a young man from down the street. Neither marriage worked out but still, it showed how close we once were.

The 70s also brought in a new culture of nightlife and fashion. It was the time of afro puffs and Soul Train. It was a time of rebellion and deflection. At 15 years old, I was trying to figure it all out. I guess my one-word description of myself during this time, would be *confused*.

When I was old enough to hit them streets, dressing was something I did and did well. The nights were filled with us! We dressed in our real leather and snakeskin shoes, alligator belts and bags, real fur coats, and silks. Winters in Ohio were harsh, so those furs were not only for show but to keep that serious wind off you! It was only after I moved to Los Angeles that I heard of a group of people who would throw paint on your furs or leathers. This was truly not a Midwest or east coast vibe because an action like that would find you with a whipped ass or worse!

We took pride in the way we stepped out of the house. We would not be caught dead going out in jeans and gym shoes, no matter what they cost. Our men wore suits and ties, and the ladies were magazine perfect. I cringe now, every time I see a young lady in a bonnet and pjs in public passing around joints and cussing. Don't get me wrong, back in the 70s, we smoked and cussed, but ladies did these things behind closed doors, and never in front of an elder. We stayed cute and sophisticated with it.

Those were the last years that we presented ourselves as queens, the last years of getting respect from our men and for ourselves. Now, we need to remind each other of who we are. We want to use the terms 'king' and 'queen', and rightly so, but we also need to live up to that title. Some of us have let the crowns slip off our heads where they were once placed. Some of our crowns have fallen down into mud puddles we made. Some of us don't know how to retrieve them and some of us are satisfied with that.

But whatever happened to the respect we used to show to our elders, to our church-going communities, to our Black Muslim communities? There used to be a time that if you dreamt of doing or saying something to a Black Muslim sister you'd wake up apologizing.

For example, I remember the Shabazz Restaurant in East Cleveland was robbed, and the young Muslim sister who worked there was killed. The men responsible for the robbery and murder were found and convicted. They went to prison, but didn't last long. After maybe a month, something unfortunate happened to them. Let's just say they didn't do the time sentenced by the court. They were administered a short life sentence. It sent a strong message to our community on who not to mess with. Like I said, back in those days, we had a strong sense of community.

Within the Black community at that time, we felt safe, and we were unified. But the ball was dropped somewhere along the line. Our Black men came back from the Vietnam War as junkies with mental health issues and no resources to help them navigate through the awful experience of war and the things they had to do.

The 70s was also the era of the free love movement, and this did not work to our benefit at all. It had us having children out of wedlock at an alarming rate, many of us just children ourselves. And not being employable made us dependent on the welfare system. I could go on, but this message isn't about that unfortunate time in the 70s and what made it so bad. We were having fun and making bad life decisions that would affect ourselves and our children to the point that our next set of youth would never fully recover from our blunder. I will forever be upset with the harm the next generation endured when we dropped that ball. They picked up such disrespect, low self-esteem, and a disregard for themselves and others. The social connection we once had left the building. Even among the criminals there had been the 70s term, 'honor among thieves.' But that died. Yet all was not lost. God, in His infinite wisdom, showed some of us the way out.

Hey! Are ya'll still with me? Need a break?
OK, take one then come back...

Let's continue.

Chapter 3: Young Heartbreak

The Vietnam War ended April 30, 1975. A lot of brothers were coming home, many who did not go to war by choice. They were drafted. There was a time when young men had no choice but to register for the armed services and Uncle Sam decided who was fit to serve and who wasn't. If a person decided not to enlist, he would be sent to prison, as did our beloved Muhammad Ali. Muhammad refused to fight a people who never did anything to him. Today he is respected in our community for standing up for what he believed in, and of course, for being our champ!

My hometown of Cleveland had a lot of firsts. It had one of the country's first Black mayors, Carl B. Stokes, and we were all proud of that accomplishment. Looking back in time, I can remember both of the Kennedy assassinations; President John F. Kennedy in 1963 and his brother, Senator Robert F. Kennedy in 1968.

In 1968, the same year Robert F. Kennedy was killed, Martin Luther King was assassinated. After the assassination, I recall the Glenville riots. This was a section of town in Cleveland. When news of Dr King's death spread, the riots broke out. I remember being called into the school gym. I was about eight or nine years old. We listened to the news on the school's loudspeaker and afterwards we were sent home. I didn't understand what was happening because I had never heard of King until then. When I got home, I could see my parents' faces and knew they were upset. Still, I wondered what was going on? Mommy was crying and Daddy just sat there. We were told to go to bed, but we could hear the commotion coming from St. Clair. After the night of looting and mayhem, we still got up for school.

When we got to the corner of 109th and St. Clair, Army tanks were all up and down St. Clair. We were all afraid to walk past them but we had to in order to get to school. I kept thinking, *are they gonna shoot us?* Later, we learned Carl Stokes had called in the National Guard to keep the community safe. This move helped him get reelected. At the same time, it was a move to keep us as a community in line.

At the end of the 70s, I was in my teen years. By the time the 80s hit, I had been married twice, divorced once, and widowed at 20 years old. Back then that was unheard of unless you were a young woman who lost her husband in the Vietnam War, but we didn't actually know anyone in this situation. In fact, at that time, I had never even known of anyone who had died. My thoughts were that widows were little old ladies, not girls barely out of their teens.

Thankfully, I still had my parents, and both sets of grandparents. I am blessed to have my parents even now. *[1] My parents divorced when I was 10, but at no time did I ever hear an argument of any kind. I thought this was great! I would hear other kids getting upset that their parents argued and fought (not physically). I would brag that my parents never did. But still today, of all the families that made up 109th street, mine was the only one to get divorced. I was hurt and ashamed.

Remember the movie *Soul Food*? That was how I saw my life. We had warm, inviting family dinners: Sunday dinners in the dining room at the table, set with Mom's best China, all of us eating together. Not like today, where everyone grabs a plate and stares at the TV or their phone.

Mommy wasn't the emotional type, so when things happened, good or bad, hugs and kisses were not what we got. However, I can't remember any real emotional pain until Daddy left the house after he and Mommy divorced. But Daddy really never left us. We saw him almost daily; he was still in our community delivering mail.

Later, Daddy remarried. My stepmom's name was Brenda. She worked for Ohio Bell. They lived on Earle Avenue, which was within walking distance from my junior high school, Franklin Delano Roosevelt. The school was on Parklawn and was halfway between Mommy's house where I lived. Sometimes, I would walk

---

[1] The author has had family deaths since the writing of this book. See the appendix for their dedications.

over there after school. Brenda had two boys which instantly gave us brothers, Mark and Shawn, then a short time later came the baby, Barbara.

Mark and I went to school together along with his cousin on my stepmom's side, Diane. I loved having siblings at the same school. Yvetta and Felicia attended a different school. Mark and I would meet up for lunch, then on to recreation which we called Rec. I loved Rec. We were allowed to play music and dance until our next class. We would try to imitate the moves we saw the dancers do on the TV show, Soul Train. We would break into a Soul Train line, and nobody could tell us nothing!

After graduating from high school, my beloved brother, Mark, tried out for the Marines, but he didn't make it. He had just been diagnosed as bipolar and schizophrenic. Uncle Sam turned him down at the same time life had. Mark was misunderstood by some, but he was my hero. He was close to my heart. We really don't know what happened to my big brother. He was in a program that offered him an apartment. After not responding for days, he was found in his home. He died alone. Something happened inside Mark after the Marines rejected him. It is as if he gave up on everything.

I still had a little brother, but I would spend the rest of my life collecting big brothers.

Chapter 4: Shitterlings, Possums, and Cornbread!

Me and Mommy (Age 16)

Getting pregnant and married at an early age really took a toll on my life, and this big change was about to hit me square in the face. I can still remember the day I told Mommy I was pregnant; still a child myself and pregnant by a boy with hardly any future in sight. I was scared stiff, and I definitely didn't want to tell Daddy and see the disappointment on his face.

Although my first husband, David Ronnie showed no hope for a successful future, he did have the most amazing mother, Clara. She took to me instantly. But for some odd reason, she could never say my name, so she called me Sheryl, and to this day she calls me Sheryl.

Clara felt sorry for me. I didn't know how to do much. She taught me how to prepare southern dishes and meals I had never heard of before. I didn't grow up eating beans and rice, and I had never had neck bones, homemade mac and cheese, grits, greens, fried fish, banana pudding, or peach cobbler! At Mommy's house, we ate spinach and kale. It's funny how people jumped on kale like it was a newfound vegetable. Anyway, we didn't eat much rice. We ate potatoes every way you could fix them: fried, boiled, or baked. Corned beef and cabbage were actually one of Cleveland's specialties. Just like every corner in Los Angeles has a cart selling tacos, Cleveland has corned beef on every corner! We ate pork but it was bacon, chops, ham, and roast. We ain't known nothing 'bout no pig's feet, tails, or chitterlings. And can you believe this? We ate pumpkin pie and liked it. Don't come for my Black Card! It would be years before I ate any sweet potato pie. I always liked to cook though, and Daddy wasn't a bad cook. He would try all kinds of foods and recipes. When Daddy and Mommy were married, he didn't cook much, but he did for the short time that he was a bachelor. I learned a lot from watching him and my stepmom, Brenda.

While living on 109th street, we had some neighbors who lived in the apartment building right next door to us. Two young women, who were sisters, lived there. I remember them inviting Daddy over to try some 'fresh meat'. Well, I was nosey and wanted to tag along, and I was given permission to do so. I was around nine years old then and didn't understand what fresh meat was and wanted to find out.

The apartment was small and dark compared to our home. Even though it had always been right next door, I realized it was my first time in an apartment, it was kind of spooky. This was a nicely kept building, the apartment building across the street was not. The building across the street looked so bad the whole neighborhood talked about its appearance. It made the entire corner look bad. Anyway, I held daddy's hand tight 'cause I was scared.

"What's that funny smell?" I asked Daddy.

"Shhh, be quiet," Daddy said, "Don't make people feel bad."

"OK," I whispered back. But it really did stink.

The two sisters greeted us warmly and began to show Daddy their fresh meat cuisine. I was too busy being nosey, looking around the apartment, trying to take everything in. I almost missed Daddy offering me some of the food.

"You want to try some?"

"Well, okay. What is it ?" I asked.

"Meat." Daddy said. "Fresh meat." Well, at least it's not old meat, I thought to myself. One of the ladies proceeded to inform me what each type of meat was on the table.

"This here is venison, this is coon, and this is possum."

Now, ya'll know I didn't realize I was eating racoon, deer, and opossum! I vaguely remember liking the taste of the deer. But recalling my feelings after eating rodents, makes me feel like passing out. Ugggh.

Big Ma and Clara

Years later, I remember eating chitterlings for the first time. One Sunday, Clara, my first mother-in-law, and her mom, Big Ma, were sharing some chitterlings while I was visiting. Clara was from Mississippi and her soul food was different from anything I had ever experienced. I must say that I loved them chitterlings, but I didn't know what part of the pig they came from. I ate chitterlings, cornbread, and fresh collard greens from Big Ma's garden. I couldn't wait to cook some for my family. *Why haven't we had this before, I wondered?*

I went into the garden with Big Ma, and she pulled up some greens.

"Wash and cook these," she directed. Big Ma didn't know that I had never had greens before.

"Yes, ma'am," I said, "but how do you fix chitterlings? I want to cook them for Thanksgiving." The Thanksgiving holiday was coming up.

"Girl you got to really clean them. They are not hard to cook, just gotta get 'em clean," Big Ma said.

I thought I would help with the upcoming Thanksgiving dinner and add some new food to the menu. I was becoming a good cook. I took some money I had saved up and went and bought a bucket of chitterlings. I got them home and thawed them out, but when they were all thawed I saw and smelled what Big Ma was talking about. The smell let me know they were dirty, real dirty.

I called Big Ma from the dining room desk phone.

"Big Ma," I said tearfully, "I think they are spoiled. They smell bad." She just laughed.

"Gurl, they are supposed to smell bad, just make sure you clean them right," she told me.

"OK," I said, "I have the greens too."

"I cut them into small pieces," she said to me.

"OK, Big Ma," I said.

"Just make sure everything is clean," she shot back at me.

So now what did I do? You guessed it, I poured some powdered Tide detergent in the water and kept swishing the chitterlings around until there were no more soap bubbles. I threw them in a pot with onions, bell peppers, celery, and garlic. *Oh boy, this is going to be a fantastic meal.*

After convincing my family to try it they started with the gritty greens. You could feel the sand on your tongue. *Hmmm, Big Ma's greens didn't taste like this. Maybe a little hot sauce. Naw, they still got something gritty on them.* Moving on to the shitty chitterlings, I watched everyone's faces while they ate, waiting to see the smiles, indicating that I had thrown down. The smiles never came. As I looked around the table, facial expressions were changing. Smiles turned to frowns and friendly chatter turned to lip smacks of disgust. About 20 minutes later, we were all trying to get into the only bathroom we had!

"Big Ma! They saying my food made them sick. I washed the greens like you told me," I cried, on the verge of tears.

"How many times?" Big Ma asked. "Gurl, I said to clean them greens good!

"I just rinsed them off and put them in a pot," I stated. I could hear her laughing and shouting at me at the same time.

"You can't just rinse no greens right out the yard like that," she laughed loudly.

"I said wash them, not rinse them. Oh Lawd, next you gonna tell me you rinsed the chitterlings," she said sarcastically.

"No ma'am. I put a little Tide in them until the water came out clear." Big Ma wasn't laughing anymore. She got really quiet and said, "Chile, did anyone have to go to da hospital? Did you pull the lining off dem chitterlings?" I could hear the worry in her voice.

"What lining Big Ma? I didn't see any lining. I just washed them." Well, I didn't kill anybody, and the next few times I went to my future mother-in-law's house, she and Big Ma would show me something different to make. I loved those lessons. There would be many a day I longed to sit at their table, listening to those two wonderful queens talk about life.

My Thanksgiving meal was a flop, but one thing that came out perfectly was my cornbread! It was the first time I had ever made cornbread that didn't come out of a box. Funny thing though, cornbread is not something I care for. Go figure!

Even after Ronnie and I divorced, I was always treated like family, even up to this day. It was actually Clara who introduced me to my next husband... but let me get back to my own queen mother.

Chapter 5: Mommy Dearest?
Daddy Nearest!

Mommy was breathtakingly beautiful. Her looks reminded me and others of Nancy Wilson and Diahann Carrol. She was quiet and didn't have many friends. She kept her hair and nails done at all times. Back in those days that meant polished and filed, we didn't have nail shops. Her hair was always combed, and she always had her lipstick on. She wore pants, but not often. We never heard her cuss or raise her voice, even when we were in trouble. We got an occasional spanking. Honestly, we didn't do much to get spanked. But punishments, OMG! If you saw the light of day again, you were lucky! A bad report card carried a lengthy sentence. Any one of us would be confined to the room until the next report came out. We didn't have anything in our rooms back then, no computers or TVs. But we were allowed to get a phone in our room with our own number. That was a big deal in those days. The phone was taken out of the room when we were in trouble.

The TV was in the living room, and we all watched it together. All we could do was read or write, and I did both. I would also pick up my hairbrush mic and sing in the mirror, pretending to be someone famous. Momma may not have realized it, but I loved being alone in my room. Some of my most creative moments occurred while under punishment. I put together many talent shows in my mirror and played all of the parts.

As I mentioned before, I got pregnant at a young age. Mommy didn't know how to relate to the idea of a teenage daughter being pregnant. Often, we heard stories of young Black girls getting pregnant and then going to visit family down south.

They would come back to Cleveland with nephews, nieces, little sisters, brothers, or cousins. There was no one to send me to because I didn't have any family down south. When I told Mommy I thought I was pregnant, she looked scared and shocked all at the same time. Our relationship changed instantly. I felt like I lost part of her right at that moment. Have you ever experienced the loss of someone who was still around? Sometimes that can be worse than death. I didn't get Mommy back for years. In fact, I got my mom back right before I lost her again. She is still the most beautiful woman in the world to me.

I would often feel things in my gut, and they would manifest themselves in different ways. My feelings always meant that something or somebody would be hurt, but it would never be the person I thought it was. One day while in class at FDR, I got this feeling that something wasn't right. The feeling got so overwhelming that I walked out of school. The closer I got to home, the worse I felt. I stopped to collect myself by the side of this big tree on Parklawn, close to Forest City Hospital. I was halfway home when I got some glass stuck in my shoe. I had to stop and rub my shoes in the dirt to dislodge the glass. As I continued on my nausea subsided a bit, but by the time I got home the feeling was back like a flu.

I didn't know how to process that feeling, but I knew something was wrong. I found out later that day that Daddy had been in a terrible car accident and totaled his car around that very tree where I had stopped. He was in Forest City Hospital. Both of his legs were broken and he sustained other injuries as well. Daddy and I had always had a special connection.

I still get those feelings sometimes, and it's still never who I think it will be. I can't remember who called us that day to tell us about Daddy, but it hurt me to my core.

I loved my father immensely and he was the one person I never wanted to disappoint. I didn't want him to stop treating me like I was special. That would be unbearable. I was always Daddy's girl. So, him finding out I was pregnant was one of the worst feelings I had ever felt. I just knew he was going to be so angry that he would reject me. And his rejection was something I knew I would never be able to stand. Thank God I didn't have to go through a test like that.

Right next to Glenville High School, in walking distance from my house, was the John Glenn Free Clinic. Mommy took me there to get a real pregnancy test. When it came back positive, Mommy and the nurses went into a huddle. I could hardly hear what Mommy and the nurses were saying because I was still up in the stirrups. Finally, someone started talking to me. I could feel a smile on my face, I was just beginning to understand that I had a life inside me.

"If you want to terminate this pregnancy, then you must sign this consent form," the nurse kept telling me over and over.

"Sign what? What is termination? What are you talking about?" I questioned.

"Termination is an abortion," the nurse yelled at me.

"Sign the papers," Mommy kept saying to me.

I didn't fully understand, but I didn't want to kill my baby. I remember pushing the doctor really hard as I pulled up my pants and ran home. *Mommy wants me to kill my baby, or was it me that she wants gone?* We did not speak or look at each other for weeks. I felt so alone. I really didn't have many close friends, but I guess the closest to me were Miss Trufinya and Niecy. There was also Jan Sweeney who was pregnant too. Jan and I would have our sons back-to-back. Trufinya was my very best friend who passed away some years ago. I really miss her. Niecy and I are still friends, and she keeps me updated on the old 109th street crowd. I would call her the historian of the old crowd.

In our household, I had two sisters who kept me company. Yvetta, the oldest, and Felicia, the youngest. I was the middle child of course. Our auntie, who had lived with us for some time, now had her own place. She was more like a big sister to us. We didn't see Daddy as often, but he was always around. I felt as if I had broken his heart. It's hard to live with the shame and heartache of disappointing yourself and those that you love. Mommy and I remained invisible to each other. I often thought that the day she found out I was pregnant was the day she stopped loving me. Still, she was my beautiful queen mother, and I wanted her to like me again.

I was dealing with this enormous pain at 16 years old. It was a feeling I couldn't quite comprehend. A lot of trauma went unrecognized. I could not deal with the pain I put her through. It showed on her face, so I just put my own pain on the back burner. It never crossed my mind that she could have been dealing with her own issues. Being divorced had to cause Mommy her own trauma, something nobody thought about at the time. Nobody views their mom as anything less than perfect, or at least I felt mine was. No, I knew mine was.

Sometimes I feel like a motherless child. Sometimes I feel like a motherless child, a long way from home.

Does anyone remember that old Negro spiritual? There would be nights, I would sing this song, hoping she would hear me, hoping she would come into my room and hug me and tell me it would all be okay, but that never happened. So I would hug myself and rock until I fell asleep. I don't think I ever got another hug from my mommy. I vowed not to let anyone that I loved feel so alone. Though unintentionally, through the years, you know I did.

Chapter 6: Mommy, I'm scared!

Oh my gosh, of all things, I think I peed on myself. No, I think my water just broke. Should I tell Mommy? She's still sleeping.

I finally got up the nerve and went across the hall to inform her my water had just broken, and that's when I got the first hard pain. I was totally unprepared for it. That pain almost knocked me down.

Mommy got up and got dressed. She drove me to Kaiser Hospital at University Circle, and she dropped me off at the ER entrance.

"Are you staying with me, Mom?" I asked her, fighting back tears.

"No, I have to go to work," she responded, coldly.

"Please, don't leave me here alone," I whispered. *Is she really gonna leave me? Do I tell her I'm scared?* I just stood there in the cold March night. I stood there and watched her drive off, as another pain hit me, both physically and emotionally.

Before going to my hospital room, I asked the nurse if I could call my child's father. Of course, there were no cell phones, only public pay phones, or the phone at the nurses' station. I tried calling David to tell him I was in the hospital, but I guess he was asleep because I didn't get through until the next day.

The nurses were all nice except one very nasty, mean ole bitch. When a pain hit me I heard her say, "That's what happens to girls that have a baby with no husband." I always wondered why the girl who gets pregnant or is having sex is called out, humiliated, and shamed. No one ever said anything to the boy. When that old crone spat her venom, God blessed me so that I didn't feel another labor pain. I had my son, David Ranel Jr., all alone but with very little pain.

When I was released from the hospital, I went back home to 109th street. David Sr, AKA Ronnie, and I got married a year after

Ranel Jr. was born and we moved in with Clara, who had become my second momma. Clara and Ronnie lived in a housing project on Kinsman, not far from Big Ma. Both lived far from my neighborhood and on a side of town that I knew nothing about. Clara bought a house shortly after, a duplex, and David and I moved into the bottom half. After 40 years, Clara still lives on Scioto in East Cleveland, behind where the old *Hot Sauce Williams* used to be. If you know Cleveland, then you know *Hot Sauce Williams*. I would use his Polish boy recipe to launch my Al Madinah Dog in Los Angeles in the future. Clara is still living there today at 92 years old.

There were some moments when Mommy and I actually smiled at each other. She would hold her grandson and play with him from time to time. It would be years before I totally understood why becoming a grandmother was so hard for her. As I look at her picture holding Ranel, clearly he could have been her child. This was at a time where grandmas were rarely in their 30s and 40s, and my mom was just not ready.

It's a heavy weight to carry as a child, to be the family's shame, and even heavier when you believe that you are not loved or liked by the mom that you adore. Feeling like this, I learned how to scream from inside and cry with no tears. And through that fake smile that I developed so well, I learned how to love people. Loving people was easy. I would just give them what I always wanted.

That was my rose passing over the thorns. Still, I felt isolated and alone.

Chapter 7: No Food, Really

Ronnie (My 1ˢᵗ husband)

When I got pregnant, I applied for food stamps. I was so happy to bring the food stamps home, but the look on Mommy's face stopped me cold.

"And just what are you going to do with those?" she asked.

"These are food stamps to be used to buy food for all of us," I said, happy to be able to contribute. Mommy's face turned so red.

"Get those things out of my house," she said, clenching her teeth, "We have never been on food stamps, ever! And we are not starting with you!"

"But how am I supposed to buy milk for my baby, Mom?" She never said another word.

After being married for a few months, Ronnie and I moved in with Clara. It was the first time in my life that I had ever experienced any kind of hardship. It was difficult to get money for things like food and laundry bills. I had never been to a laundromat in my life. I found we didn't have enough money for simple things like milk and diaper service. Back in those days we used cloth diapers. For the first time in my life, I saw roaches and mice.

Well, on this particular day, we set out to visit my mom and we were super hungry. We packed up Ranel, some dirty laundry, and headed out. We didn't own a car, so we had to use the public bus system. It took four buses to get to that side of town.

"Hey Mom." We half smiled at each other.

"Hi, what's up?" Mommy said, as she took Ranel out of my arms and began to play with him.

"I am so glad that you are home," I said to her, "We are so hungry."

"Hungry? Why are you hungry?" Mom said under her breath.

"Umm, we used up all the food stamps."

"Humm, food stamps," she muttered.

Mom put Ranel down and went into the kitchen and started fixing a meal. To this day I don't remember what it was. We were so hungry we didn't care. It was a time before microwaves, so when you went into the kitchen to fix something, you really did have to cook it.

"Oh, you have laundry," Mommy said. "Well, separate the baby's clothes from yours and wash the baby's clothes first," Mom directed.

"I am, I don't wash his clothes with ours anyway," I responded.

I began to hang the clothes on the line and then began to fix plates. Mommy picked Ranel up and began to feed him.

"What are you doing?" She said, under her breath without looking up at me again.

"Oh, I'm just fixing me and Ronnie..."

"Put it down," she said, before I could finish my sentence. I laughed and turned to meet her eyes. They looked stern and serious.

"Put the food down!" she said again through clenched teeth.

"You are a grown woman with a child and husband. Why are you hungry? I'm gonna feed my grandson, but you, you go have your husband get you some food." Mommy said, seriously.

How shocked was I? *How can she be so mean?* She fed Ranel until he was full, changed his diaper and his clothes, and handed him back to me. It would be a long time before I saw my mom again. I did not understand this harsh lesson. I was so mad and hurt at the same time. Just how many pieces can my heart break into?

But through this madness, I never went back home again; hungry or broke. It took me years to understand this lesson. Not only did she try to teach me a lesson, but she taught me a LESSON! And I never had another man the rest of my life that couldn't buy my food or pay my bills.

Mommy and Ranel

Chapter 8: The Bond Court Hotel

Clara had gotten me a job at the Bond Court Hotel in downtown Cleveland. We were the Salad Girls, we made the food setups for all of the restaurants in the hotel; *The Bistro, The Gourmet Room,* the coffee shop, and the *Banquet Ballroom.* That job taught me how to prepare food for a large crowd, skills I use to this day. The *Banquet Room* could hold about 1500 people by itself and was used for breakfast, lunch, and dinner. The Bond Court also had a formal dining room where steak, lobster, and caviar dishes were served. We did all the prep work for the chefs, the cutting, and chopping. We made all of the salads for each restaurant, and we also did the prep for the baker.

Once I started working, Ronnie and I didn't stay married long. He just couldn't keep a job. Clara and I would trade off days in order to watch Ranel. Someone had to get the bills paid, and Mommy's lesson was beginning to sink in well. It did not take long for me to understand that my marriage was ending, and all before I turned 18 years old!

Curly, Larry, and Albert

Larry Albert (Curly)

I met and married my second husband while working at the Bond Court Hotel. He worked there as well, as a dishwasher. He was a very handsome man and would watch me as I tried to ignore him while making my salads. I had been promoted to head salad girl, and we would experiment with different food combinations and ask the other kitchen help to taste. Every time I looked up, Curly was staring at me, so much so that my ex-mother-in-law would notice and tell me to look over at him. Even though I had been married and had a child, I was really shy and had never had a lot of boyfriends. In fact, I married all of my boyfriends! It was a family joke that I married every man I had ever met; not funny and not true.

Curly's name was Albert. We called him by his middle name, Larry. I ignored him, mainly because he was 10 years older than I, but then so was Ronnie. But talk about a fine old man, Baybe! Curly was fine. He got the name Curly from his beautiful shiny black hair. With his reddish-brown skin and full beard, you'd expect to see his horse run up to him and sweep him away. His Native American features were so dominant. We were married almost a year from the time we met. We moved to 123rd street, off of St. Clair; not far from Mommy. Curly was a troubled soul, with a dark past. He was the first gangster I had ever met. Well, ever met up close and personal. I did meet a few during my childhood. My Aunty Olga and the friends she had? You did not mess with her and imma leave that right there.

My husband was three men all wrapped up in one. His co-workers called him Larry, the streets called him Curley, and Albert was the charming gentleman that loved his family dearly. Curley was an undercover gangster. He could be dangerous, but that made him all the more appealing. I would often find him sitting and crying when alone at home. He would wake up in night sweats, screaming. Sometimes he would be at my throat, and I would have to tell him that it was me. His face would seem distorted until he would come back to himself.

"Allahu Akbar. Assalaam alaikum. Alhamdulillah."

"What? What are you saying? Are you speaking in tongues? What is this gibberish? And what's wrong with you?" I would ask him.

Larry would sometimes look at me, stare, and say, "You don't know what I've done to people." When he had been drinking, his skin tone would get even redder, and his eyes would gloss over, but he'd tell me that more than once.

"You don't know what I've done. I'm just here to prepare you for your next man. I'm not gonna be here long."

When he said things like that it made my blood run cold. "Stop saying that." I'd say.

When he made statements like that, it made me think he was going to leave me. Larry fell deeper into a depression and began drinking more heavily than normal. Me on the other hand, I was enjoying my life with my new sisters-in-law. We were hanging out, doing things I had never really done. I was never a drinker, I couldn't stand the taste of that stuff, but I loved to dress up.

One night, we were planning to go out, and I had picked out the dress I wanted to wear. It was a white wraparound dress with a slit that went all the way up the side. I mean I was *wearing* that dang thang. We went to a local club that was having a pantyhose contest and guess who won? Me! I won the Terri Lynn Pantyhose contest, and you couldn't tell me nothin'. My legs were flawless (you couldn't see how knocked knee and pigeon-toed I really was if I stood still). The cute wraparound dress was knocking eyeballs out!

My husband had told me he didn't want me to wear the dress, but being a little hardheaded, I did it anyway. *I am going out with my sisters-in-law and going to have fun and he will be asleep when I get back, so imma wear my dress.* And I sure did. And of course, when I got back in, he was there waiting for me.

"I thought I told you not to wear that dress," he said, as he was standing up, trying not to lose his balance.

"Well, I wanted to wear my dress and so..."

Before I could get the words out of my mouth, I was sent flying across the room and landed under the dining room table. I had never been hit before in my life. My dad had never hit me, and Mommy only spanked me once or twice. Larry not only hit me, but he also smacked the hell out of me, then went to bed and left me on the floor, mouth bleeding and my dress messed up. It was ripped in three places in the seams. After I got over my crying spell, I called my friend Trufinya. I knew she would tell me what to do. The next day, I met her, and we went shopping. When I returned, Larry was awake and up looking for me and had a major attitude.

"Who told you to leave?" he growled. "Go straighten up that room, then fix me something to eat," he barked. All this was new to me, he had never acted like this before, towards me, anyway. If I did something he didn't like, I'd hear about it, but never was there violence towards me. I held my head down, went into the bedroom, and started planning my revenge. When I came out of our bedroom, I went into the kitchen and began to prepare mashed potatoes, cornbread, chicken, and string beans. I made Larry's plate. I heard him getting out of the shower and stumbling into the kitchen.

"Your food is on the table," I said, in my sorriest voice.

"I didn't want to hit you, but I told you not to wear that dress," he said, as he gulped the food down, all the while he was squirming in his seat. "Damn, this don't even taste good. I know you mad at me, but you really f****ed this food up. Dang." Suddenly, he jumped up and grabbed and scratched his crotch. "Why you ain't eating?" he said and started to scratch himself again. I looked him in the eye and said, "You slapped me, but I just killed you."

When he jumped up this time, I jumped up too. I ran down the stairs and out the door. We had left Salina in the bed sleeping. *At least now, if he hits me, I'll be outside.* He was gaining on me; he was right at my back. As he began to pass me, he kept running. He ran from 123rd in St. Clair to 105th in Parklawn, to the Forest City Hospital.

He thought I had poisoned him and was running to the hospital to get his stomach pumped, but the itching in his crotch lasted for days. I had put BC aspirin powder in his food. I confessed to what I had done since he was at the hospital, and the doctors wanted to know what kind of poison I had used. Oh well! But the itching in his crotch came from something else. After being slapped silly, my friend Trufinya and I went shopping. We went to a novelty store in downtown Cleveland and purchased itching powder. I rubbed it all in his clean underwear. His itching went on for about a week. I never told him that part!

Larry and I had one child together, Nel'Salina. He would rock her and just stare at her.

"This is my baby, for real?" he would ask.

It was not that he didn't believe me, she was just so beautiful to him, and she looked just like him. Every morning he'd pick her up and take her to the window and shout out, "Hello world!" She would just squirm in her daddy's arms. He adored his baby girl. He had two other girls from a previous relationship, but Salina was his baby, and mine. Nel'Salina was named after her dad's two favorite uncles, Nelson and Rockwell. We had a hard time trying to find a name for her. He gave me two choices, Nel'Salina or Rockola. Need I say more?

Salina was always quiet, and she liked who she liked. My friend Denise, who lived down the street, became her babysitter. It was Niecy, as we called her, who told me that Salina could talk, and talk in whole sentences. Denise would call me on the phone and let me hear her talking, but when I showed up she would stop.

Larry would disappear from time to time and come home upset and withdrawn. Even though we were still working at the Bond Court, we had more money than our paychecks. I never asked where the extra money came from. I would whine for clothes, jewelry, and shoes. One day, after asking one too many times for a pair of shoes, I was ordered to get in the car.

"Where are we going?" I asked, a little scared because Larry wasn't answering me. We drove for a while until we got to a field. There was a car hidden in the bushes, and it smelled awful.

"Where are we going? It stinks over here." Larry opened the trunk and walked away. The smell made me vomit. I could see human feet and that was all I needed to see. As I ran past him, I could hear him speaking.

"You don't know what I got to do for shoes," he said in a low, muffled voice. From that day to this, I could care less about a name brand anything. Ninety percent of the time, I am barefoot. We never talked about what I saw, ever!

Are ya'll still here? Well, I hope so. Close your mouth, I ain't finished with my story yet. This recalled trauma had to sink in a bit. This was a forgotten memory too. OK, ya'll ready? Let's continue.

Chapter 9: Dead Is Just Dead

Larry 'Curley' Albert was very protective of his sisters and brothers. He was the one person who you absolutely didn't want to mess with. When he got in an ugly mood, only his mother could calm him down.

"Dang," Albert said out loud.

Someone had just put hands on one of his sisters, and Albert wasn't having it.

"Now I got to go and kick some nigga's ass about my sister," he said.

"Oh Lord, here we go," I said. Albert had a best friend, Walter, who lived right next door to us. We lived in a two-family duplex in the upstairs unit. Walter and his family lived in the bottom unit of the house next door. Most of the houses on the street were made similar.

Our baby, Salina, who was about four or five months old, would play with the neighbor's young child. Walter and Albert were always in some sort of friendly or unfriendly competition or argument. I stayed out of it, mainly because oftentimes they were both drunk when these disagreements broke out. Walter's wife, Sarah, and I were friendly in a next-door neighbor type of way. We were not friends.

Later, after much complaining, Albert got up and went to the aid of his sister. He returned a few hours later. I was notified of his return because of the yelling that came from outside.

"What is it now?" I said out loud, to no one in particular. I went out on our porch balcony, only to see Albert on the ground next to the fence and Walter standing over him.

"What the hell ya'll fighting about now?" I yelled at Albert and Walter. Walter just looked up at me, and Albert stayed down on the ground. Sarah, Walter's wife, appeared on her downstairs porch and did the same thing I did. We went back into our houses. These two were always at it, and it did not make sense for us to get involved.

After a while, Albert made his way back upstairs into our unit.

"What happened?" I asked.

"Don't worry about it," Albert said, "Imma get him tomorrow." Albert looked dazed and wild-eyed, as he usually did when he had been drinking. With his native blood running wild through his veins, the last thing he ever needed to do was ingest alcohol or any substance, for that matter. Over the next few days, Albert appeared as if he was catching a cold. He had chills, was vomiting, and had a headache.

"I don't feel well, hon," he said to me.

"You don't look well either," I responded. We were both due to be at work at Bond Court the next day, but we decided I'd go, and he'd stay home and watch the baby. Our neighbor, who lived under us, sometimes babysat for Salina. Her name was Jean.

"I'll ask Jean to look in on you both while I'm gone. Make sure you feed and change the baby." I gave Albert a big kiss on the forehead and then gave the baby one and headed out to work. We had a car, but I didn't drive. I was on the bus. Back then, there were no cell phones. We made phone calls from the pay phones that were on every corner and in every store. There wasn't an Uber service either. We had a yellow cab and that was about it.

On my lunch break, I called home to check on Albert and Salina. I'd called about three times already, and Albert had not picked up. I wondered where he could have gone with the baby, with him feeling so bad. But then I got an uneasy feeling and tried one more time. Albert answered the phone.

"What? What are you saying?" It was total gibberish. I couldn't make out what he was saying. "Where is the baby? I screamed into the phone. Albert let out a screeching sound and would not answer me. I could hear Salina crying in the background.

"Albert!" I yelled, "What's wrong? What happened to Salina?" No answer. I finally hung up and dialed the downstairs neighbor's house. "What's going on? Is Salina OK?" I was in total panic mode now.

"I don't know," she said, "but there is a lot of bumping around coming from your house. Do you want me to go see if I can peep through your curtains?" Jean asked.

"Please, I'm so scared. I'm trembling, Jean. I think something happened to Salina and Albert can't tell me." Jean kept me on the line with her cordless house phone, I could hear her run up the stairs and bang on the door.

"Albert," she screamed, as she continued to bang on the door. "Oh no, sis!" She yelled into the phone. "Albert is on the floor and Salina is lying on top of him crying."

"Dial 911!" I yelled and hung up the phone. Then I called 911 myself. I slammed the phone down and ran to my locker for my purse. Since I worked in downtown Cleveland for a major hotel, cabs were always lined up outside. I jumped into one and started for home. It was a long ride. Jean didn't have a key to get into my house, so she could only wait and watch from outside the door through the window. The cab got me home at the same time the ambulance decided to show up. I ran up the stairs as the fire department was breaking my window out in order to get into the house. I could hear Albert moaning and groaning. I grabbed Salina and began to check her out. At the same time, I started asking the paramedics about Albert.

"What is wrong with my husband? Why is he making those sounds?"

"He is having a seizure," the paramedic informed me.

"A what? What's that?" They didn't answer me. They put him on a stretcher and started down the steps with him. I don't remember how I got to the hospital. When I finally got there, I was rushed into a small room where I was told that Albert had a brain bleed and they needed to operate right away. I wanted to call my mother-in-law to ask her what to do, but the doctor said my husband would be dead in an hour if I waited, plus I was his legal next of kin and the decision would have to come from me.

"Where did he get this brain bleed?" I asked the doctor.

"He must have been hit in the head with something or fell hard onto something," the doctor said.

My God, the fight. Walter and Albert had a fight.

I gave the doctor permission to operate on my Albert. I also had the very emotional duty of telling his mom and family.

Nobody liked the decision I made to allow the doctor to operate, but who makes decisions like this at my age? I was 19.

I called Walter to ask him what happened, and he hung up on me. I tried again to talk to him. Since I'd told the doctors about the fight, the hospital called the police. Walter was arrested. Albert woke up for a short while after being put into a medically induced coma for a few days.

"Alhamdulillah," he said softly. *There is that word again, that gibberish that I don't understand.* "You shot me," he whispered.

"What? What did you say?" I asked, in astonishment.

"You shot me," he said again.

"I did not shoot you, Albert." The look of fear that was on his face really bothered me. He was afraid of me. He kept repeating to me that he thought I shot him. The doctor said it was normal for him to act like that after having surgery on his brain. His head was healing nicely, but Albert had developed pneumonia and that was bad. Now he had tubes in his nose to suck the phlegm out of his lungs.

"I'll check on you tomorrow, hon," I told him as I went out the door, but he'd already fallen to sleep. I went home to check on Salina. I had not been going home much. I would stay at the hospital or a friend's house because I didn't want to be alone. I kept calling Walter and for some reason he would not call me back. His wife had stopped speaking to me, and they would turn their heads whenever we were outside at the same time. Sarah thought I had her husband arrested, but that wasn't true. I told the hospital about the fight, and the hospital called the police. I told the authorities they were friends who often fought and made up.

But this time, for some reason, Walter never called. He never asked how Albert was doing. I felt a resentment build within my soul for Walter. The more he ignored me, the more I started to hate him. Now, I began thinking that maybe he meant to harm my husband. Albert and I never got the chance to talk about the fight.

The next day, the hospital called me several times to come right away but I did not get the message until hours later. I arrived at the hospital in time for regular visiting hours and walked right into Albert's room.

"Hey sleepyhead," I said. He was sleeping peacefully. His natural color had returned to his face and all the tubes were gone. I was smiling and rushing over to wake him with a kiss, when the nurses ran in behind me.

"Mrs. Davis, we are so sorry that we couldn't reach you in time. We didn't want you to come in before we had a chance to talk to you and prepare him." I looked over at my husband's peaceful face and it was then that I noticed he had not moved. I stared blankly at him and then his sisters came in. I don't remember which ones; everyone was talking at the same time and I zoned out.

"What are you going to do about the funeral?" *Funeral?* I don't know who or how the service details were put together; it may have been me. I just kept remembering the preacher (who kept saying over and over again, that if Albert was here, he'd tell you to run, not walk to church. But, what I heard was 'a salaam alaikum,' but that voice was in my head, no one else heard it. Everything else was ... blah blah blah. What I heard next was Allahu Akbar, Alhamdulillah. Why of all times do these unusual words keep popping up in my head, and why now? I could hear these words in my head in Albert's voice, saying, "Imma die, I'm not going to be here long. I'm getting you ready for the next one." My husband was dead. Yet, it was I who wanted to kill.

Chapter 10: Till Death Do You Part!

After the funeral, I plotted my revenge. After losing my husband, I had to see Walter and his family every day. *I hear ya'll laughing and joking as you leave the house. You have moved on with your life, and still, he won't even say good morning to me.* The court had let Walter out of jail and deemed him innocent of all charges.

My front porch was upstairs and semi-enclosed. Walter's porch was ground level, and I could see a side view of people entering and exiting his front door. I would watch Walter come out of his house, along with his family. How dare they be so happy when I'm so miserable? While I was packing up some of Albert's things, I found about $10,000 in cash in a sack with a .32 pistol in the back of the closet. It was loaded. I had only held a gun once or twice when Albert was trying to show me how to use it. I guess that's why he thought I had shot him.

I would sit far back in the corner of my porch, gun in hand, where I could see Walter and his family, but they couldn't see me. I would aim that gun at everyone in his family except him. I didn't want to kill Walter. I wanted him to feel the same pain that I did, so shooting someone he loved seemed like a good idea. I sat there with Albert's pistol. Now, my pistol was aimed at his wife as she came out of the door with their son. This was an opportunity to hurt him for taking the life of my beloved.

My crazy ass was standing there on the porch holding Salina. She'd started to fuss and squirm on the porch floor, so I'd picked her up using only my hand and arm. In the other hand, at arm's length, I had that gun, still trained on Walter and his wife.

As I followed them with my eyes, all I had to do was squeeze the trigger and I would have hit one of them for sure! Salina started to fuss even more, which caused me to drop the pistol. It fell to the floor of the porch and it felt almost as if it were slapped out of my hand. I stepped back where no one could see me and looked at my baby. Whatever made her jump and squirm like that truly saved a life. Salina looked at me as I sat down. Looking into her little face I began to rock her to sleep. Yes, like one of the crazy, mad women in the movies, I just hugged and rocked my baby while sitting on the porch floor with my silent tears. She stopped being fussy almost immediately.

The impact of the pistol hitting the porch floor made enough noise that it caused Walter and his family to look up. 'An eye for an eye' is what I'd wanted to say, but God had sent his angels down on that day and protected me and them. Languishing in my grief, I didn't let the devil win that day. Once again, God protected me when I didn't realize I needed protecting. I pushed it all back and tucked it away, leaving behind all thoughts of what I almost did on that porch. I could never figure out why I always suppressed being angry. There have been times in my life where I was called soft, a pushover, and weak, and I was OK with that.

It took me years to understand that it was a possibility that Walter could not face me because maybe he was hurting from taking the life of his friend. Maybe he was truly sorry.

And after all these years, I often wonder what would have happened if I hadn't looked at my baby girl. If she had not started to cry, if I had not picked her up and stared into her little face. Sometimes the life you save may be your own!

Chapter 11: Life Goes On

I continued to work at Bond Court Hotel a few years after Albert's death. My older friends from there, including a married couple named Carole and Cleo, became my street mentors. I started singing around town at various night clubs and in competitions. We had events called gong shows which were handled similar to talent shows, and the clubs would hire a house band. Most of the talent showcased on the gong shows were singers.

These shows were very popular. The Dazz Band, whose hits were *Let it whip, Joystick,* and *Swoop* used to come to some of these shows around the Cleveland area. They were called the Kinsman Dazz at one time, named after a street in Cleveland called Kinsman. A lot of housing projects were in this area and it was known to be a rough side of town. The comedian, Arsenio Hall, was from that area as well.

I don't know why I always kept older friends, but I got the nickname Baby Sister from always being the youngest in the crowd. It had its perks, everybody looked out for me. The drug dealers, the drug addicts, the pimps, and the prostitutes all seemed to like my voice and tried to use it as a means to make themselves some cash by being my manager. I had so many street managers I can hardly remember them all.

Prior to singing in the clubs, I tried singing in the church choir, then in a gospel group. I guess I was around 14. I was introduced to gospel groups by my neighbor on the next street. His name was Ricky. Ricky was another young man whom I considered a brother. He was handsome and could sing his butt off. He was in a group with his brother Tony and a few others. I would go from church to church with them, just to watch how they stirred up the crowd with their songs of spiritual enlightenment. They called themselves the Mighty Revelators, (I have no idea what that means). The girl group I was introduced to was called the Gospel Fabulators. I was with them up until I was taught how to pretend to have the holy ghost fit and fall out.

I was thrown out of the group just like I was thrown out of the church choir. Years later I would sing at my little sister's wedding. I sang a duet with our neighbor Calvin Goodman, who had a voice like LeVert, and I must say, we sounded great together.

My dad and my stepmom, Brenda, belonged to Cory Methodist Church on 105th Street. It is Cleveland's oldest Black church and was a common stop for civil rights dignitaries in the 60s, Martin Luther King being one of them. The Glenville section of Cleveland was once a Jewish area. The church had once operated as a holy place for Jewish people to worship. It was built in 1875 and is still around today. Cleveland has a rich history, if you are into that type of thing.

I really wanted to sing in that choir, but it wasn't meant to be. I had been going to Bible study with our neighbors, the Macks, from across the street. They were Jehovah's Witnesses. I went to Cory Methodist Church because that's where we'd go if I went to church with my dad and Stepmom. If we went to church with Mommy, it was St. Mark's. Before you could be in any of the choirs, you had to be a member of the church, which meant you had to be baptized. So, when it was my turn to be baptized, I tried to talk to the Pastor. They wanted me to say that Jesus Christ was my Lord and Savior.

"Where in the Bible did it say anything about Easter and Christmas? The only thing I know is that it says, 'to remember the Sabbath and keep it holy.'" Well, instead of answering my questions, my dad got so mad at me.

"Who do you think you are?" Dad said to me. An absolute look of embarrassment was on his face.

"You think you know more than the preacher?" my father asked.

"She doesn't understand yet," the Pastor said, "bring her back after Bible studies."

Well, I was already attending Bible studies with the Macks from across the street. They were Christians, I think? They were Jehovah's Witnesses, studying the Bible. Anyway, I pretended to understand because I wanted to sing in the choir. I let them dunk me, and I got to sing my solo part. Afterward, I asked a few more questions.

"Since Jesus died for my sins, does that mean that I can do anything I want and still get into heaven?" I was overjoyed with their answer. "Well," I shouted, "This is good." I had quite a few transgressions I needed to be saved from, and later on it would *include trying to take a life.*

Needless to say, I got kicked out of the choir.

However, I did continue with my studies with the Jehovah's Witness community. Their doctrine was kinda shaky too. They told me I couldn't listen to music and that there would be no kids in heaven. They said if my parents were not Jehovah's Witnesses, then it was a wrap, none of my family could get into heaven. Now this may not be the true teachings of the Jehovah's Witness faith, but this is how my childish mind processed what was said to me.

I loved the night life Carole, Cleo, and I had. We could party all night and get up and go to work and start all over again. There were a few alcoholic drinks that I tried, but I didn't like the taste of alcohol and the worst thing I saw in these clubs were drunk, unruly women. Something I wanted no part of. Cocaine was the drug floating around the people I hung out with.

"Wait! So, Carole, you mean you put this in your nose?" I asked.

"Yes, Baby Sis, just sniff." Carole urged.

"I can't do that," I told her, "I can't stand to let the shower water hit me in the face, let alone anything else."

I definitely crossed drug addict and drunk off my list of things to be. God protected me from having a liking for either. I did, however, smoke cigarettes, and being an 'entertainer', I had an image to maintain. So, I smoked cute, expensive cigarettes from a brand called Dunhill. Dunhill's were designer cigarettes and came in different colors; I even used a cigarette holder. I was the original booshie woman. I was always in heels and had a private hairdresser and makeup person. That's not anything to talk about now, but back then, it was lit. My shoes were custom made and yes, they were real snake and alligator. I would go pick out the skin that I wanted, and the shoemaker would make me a pair just for my feet, but I didn't do this often. I usually got a cheap pair of shoes, because I was trying not to relive what I saw in the back of the trunk of that car with Larry, years ago.

We would equate being an entertainer with money and expensive things, but in reality, most of us were really broke. I would sing in various bars on Euclid Avenue; *The Name of the Game, Tucker's Casino*, and *TuJague's*, to name a few. I would usually sit at a table by myself and just watch the other contestants in the crowd and see what all the other people had on. I observed whether their furs were real or fake, same with the shoes. I think most people in the clubs did not relate to me because I neither got high nor drank alcohol. They didn't really know what to think of me. Shoot, give me Tylenol and it will make me high. I had an occasional champagne cocktail or a Brandy Alexander that was watered down until there was no taste of alcohol. I really hated the taste of alcohol.

Carole and Cleo were always somewhere around, trying to hook me up, or to hitch me to their wagon. I didn't understand my 'street value' back then. I thought that my best interests were being looked after. I believed they were my friends. For years, I would make this mistake over and over again in my life. In fact, I would make this mistake with most of the people around me.

I never did the things a lot of young women got a chance to do as teens. I did not grow up hanging around 'street people'. This is something I picked up after I left home. Everything in Mommy's house was quiet and sterile; we never heard any cuss words, and when we did, we didn't know what they meant! I wanted to fit in somewhere, but there was always something or someone that prevented me from jumping all the way to the other side. I still didn't have any close friends my age. Even Trufinya and the rest of my childhood friends had all gone their separate ways. I didn't go shopping, to movies, or lunch. I did none of it. And I still don't.

I would watch Carole and Cleo prepare drugs for their consumption and then begin the ritual of passing it back and forth on little gold coasters. People who did cocaine thought they were better than the ones who shot heroin. I don't know why. Maybe it was because most of the people we saw that shot up were junkies on the street. We didn't perceive people who snorted white powder up their noses on gold trays as junkies. How could you? They had on furs, drove expensive cars, and had pockets full of money. Or was this just my perception?

During this time in my life, I rarely went to see my parents. I would pop up every now and then but I cannot recall anyone ever visiting me either. My mom reached out to me when Albert died. I went home for a few weeks while I waited on my new place to get ready. Albert and I had rented this house on 123rd in St. Clair from Daddy's friends, the Tindells. After Albert's death, I couldn't bring myself to stay in the house we'd shared. Look, because of my extreme grief, I had almost killed someone! To see these people every day was more than I could bear. I never wanted to feel like that again. Unfortunately, I would get that feeling again in my life, but not for the same reasons.

My children were with me most of the time, but it was Clara or Denise who watched them for me while I worked or went out at night. Even though I had been married and divorced her son, and married another man and had a child with him, Clara still remained close to me and was so good to my daughter that Salina would call her Momma Clara.

"Where are you going tonight, Baby Sis?" Carole asked.

"I don't know, maybe I'll try the gong show over at *TuJaque's*," I replied.

"OK, meet us at Tucker's afterwards. I got someone I want you to meet," Carole said.

"Who is it this time?"

Carole was always trying to hook me up or use me to get out of the house without Cleo so she could sneak out with some dude. After the show, I walked on over to *Tucker's*, took a seat at the bar, and ordered my usual watered-down pop (some say soda) with a splash of Hennessy, and I do mean splash, and that was too much. *Whew, this stuff could gag a maggot! How does anyone actually swallow this? Ugh!*

It wasn't long before Carole showed up with her date, Fats or Fat Daddy. That was his street name. Fats wasn't a very attractive man. He was short, round, and loud, but he was funny. Next to him stood a figure that captivated the whole bar. He stood there and looked around as if he owned the joint and walked over to where I was sitting, after Carole had pointed me out. He seemed to glide over and sat beside me, then put his arm around my chair. *Wrong move.* I didn't like him putting his arm around my chair like that.

"Hey, I'm Reese. Carole tells me they call you their baby sister. What's your name?" he questioned.

"Baby Sister, like she said," I said in my smart alec voice, "Excuse me, but you have your arm around my chair."

"You don't want my arm around your chair? OK, cool, I'll move it."

By now, I'm staring a hole into the side of Carole's head.

"Who is this rude old man you got me hooked up with?" I whispered in her ear.

"Aw, Baby Sister," Carole began to whine in that voice when she wanted me to do something. "Just hang out with him for a few hours. It will be fun. You know I can't go home without you." Carole and I lived in the same duplex. "Cleo will get suspicious," she went on to say.

"OK girl," was my reply, "but how do I always end up in these situations?" After a long while, Reese broke the silence between us.

"Carole also said that you were looking for a manager," he stated.

"Oh, so you a manager?" I asked. "You haven't even heard me sing. How do you know I'm any good?" I questioned him, still getting smart.

"Well, are you? he asked. I just ignored the question. "You sound alright," he said, "I've heard you sing before, you just need some grooming. You are about to sing now anyway, so I will hear you then."

"How do you figure that?" I asked again in my ultimate smart alec voice. Frankly, Reese was getting on my last nerve.

"Because," Reese said, "I just slipped the band $500 to let you sing whatever you want."

"Wait a minute, you just gave the band $500 to let me sing? That's more than they were making all weekend," I muttered out loud to myself. "But they don't know my songs do they?"

"Look, Sis," Reese said, "either you are singing or you ain't. But don't waste my time."

Now I really had an attitude. Carole was so involved with Fats that she wasn't following my conversation with Reese. I flounced myself up to the stage and asked the band if they knew any of the songs. They knew *Inseparable* by Natalie Cole. This was what we ended up going with.

Me singing in a nightclub

I didn't know then that this song would be the beginning of a more than 25-year ride. I met Reese every single day for a week, going to one nightclub after another. I met him in downtown

Cleveland one day because he said he wanted to buy me some shoes and a few dresses because I wasn't dressed well enough to go out in the streets with him. *Really?* Reese introduced me to after-hour clubs, where all kinds of situations that I had not been exposed to kept popping up. I was sure that in the bars and nightclubs there were gamblers, pimps, and prostitutes, but I never knew who was who because I was always in the corner by myself.

Reese was a gambler. He took me to this spot in the Kinsman area of town. I had never been over there before. It was dark and scary but there were cars parked everywhere. We got out of the car and walked around the side of the building, which was still dark and abandoned-looking, but we could see people standing by the door. Ladies with long furs, men with apple cashmere hats, and all this jewelry dripping from everyone's neck and finger. This made me look at Reese's hand. He had a simple silver band on his finger and only one chain of silver around his neck, *or maybe it's white gold.*

After that night at the club with Carole and Fats, Carole asked me questions about Reese.

"Did you notice that Reese was carrying a black leather bag?"

"Yes," I answered.

"Well, that's where he keeps his stuff," Carole said.

"What stuff?" I asked.

"He's a jewel thief and a bank robber," she said.

"Who's a jewel thief and a bank robber?"

My dumb butt kept asking, "You said he was a manager?"

"I just said that so I wouldn't scare you off. I needed you to get out of the house so I could be with Fats. I bet if you went in there and took something, he'd probably never notice that you did." I couldn't believe Carole, who I'd trusted to have my best interests at heart, was trying to convince me to steal.

"I'm not a thief, Carole. I'm not going in that man's bag. Besides, he just got me this outfit and it cost more than anything I have ever owned. The old dude is beginning to grow on me," I said.

"He always has that bag with him. The only time he leaves it is when he goes to the bathroom. Look through it then," Carole whispered. I knew when she said it that I wouldn't be doing that. No way.

Later that night, Reese and I went inside what looked like an abandoned building. It was like something I had never seen before. Inside, the music was blaring, women were dancing in cages, and they had a full bar. People were being served food, just like the elegant dining room at the Bond Court. Upstairs, people were shooting dice and playing cards. I was trying to act like I wasn't impressed, but I was really mesmerized by what I saw. Reese wasn't from Cleveland; he was from Detroit by way of New York and Pittsburgh. I was trying my best to act normal.

"Baby Sis, I got a meeting in the back. I'll be right back," Reese said. "They gonna look out for you and make sure nobody messes with you." He pointed to two men in suits.

Why would somebody mess with me? I just sat down, agreed, and tried to look cool and cute like all the other ladies.

"As salaamu alaikum," I heard him say to the man closest to him.

"Wa alaikum salaam," the man replied back.

"Keep an eye on her 'till I get back. She doesn't know what's happening." My head whipped all the way around because I had not heard those strange words since Albert died. Now my head is all messed up. *Was this some code or foreign language?* The two men stood on each side of me with their arms crossed. They both had on leisure suits, now they are called sweat suits. They didn't talk to me, they just stood there 'till Reese came back. When he did return, he took me upstairs to a room with a peephole. He knocked and they let us in. Inside was another elegant room.

Ladies were sitting on the sidelines of the big crap table while some were playing. I was told to stand next to Reese at the crap table. I had never seen any of this before. I didn't know if Reese was winning or losing. After a while, he handed me the dice. I threw the dice like he told me to and every combination he shouted at me was the numbers the dice landed. People thought we were cheating. He may have been, I don't know. What I do know is that he won a lot of money that night and I didn't get a dime! It was then that I saw him go into his little bag and pull out some rings and watches and sold a few. I stopped counting at $2200, because he could see how my mind was calculating all that money.

From the gambling and the jewelry sales, I estimated at least $5000 profit in that one night.

We left there and went to another spot. All night, we went from one run down building to the next. We were on the Eastside of Cleveland, and by day the buildings looked abandoned. On our drive to the next location I asked, "So why do you wear silver when you have all that gold?"

"Real men don't wear gold," he said, "gold is for the ladies."

"Huh." I was confused at what he said.

"Besides, this is not silver," Reese said, "it's platinum and it is more expensive than gold. Your so-called friend could have gotten you into trouble with the way she was advising you," he stated. My head whipped around to see his face. I was shocked at what he had just said. "Fats heard her tell you to go in my shit and take something and you didn't."

"I am not a thief," I said, "and if I was, you don't do that to friends."

"Well, since you didn't, you can go through the bag and take anything. I'm gonna let you pick something out that you like. You can pick any one thing out you like."

I chose an emerald and diamond ring. I chose it because not only is emerald green my favorite color, it's also my birthstone. When I saw Carole a few days later she was sporting some oversized sunglasses in the dark! All I am going to say is that Reese wasn't the cause of her having to wear the dark glasses, but imma leave that story right there.

I had to pick up Salina from Clara's house and take her to get some shoes. Reese was still in town, but he had told me he would be heading back to Detroit in a few days. He picked up his son Hassan from someone who had been watching him. Reese pulled up and got out of the car. Salina let go of my hand and ran up to him and said, "You my Daddy?" Salina was two years old. He looked at me.

"I didn't tell her that." She just looked up at him until he picked her up. He was aware that her father had passed. Salina had never said that before and there were other people she could have said that to, including my own Dad. Salina never did a lot of talking to me, it was Denise who told me that she could even talk.

"You want me to be your Daddy?" he asked her, as he tossed her into the air. She just squealed.

"From now on, I'm your Daddy. While I am gone, if she needs anything, tell me," he said.

Well, on that shopping trip, I didn't get the chance to ask Salina what she wanted because everything she pointed at that day went into the bag. I think I got some pantyhose.

Reese was due to turn himself in in Detroit. He was wanted on a parole violation from a bank robbery that he had committed several years back.

He'd told me that he was in Cleveland visiting relatives. One relative was his aunt, Lillian Walker Burke. She was the first Black female judge in the state of Ohio and in the city of Cleveland. He had to downplay who they were to each other. *How are you going to be a bank robber with a judge for an aunt?* Nothing improper ever happened between them. They maintained a healthy distance and were never involved with each other legally.

Boy was I sad Reese had to go away. I think he had to be gone for 18 months. I would write to him and send pictures of me and Salina. After about 6 months I received a letter from him saying that I had not sent him any commissary money, and that he required $100 for every month that he had been incarcerated and that would be the ongoing arrangement. Well, up until then, I had never known anyone in jail or prison. I thought this was a requirement, so I just stopped writing and went on with my life.

Chapter 12: Life Goes On and On Some More

I was living at the Parklawn Apartments in Euclid, Ohio but decided to move to East Cleveland. My career wasn't going anywhere. I sang at every chance I got, trying to make a name for myself. I even had a new boyfriend, Terrell. He was the only one I didn't marry. I had moved into this big spooky house behind Boyd's Funeral with Salina. Ranel spent most of his time with his dad and Clara. They didn't live that far away. I often rented out rooms to make ends meet. The house had five bedrooms, and was big enough for me to do this easily. My best friend, Trufinya, lived next door.

I found out that Terrell had a whole family tucked away, and that I was the other woman. We went through the usual, 'I'm leaving her blah blah blah.' My 22-year-old head and heart were saying otherwise, and he convinced me to believe the lies for a little while. But when I caught on, I knew I would have to make a change. I grew up in the church (well, most of the time), and I knew that this relationship was wrong.

Ranel staying with his father most of the time gave me a chance to be a little more independent without having to find a sitter for two kids. I thought it best that a son stay connected to his dad.

Mommy had married James. He was a standoffish person, whom we never felt at ease with. He did not care for us and in turn we didn't care much for him. It's funny how life turns lemons into lemonade. Years later, James would be our lemonade, taking care of Mommy and all of her needs. He still takes care of her today, and we thank God for him. My oldest sister, Yvetta, had remarried a very nice man and had a daughter, Nicole, who reminds me so much of myself it's scary. Nicole is just smarter and more beautiful than her ole aunty. She would marry a third time, to my sweet brother-in-law, Taft. We all love him to pieces, and thank God for him. My younger sister, Felicia, would marry

Donelle later, and they would stay married forever and they have the most amazing sons. Donelle was another Godsend who took care of Daddy in his later years, which was truly a job that he didn't sign up for. We would lose Brenda, Daddy's wife, along the way, but not our family. We stayed close. Aunt Olga was always there for us throughout our lives.

Even though I lived next door to my best friend, Trufinya, she and I were very different people. I didn't have a lot in common with her. To be honest, I didn't have a lot in common with hardly anyone. I believed in my boyfriend but didn't want to be in a relationship with a married man. My ex-in-laws had stopped communicating with me much later after Albert died. Somehow they held me accountable for not doing more to bring Walter to justice. I often wondered what would have been my story had I pulled that trigger.

Before Reese, my old friend I'd met while singing and who went away to prison, and I stopped writing, I would love to get letters from him. Maurice (Reese) was, and still is, the smartest person I have ever met. He made you go get a dictionary; you couldn't just skim through a letter from Reese. He had beautiful handwriting and always found something poetic to say. Reese had a photographic memory. I mean, really, he did. He read all the time, and if you wanted to know about a book or what was in it, he could tell you what page and what line to refer to. And if he had a question about what he was reading, oftentimes, if the author of the book was still alive, he'd call them or write to them directly to get the answers he was looking for. This is something I learned to do from him; go straight to the source if you have the opportunity to do so. But I don't have a photographic memory, and it used to annoy the hell out of me, how when I asked him any questions he made me look up the answer. Reese had gotten a BA from Wayne State University while locked up but because he was now an ex-felon, he couldn't use it anywhere.

After I thought I had broken it off with Reese, I got with Terrel, and he was a drug addict. I don't know what he was using back then. But people used reefer, pills, cocaine, or heroin. Funny, with all the drug users I was around, I never really saw people do drugs. On occasion, I did see some folks sniff that white powder up their noses, but seeing that was enough of a deterrent for me.

After all of the, 'I'm really leaving my wife' stories and 'It's the reason I get high' stories, I wanted out, but I couldn't figure out how to do it. Terrel was a means of income for me and my daughter.

I rented out some of the rooms to a family of four, a husband and wife with three small kids. Terrell's uncle, a shell-shocked old veteran in a wheelchair, rented a downstairs room. He suffered from some type of mental disorder.

The wife was a nice-looking young woman who was older than her husband, but the couple fought all the time. I mean, he would beat her up! I had to ask them to leave because this was something I was not used to seeing at all, and I didn't want Salina seeing it. I once asked the wife why she stayed in such a miserable relationship. She told me that she was a witch and had put a spell on him so that he could never leave her! Now, I was thinking in my head, if she was the one that put a spell on him, couldn't she unspell him? Hmm.

So, now y'all know I'm looking over my glasses, trying to figure out how to get this 'witch' out of my house and stay on her crazy-ass good side. When they moved in, they paid me three months' rent in advance, so getting them out would not be that easy. The crazy uncle had to go as well. He was some kind of pervert in a wheelchair. If any lady walked past him, she'd have to go fast because he was a grabber. I felt bad socking pops in his jaw, but I had warned him several times.

"Terrel, why is it that your uncle can't go to your house where your wife and kids are?" I asked him.

"Because," was all he could answer. I began putting two and two together.

"So, you hang on to me so that crazy uncle has a place to stay, because he cannot stay at your house. But check this, crazy uncle gotsta go, along with this crazy family. After all, I got a small child here," I said.

"Well, my uncle is not going nowhere until I say he is going, and for that matter, you not either. I told you I was leaving my wife and family just to be with you." Yeah, so the 'all day sucker' sign was lit up across my face, and I fell for the okey doke once again.

Mommy and my stepdad, James, had moved from 109th to Shaker Heights. This neighborhood was a really nice area in the East Side of Cleveland. Mommy and I spoke on occasion, but she rarely saw her grandkids, not mine, anyway. You just didn't drop off any kids at Mommy's house, you made appointments to see her. She'd take all the kids, mine and my sisters, from Friday to Saturday, sometimes to Sunday. She'd spend time with them, but you had better not be late picking them up. Period! And there was no babysitting. Oh no, you didn't get that, and we just didn't drop by Mom's house. But somebody did, somebody who didn't know the rules absolutely did.

Chapter 13: Return from Outer Space

"Hey Baby Sis, what's happening?" said a familiar voice on the phone. I looked at Terrell, who had just answered and given me the phone.

"Who is this?" I asked.

"I know you didn't forget my voice. Where's my Baby Girl? She must be so big now." The caller questioned. Terrel was staring at me, and I was gazing in disbelief, off into space. I know my mouth was wide open.

"How did you get my number?" I asked in shock.

"From your mom. I'm over here now, she called you for me. Look, I'm on my way over there. Your mom gave me your address," Reese said.

"She did what?" I asked, feeling like I was about to pass out. Terrel kept asking me who I was talking to, talking loud enough for Reese to hear.

"I will be there in about 30 minutes. You'll be home, won't you?" he said.

"Wait, I thought you said if I didn't send you any money while you were locked up for me to stop writing to you."

"Yeah, I said that," Reese replied, "and I also said that to you and two other women. You the only one that didn't send nothing," he laughed out loud, "so I had to come back and claim what's mine and see my baby. I made a promise to Salina, and so, I'll be there in a few." Salina would sometimes say, "Daddy Reese coming?" To this day, some 40 years later, I don't know where that came from, that instant bond that they had lasted a lifetime.

After almost two years, Reese shows back up and ends up at Mommy's house.

"Wait, how are you at my mom's?"

"Who's at your mom's house?" Terrel kept trying to be heard in the conversation.

"I remember dropping you off here the day before I left. I went to your old apartment and found out that you had moved, so I came here and knocked on the door, and bingo, your mom dialed your number for me."

"Wait, my mom?"

We hung up, and I just sat there not knowing what to do.

First of all, I looked like a hot mess. Second of all, what am I going to tell Terrell? Another man is about to come visit me who claims my daughter is his child, and don't give two shits about him. Humm.

"Oh," I said, after coming back to life, "that call was from an old friend of mine at my mom's house and my mom called me for him."

He was mad.

"Well, it's not like she knows anything about you, Terrell. I cannot tell my family about you. We don't do things like this. I have been isolated for over a year from my family, afraid they would find out about you and find out about your story," I explained, defending my mother's actions.

"Well, he not coming over here," Terrell said. "Oh, just wait 'till he shows his ass up over here."

All shucks, why am I always in trouble? I called Trufinya and told her the situation.

"You mean that old man that you used to go out with last year? The one with jewelry? Gurl, don't mess up what you got going on for that old man," she advised me.

"But, I don't have anything going on. This man is married."

"Yeah, he may be married, but you don't pay no rent."

"Look Fefee, (Trufinya's nickname) I wasn't raised like this. I'm not hanging around Terrell much longer. This ain't right, besides, Reese lives in Detroit or Pittsburgh. He just pops through every so often."

"Well, you better figure something out because there he is," Trufinya said, as she hung up the phone. I looked out the window, and I saw a car pull up. Omg, I ran to the bathroom to fix my hair, threw a clean top on Salina, and started for the steps. When I heard his voice, my heart stopped.

"Hey, Man, I'm Reese," I heard him say to Terrell. "I'm here to see Baby Sis. Oh, I see her," he says as he opens the screen door and walks past Terrell.

"Hey!" Salina turned around in my arms, broke free, and ran over to Reese. He scooped her up and before I could say anything, with his other arm he grabbed and hugged me! Terrell was standing by the door. He hadn't moved an inch. I don't even remember the conversation.

Reese had his son Hassan with him; he was asleep in the back of the car. He went to get him to wash him up, because they had been driving from Detroit on their way to Pittsburgh. "You better get rid of that nigga quick," Terrel said.

In my head I'm sayin', *you get rid of him*. When Reese returned, he asked for the bathroom and went to clean up Hassan. Hassan was Reese's only child and he had developmental issues. It hadn't been noticeable at first. Hassan just laughed and hugged us as if he had known us forever. After coming out of the bathroom, Reese picked up Salina.

"You wanna go with Daddy?" Reese asked her.

"Yes!" she squealed.

"And how about you, you wanna go with me or stay here?" he asked me. I was shocked out of my mind.

"Huh, what?" Terrell and I kinda said at the same time.

"Look man, no disrespect to you. I'm thankful that you took care of my family while I was gone, but I'm back now. Sis, I asked you a question," Reese said to me, "do you want to go with me or stay here?" I'm looking at Terrell who ain't said spit.

"I'm gonna overlook any mistreatment towards my family because you didn't know about me. But for the last time, Sis, are you going or staying?" he said, "You can tell me what you want to do tomorrow, if you need time, but I'm leaving tomorrow night about 9 PM. I'll be here with a truck."

"What you mean you will be here with a truck, Reese?" I asked him.

"Me and Hassan are moving to Pittsburgh. If you want to come, have your stuff ready. I'll be here to pick you and Salina up. If you want your son to come, have him ready too," he directed. "And hey man, look," he turned to look Terrell in the eyes. That was the first time I saw his eyes turn colors right in front of me. He handed Salina to me and said, "When I get back, if she wanna stay then so be it. I will just leave something for my daughter and be out. But, if she wants to go, either way, there better not be a mark on her or her things. You don't want me to come back here and find out she hurt, or her things messed up."

This punk ass Terrell would talk crazy to me all day long, but ain't opened his mouth once to Reese.

I'm going. You gonna let somebody you don't even know waltz up in here and tell you we his family? Whew.

"Yeah, I'm going. What do I need to pack?" I asked.

"Whatever you want to take, or leave it all, but we are not coming back," said Reese. "So anything important you need, get it. I got some business. I'll be back at nine tomorrow night. Man, I hope for your sake, you don't put your hands on my wife and family."

"Wife?" Terrel and I both said at the same time.

Terrel and I must have sat still for all of 10 minutes trying to process what just happened.

"Who was that nigga?" Terrell said in his forceful voice. Hum, funny you didn't say nothin' to him about who he was when he was standing here in your face.

"You had a boyfriend all this time and wanna talk about me having a wife?" He was just ranting and raving, going on and on about what he was going to do if he ever showed back up. Again, I'm wondering why he didn't say all that when he was standing here. I think I may have made my decision to really leave when Terrell let this man come into the house where he helped pay bills and punk him out like that in front of me. While he was still sulking around, I went in the kitchen to call FeeFee. Any other time, Terrell would be nowhere to be found. He was sticking around now.

"Gurl, he said he'd be back tomorrow at 9 PM."

"You sound like a fool, Baby Sis. I know you ain't leaving to go nowhere with that old man," FeeFee said.

"I wish you would quit calling him that."

"Oh, you're mad? I know you like older men, and he is fine, but girl, old men are possessive."

"Salina loves him, and I don't know how they got so connected, she never acted like that around Terrell. I think I'm gonna do it."

The next day was awkward. Around 6 PM, I went upstairs and started putting all my personal papers in a bag. I had three empty suitcases that I began to fill up with Salina's clothes. I put mine in a garbage bag. I went to find my personal items and noticed that my jewelry box was gone, so was my purse.

"Where is my jewelry box and purse, T?" I asked.

"I know you ain't going nowhere." Terrell tried to use his sexy voice, but he had already let Reese punk him out, so he could have been butt naked and nothing would have ever turned me on again. As I put my bags by the front door, I went to put on Salina's coat. Just then, Terrell opened the door and threw all my bags into the yard in the snow, along with my purse and jewelry box, which had my diamond and emerald ring that Reese gave me. The box hit the ground just as Reese showed up with the U-Haul truck. He got out of the truck with that devilish grin. He softly said in a deadly sort of way, "Salaams."

"Huh?" was our reaction.

"Hey Baby Sis, you OK?" he asked.

"Yes," I replied.

"Where's Salina?"

"In the house by the door."

"Get her and you two get in the truck."

"Say dude, bruh, don't move," Reese said to Terrell. I got Salina and got in the truck and noticed that bruh didn't move.

"I think you misunderstood me when I said that it better not be any marks on them," he said, looking Terrell up and down. "Baby Sis, do y'all have any marks on you? You or the baby?"

"No," I said.

"Well, as soon as bruh, what's your name again?"

"It's Terrell," I said.

"Thanks, but I wasn't talking to you, Sis," Reese said, "Anyway, as soon as Terrell picks your stuff up off the ground, wipes it off, and loads it on the truck, we will be on our w—"

"Let me get my coat," Terrell interrupted.

"Naw man, you need to get my wife's things off the damn ground right now because I'm losing patience."

I'm bracing myself for the fight that is about to go down, turning Salina's head so she couldn't see. But to my surprise, Terrell started picking up my things and putting them on the truck. It took all of five minutes tops.

But wait, why does he keep calling me his wife?

Chapter 14: Pittsburgh

Me and Saud

Six hours later, we arrived in Pittsburgh, the Steel City. We pulled up to 3202 Iowa Street, and a cute little brown-skinned girl met us at the door. She was talking a mile a minute, and I was trying to find out just who she was. The house was right next door to a church. It had a nice porch and front yard. Upon entering the house, it opened up to a medium-sized living room and dining room, but its furnishings reminded me of my grandparents' home in Jersey. The house belonged to his father who had inherited it from his parents, and it was their family home. On the left side were three bedrooms, one with a lock, and two open. The big room in the back had two beds and that was where Salina and Hassan would sleep. Hassan was developmentally the same age as Salina, and for the most part he was non-verbal. He still needed help eating and going to the bathroom himself. He played with some toys but basically sat and watched everybody. Forty years later, he is still doing the same thing, only now he's full-bearded and gray! The middle room was full of antique bedroom furniture, but I loved it. It had a big dressing vanity with a mirror and hassock, you could smell the pine wood.

"Hi. My name is Sandy and I'm the housekeeper," the lady said, interrupting my visual scan of the house.

"Reese told me to have this place cleaned up by the time he got back with you. Aw, the baby is cute," she said, talking a mile a minute. "Where did you come from again? What's your name?"

Dang, my face must have looked really messed up by Sandy's reaction.

"Cleveland," I said. While she was chatting along, I noticed that Reese had left. *He has probably gone to take the rental moving truck back.* Sandy started telling me about Pittsburgh and its nightlife and about the bars and clubs that Reese's family owned.

"You ain't never heard of them?" Sandy asked in disbelief. "Everybody knows about them, the Walkers. Reese's father owned Walker's vending company; it was the first Black-owned vending company in the state of Pennsylvania. What do you do besides sing? Reese said he was your manager and that you could sing. Funny he kept telling people that, because he still ain't got me no gig."

I wasn't doing so well answering Sandy's questions. I thought I was cool, hip, and into everything until Sandy said that I should know that Reese had her babysitting me!

"Babysitting me? I'm grown!" I yelled.

"You are so green and square; you better not leave outta here unless you know what's up," she said. I wasn't being held prisoner or anything, it was more about my protection, so that I didn't roam around by myself. I was unaware of those Pittsburgh streets, and everyone would've known that. We were in an area known as Sugar Top and down the way was the Hill District. Center and Herron Avenues was where I would end up a few nights later, looking for Reese.

The house had books everywhere. I had never seen so many books in someone's home. The only time I'd seen this many books was in a library. A lot of them were in a different language. The books were categorized, the top was for different languages and the bottom shelf was in English. One book he had wrapped up and it always sat on the top of the bookshelf. It had all this funny writing in it. It looked like a Bible, but it wasn't.

"When he is here, this is what he does all day," Sandy said when she noticed me looking around.

"Do you live here too?" I asked her.

"Naw," she said, "but sometimes I do spend the night when he leaves me here with Hassan and knows he is not coming back."

I was trying to process what I had just done. I left home. I'd left Cleveland and moved to Pittsburgh a few days ago with someone I didn't know to an unfamiliar place with my baby, and left one baby in Cleveland; so I knew I was returning soon, either to pick my son up and bring him to Pittsburgh, or move back home.

When I walked away from the house I was living in with Terrell, I felt rescued in a way. I had been stuck in a cycle with Terrell and that crazy family who was renting from me. But, I also left the only family I had, and relocated without a second thought, and with a stranger. If any of my kids had done something like that with my grandkids, it would be hell to pay, and needless to say, there was hell to be paid.

Sandy and I became close friends. I still had not confirmed with anyone back home that I had no intention of returning. Sandy came by almost every day; she took me all over Pittsburgh, showing me, Salina, and Hassan around.

I usually cooked dinner and had it ready, but Reese was hardly ever home and stayed away for days, which turned into weeks. He would show up sometime during the night and would leave stacks of cash, one was for bills and paying Sandy, and one was for me to do whatever I wanted with.

One day, I finally was able to pin him down to ask about where Hassan's mom was and why I was brought to Pittsburgh. I wanted to know if my role in his life was to be the babysitter of his son, Hassan.

I had thought of returning home, but really had no home of my own to go back to at this point. I tried to think of a good story to tell when I returned to Cleveland, a believable story, but who could I stay with? I had made a big mistake.

Reese's family would come by sometimes. They referred to me as 'that little girl'. They would huddle by the door and whisper among themselves. I would usually just go into the other room when they were there. If it wasn't for Sandy, I would not have had a soul to talk to. Long-distance calls cost money, plus I would have to explain myself, and I wasn't ready to do that. I did, however, call my girl Fee Fee from time to time. Other than that, Sandy was my only friend in Pittsburgh.

Whenever Salina and Hassan were sleeping or busy doing other things, I would start reading the books that were all over the house. Most of the books had strange writings; other books were on the lives of Black militant folks, most of whom I knew nothing about.

On Friday, Reese always insisted that we have a Friday meal prepared. I didn't understand why Fridays were so special. But on Fridays, he usually showed up. This in itself was strange behavior. I mean, you brought me all the way here just to ignore me?

What in the world is a Muslim?

My cooking skills had improved a lot thanks to Big Ma and Clara. I had come a long way since the gritty greens and shitterlings. I started to prepare the Friday evening meal of smothered chicken wings, string beans with potatoes, salad, yams, and cornbread. We would always have iced tea with lemon and some sort of dessert. Reese had a sweet tooth and would look for his desserts everywhere he went. He always raved about the bean pies he would get when he went to Detroit.

"It's the original recipe," he'd boast. I was a good cook, but whatever I baked came from a box mix or the bakery.

One day, Reese came home and into the kitchen where Sandy and I were working on the meal. Sandy had just made a ham sandwich and started to take her first bite when Reese went smooth off.

"WHO brought that swine in here?" he shouted.

"What's a swine?" I yelled back.

"You know I don't drink," I said.

"Swine, not wine," he shouted, "Pig! Pork!"

"Well, I don't eat pig," I said, "I told you that."

"Oh spit, I thought I could eat it before you came back," Sandy confessed nervously.

"Get that shit out of my house and don't bring it back in here. Neither one of y'all." He was heated. In all honesty, Reese did tell me when I first got to Pittsburgh, "NO PORK, NO ALCOHOL, and NO POLICE!" I didn't bring it in, and from the look on his face, I'm glad it wasn't me.

"What's so bad about pork? I don't eat it, but I'm not tripping on her eating it," I said.

"Neither am I," Reese said, "but I am a Muslim. If you eat that outside, keep it outside, but under no circumstances does pork or alcohol come in here. Do you both understand?"

"Wait what? You a what? A Muslim? What is that? You mean you don't believe in God? Oh my God, and I'm here with you?"

My mind went racing double time. *I gotta get out of here. I got to get back to Cleveland.* In the three and a half weeks I had been in Pittsburgh, Reese had never stayed here. He was in and out. He would have dinner with the kids, play with them, and leave. *Does him being Muslim have anything to do with that?*

"I believe in God, Baby Sister," he said, "Muslims believe in God."

"I am a Christian," I said, "I gotta go. I can't stay here."

It's crazy how a person can do wrong and still want to lay claim to following the precepts of a religion.

"A Muslim! Ahh, you're going to hell," I said, "and I ain't going wit ya!"

"Baby Sis, you need to calm down. You don't even know what you talking about," Reese said, "Read this book, and then we will talk. But, if you have any questions, call this sister." Reese wrote down a number and a name, then handed me a book. But before I could hold the book, He told me I had to go and wash my hands.

"Do not take this book into the bathroom," he stated, "or in the kitchen while you are cooking."

There were so many books in that house, but I started reading the one Reese gave me that night. The book was the Holy Quran. I read the entire book in about a week, I mean cover to cover, all the commentary and footnotes. I couldn't stop reading. I couldn't put the book down, and I was really trying so hard to find something wrong with it. I thought if I could find something off, maybe I could help him see that this was wrong.

Reese told me he would send us home if we didn't want to stay. He also dared me to find a flaw in what I was reading. When

I had a question, I was referred to the lady whose name was on the paper he gave me. Reese wouldn't answer anything. The lady would answer my questions, then would show me where she got her answers. We lived right next door to a church; I mean, I could touch the door from my porch. I went over to ask a few questions and got the same kind of answers I had gotten at home, years before, when I wanted to sing in the choir.

To me, their explanations didn't make sense. So, I decided to call the Muslim lady to see if she could help me understand. I stared at the phone number for a while then dialed.

"We do not celebrate Christmas or Easter," the sister said. Her name was Inshirah which means the expansion. Inshirah went on to explain more. Well, the Jehovah's Witnesses I had studied with didn't celebrate those holidays, either. When I asked her why, I was given an answer that made sense to me. In fact, everything I was reading made perfect sense to me. I agreed to meet with Inshirah the next day. I went down to where the sister was located and met her.

I saw this holy-looking woman, all covered with a long dress and headwrap. She took me inside where I was instructed to remove my shoes. I went in and we sat and talked for hours.

"Saud didn't tell me exactly what you want to know," she said.

"Who is Saud?" I asked, "Saud?"

"Oh, Maurice. Reese, as you call him. His name is Saud Abu Hassan Shabazz. That's his Islamic name. Brother Malcolm gave it to him."

"Who is Brother Malcolm?" I asked. The sister is now looking at me really strangely.

"Malcolm X."

"Ooh," I said. I had never heard of Malcolm X, and I was trying to play it off as if I had.

The sister also told me that Saud and I should not be alone because we were not married. Well, technically we were not alone, Sandy was always there. It finally hit me what Inshirah was trying to tell me. She was suggesting that we get married. I was young, a widow, and had been married twice before.

I went home and told Reese what I had learned. I struggled with it for a few days. I couldn't eat or sleep. I finally fell asleep on the couch one night while Reese, Salina, Sandy, and Hassan were up watching TV. The room had gotten dark, and nobody seemed to notice.

Am I asleep? I heard this calm voice in my ear but nobody else seemed to hear it. I couldn't figure out what was going on with me. I was asleep but not asleep.

"Why do you keep denying what you know in your heart to be true?"

"Huh?" *Where is that voice coming from?* It was a calm voice, a comforting voice. I felt as if I was being hugged. Now, I was crying in my sleep, but they were tears of joy. "Why do you deny the truth? Accept it."

Does anyone else hear this except me? I heard this being said a few more times. "You cannot deny the Truth that's in your heart."

"What's wrong?" Reese kept asking me, "Why are you crying?"

"Because I'm one too."

"One what? What is wrong?"

"I cannot deny anymore who I am," I said. "What I'm learning, I believe. I am Muslim too." Reese got up and went over to turn off the TV. He asked me to repeat what I said, and he asked about what I heard in my head. The next thing I knew, three people came through the door, two men dressed in what looked like long dresses and the sister who had been answering my questions.

"She is ready to take Shahadah," Reese said.

"What's Shahadah?" I asked.

"We thought you said she was ready?" one of the men said.

"Let her tell you what she said to me. I don't want to influence her in any way.'

The Shahadah is almost like a baptism. You are declaring before witnesses that you believe what Muslims believe.

The men went on to admonish Reese for even having me there in his house in the first place. Then one man started to ask me questions.

"Do you believe in One God?"

"Yes," I said.

"One God over everything and everybody?"

"Yes," I said again.

"That He needs no partners, nor does He have any partners, and has no children?" he asked.

"What do you mean by that?" I asked.

"Do you believe that we are the sons and daughters of Adam and Eve and that we are all a part of God's creation, that He needs no partner?" he rephrased.

"Yes, I believe that," I said.

"And do you believe that Prophet Muhammad, may the peace and blessings of Allah be upon him, is the seal of the Holy Prophets? That means that Elijah Muhammad is not the seal, but the Prophet Muhammad that died 1400 years ago is the seal?"

I had read all this in the books and in the Quran and I didn't even know who Elijah Muhammad was.

"Yes, I believe that." Reese was crying, the sister was crying. I didn't understand why at the time. I was holding Salina in my arms when the brother asked me to repeat after him.

"Ashadu La ilaha illallah. Wa ashhadou an Muhammadur rasulullah."

I repeated without hesitation, "I bear witness that there is only One God, Allah and I bear witness that Muhammad is His slave, servant, and messenger."

"Allahu Akbar," they all shouted. (God is the Greatest)

Now I was crying because I finally knew what these strange words meant. At that moment, the things I had heard from Curley came rushing back. *I'm getting you ready for the next one.* I could hear him loud and clear in my head. Reese turned to me and said, "If it's not too much on you right now, I would like to marry you today while we have the witnesses here." Marry me today?! My mind was blown. He had been referring to me as his wife and Salina his child, but he never really asked me.

"How are we getting married today?"

"We have the witnesses here. We will be married Islamically in the eyes of God, then if you want to do a legal ceremony later, you can," Reese said. The sister again took me to the side and told me not to feel pressured and asked if I took Shahadah because of Reese.

"No," I said, "I really believe what I said."

"So, if you don't marry him, will you still consider yourself Muslim?" She asked.

"Yes, I would, but I only know what I believe so far."

"Well, marry him only if you want to. You don't have to." When I turned around and saw the love he had for my baby girl and how safe he made us feel, I knew I would marry him. I still didn't feel totally accepted in my new environment, but I loved my new family. I became Muslim that day, but it would be a minute before I became Mu'min (True Believer).

Faith increases and decreases. As my faith increased, I shed old habits and walked towards the path of becoming Mu'min.

My play brother, Teddy, happened to call right around this time. I'm so glad we were able to bring him some joy before he left this earth. Right after the ceremony, Reese decided to give me a name to live up to.

"Why do I need a new name?" I asked.

"You don't," he said, "but to my Muslim family, I'm Saud. (It's pronounced like Saudi, like in Saudi Arabia. It means Fortunate.) I would like for you to call me that from now on."

"Well, what do you want to call me?" I asked.

"KHADIJAH SHADIYAH SHABAZZ," he said, loudly.

"What does that mean?"

"Khadijah was a great lady, the Prophet's first wife. She was the first one to accept Muhammad, peace be upon him, as a prophet of Allah. She was a businesswoman, she was the best of women, the best of wives. Shadiyah means the one that sings, and Shabazz is my name given to me by brother Malcolm." *Again, with the brother Malcolm!*

"Who is he?" I asked. They all started laughing at me. But that day, not only had I taken Shahadah and gained a new family, but also a new name.

*In the Name of Allah, the Most Beneficent, the Most
Merciful*

*Before I go into the next part of my journey, let me explain
something. As you can see, I am a person with flaws. Any
mistakes that I make, representing or misrepresenting any
Islamic information, are my mistakes and not Islam's. May
Allah, subhanahu wa ta'ala, forgive me.*

*My flaws in no way represent the behavior of our perfect
way of life; the only way of life for me as our Lord has laid it
out for us. I am not the face of Black Muslims, and I don't
speak for them.*

*Although there will be some of you who can relate to me,
there will be some who will not and all of it is okay.*

Chapter 15: Back to Pittsburgh

I was enjoying my new life, but still had one foot in my old life. I couldn't get enough of the Islamic material I was reading and trying to understand. I was so excited that I had found a place in my own head and heart that I could call home. I did not deep dive into my newfound religion, mainly because I was still so isolated from the community and Saud's double life didn't help me grasp what was becoming my new identity. Still, I had a sense of safety that had settled in my soul.

Nightlife still called to me, and I was all too eager to answer it. Drinking and drugs never attracted me. It was always the music and the royal treatment I received as Maurice's wife. After I became Muslim, I never referred to my husband as Maurice or Reese again, unless someone else did. I always called him Saud. As I said before, his family was very prominent in the Pittsburgh area. His father and family owned many of the bars and nightclubs in the area. They also owned Walkers Vending Company, which supplied many of the Black-owned businesses with vending machines. They supplied dispensers in the ladies' room, Pac-Man machines, cigars, cigarettes, pool tables, you name it, Walkers Vending Company had it.

Saud's job was to collect the money out of the machines and take it to the bank, then take the receipts to his dad. This is all that I was aware of. Even though I had money, I never had to spend any on clothes or household expenses. But I loved treating my friends. Whenever I would go out, whoever was with me could put their money away. I loved to treat people to a good time.

Although I was around many people, doing a whole lot of things, Saud did not allow me to sit in conversations about business, period. He handled all business affairs and with his earnings, he took care of me and the children. I didn't have to work, nor did I have to spend any money I had. My husband did encourage me to open my own business if I wanted to. But under no circumstances were my business ventures for my daily living.

I was in the loop, and out of the loop, at the same time. I justified my actions because I did not do drugs, sell drugs, or drink, nor did I see any of those things.

Every week, I received two stacks of money; one for bills, the other for me to spend as I liked. If I spent all the money allotted to me, I would have to wait until the following week to get more.

I never bought any clothes out of a store. It would be years before I went into a mall to shop. Everything that I wore came from the back of someone's car. All I know is that what came out of those car trunks wasn't cheap! I have never been into designer clothes, but I do gravitate towards quality. Back then I couldn't see myself going crazy over somebody's name across my body. I would try to take the labels off. We were all into leather, silk, and furs, and I had my share but ask me where they are today, I can't tell you lol.

Saud wouldn't wear silk or gold. For years, I didn't understand why. Saud sported a beaver-skin jacket and wore platinum and jade jewelry. I had 18-karat gold and emeralds. I even had gold pinky fingernails. Ya know, my hand had to be fly holding that mic, right? At times I would show up in spaces where Saud was hanging out. The ladies would be glued to his side as I watched their eyes roll towards me. I always greeted him with a smile and a kiss and held my hands out to receive any money that he may have earned. I'd smile at the ladies and leave. I would be hot as fish grease. I'd be so mad, but I would never let anyone see me sweat.

There was one evening a young lady showed up while Saud and I were having dinner. She attempted to do what I did and collect money from him. But when she attempted to disrespect me by leaning in to kiss his cheek, his eyes flashed, and he told her to move back. She moved a little but took another approach. She started talking loudly at him. Security came and escorted her behind right out of the building.

The next day this young lady had the audacity to call me, laughing at me, and saying things about my husband and her.

"Judy, I'm sorry you are being treated so unfairly by my husband," I said to her very politely. Today I have a very colorful vocabulary, but back then I rarely used harsh words or profanity.

I have always scared myself with my silence because when silence comes out of me, it manifests itself in unproductive ways.

She was screaming at the top of her lungs at me.

"Why are you calling me?" I asked her. "Is it something that you need? You know, if Saud knew you were calling me, he would not like it," I told her. "If you don't believe what I'm saying then when he calls you, put me on a three-way and say what you are saying." Judy continued to shout at me and the louder she got, the quieter I got.

"Listen, Judy," I said, "obviously you are upset." Low key, I was mad as hell. She went on to say what she was doing with him and what she expected. "Well Judy, if Saud knew you called me, your perks would stop today, and so what I'm going to do is send you a parting gift, you can accept it and move on, or accept it and keep your mouth shut. I don't know anything about what my husband does for a living. My day consists of watching *All My Children*, reading, and shopping. If you think that you are more than a business partner then you need to take that up with Reese, not me, 'cause I promise you, to call me is the wrong move. Your choice."

I really felt bad for Judy. I never knew what happened to her. I don't know if she continued some kind of relationship with Saud or broke it off. It was not my concern. Saud never showed any aggression, violence, verbal or otherwise towards me, in all of our 27 years. Of course, he had some bad manners and behaviors. But those changed over time through his accepting and living the life of a believing Muslim.

Listen up! People have always held Black Muslims to a higher standard than Christians, but the same things that are impermissible for Muslims are also impermissible for Christians. **Don't forget it!** I pray that before Allah takes our souls, that we get it right. In shaa Allah.

يَـٰٓأَيُّهَا ٱلَّذِينَ ءَامَنُوا۟ ٱتَّقُوا۟ ٱللَّهَ حَقَّ تُقَاتِهِۦ وَلَا تَمُوتُنَّ إِلَّا وَأَنتُم مُّسْلِمُونَ يَـٰ

O you who have believed, Fear Allah as he should be feared,
and don't die unless you are Muslim. Al Quran 3:102

Chapter 16: Time to Tell Mommy!

Enough was enough, a month after taking Shahadah, I decided to call home to tell my parents that I would not be returning home, that I had changed my religion and name, and married for the third time. The conversation went something like this: "Hi Ma, I'm still in Pittsburgh," I said. To be honest, in my heart, I was hoping that she'd ask me to come home.

"I'm fine and so is Salina." I stuttered, "Ma, do you remember the man that came by your house a few months back and you gave him my address and phone number?" I questioned, trying to jog her memory.

"What about him?" Mommy asked.

"Well, me and him got married." In that moment, the silence between us was maddening.

"You're talking about Maurice?"

"Yes Ma, I call him Saud. Saud is his other name. He's a Muslim Mommy and I am too. I have learned so much in these past few weeks about Islam. Did you know that they don't celebrate Christmas either, just like the Witnesses don't?" Again, silence. "Ma, are you there? ... Ma?"

"So, you joined a cult, huh?" my mother asked.

"Ma, what did you say? No, I didn't join a cult. It's the same God as..." I tried to say a few more words before she interrupted me.

"You joined a cult!"

"It's not a cult Momma, really."

"Oh, so you one of them Black Mooslems that hate White people?" Mommy went on to say.

"Huh, no I don't hate anybody. Ma listen..."

"No, you listen," she said, "talk to me again when you give your life over to Christ, other than that you are going to hell." Then she hung up. I knew it would be bad, but I didn't think it would be that bad. I was now hoping that telling Daddy and the rest of my family would not go down as bad.

I was still clubbing most nights. I never had an interest in drugs and alcohol though, it was the music and the clothes. I loved the way us Black folks dressed. I would step out on the town with Sandy or Freckles. Freckles was another sister I met who would become like family to me. We maintained a lifetime friendship of Sisterhood not comparable to anyone else. We would go to the clubs and after-hours clubs. We would listen to the music, and they would drink. I wasn't a drinker, but the few times I did try it, one drink, and I was stupid crazy, two drinks, and I would want to fight. And I had absolutely no fight game. I couldn't fight my way out of a wet paper bag.

Just two drinks and I was known for climbing on top of the bar, and I'd walk it from one end to the other, telling people about themselves. After this happened twice, I didn't want any more liquor and the bartender was instructed not to serve me any! There was always some female trying to pick a fight. I wasn't scared and I wouldn't back down, but I couldn't fight a lick. I was a pretty good shot though!! I'll leave that story right there!

I was getting a reputation for having a smart mouth, and Saud would hear about it and told me that after the last incident I wasn't allowed in the after-hours clubs without him, and I couldn't go alone into any bar that his family didn't own. I only went out hoping to be discovered in the first place. Saud did have a lot of connections, but for some reason he never found the time to hook me up. I made a demo tape, but it never got out.

While sitting in the Lowendi After-Hours Club, I watched as this man walked in with two girls on his arm, all dressed to sho' nuff impress. The band was playing my song and I sat there humming and singing along to *Somewhere in my Lifetime* by Phillis Hyman, my absolute favorite of hers.

"You sound pretty good," the handsome man said, as he and the two ladies sat next to me. "Do that run again. That was really clean," he said. But me and my smart-alec-self looked over my shoulder and asked, "Are you talking to me?"

"Yes," he said, "I've been sitting here listening to you. You got skills? Let me hear that run again," he asked very enthusiastically. *This is some pimp with his girls on his side. Let me get him straight right quick.*

"Look, honey," I said, "I'm glad you liked what you heard, but I don't do this for free."

"Oh, you don't," the handsome stranger said.

"No, I don't, and I also don't talk to pimps. In fact, I can't stand pimps. So, unless you got some dead presidents I don't humm or la la for free!" The handsome stranger and his two girls just looked at each other and laughed out loud.

"OK," he said.

Now the bartender is laughing at me. I am getting angrier because this overdressed pimp is laughing and everyone sitting at the bar is laughing too. The handsome stranger got up to leave and told the man they were talking to that he had to catch a plane for Hawaii and had to go.

Hawaii my butt.

"Hey, Khadijah," the bartender said, "you really don't know who that was, do you?"

"Naw," I said, "Who is he, some pimp that was trying to impress me?"

"Naw girl, wit yo dumb ass," the bartender said, "that was George Benson. Georgie. You know, who got the album *Breezin'* and has the hit *This Masquerade*? How do you not know who he was? Girl, he is looking for backup singers and you just told him off like that." I was so embarrassed OMG, and of course it got back to Saud who then told me that I wasn't allowed out at night without him, because I would cause him a problem sooner or later.

I pretended that was alright because I was really losing interest in the whole nightlife scene, but really inside I was so upset with myself, not understanding that my destiny was already formed. Sandy had introduced me to a few people and one of them was my dearest friend, Layne. To this day she is the friend that I haven't seen for years but know that she is always there. She was the only person that I would let babysit Salina and Hassan. I spent my days like most housewives, bored, but I continued reading my Islamic books.

Mommy thought I was in a cult, so I began to read more on my newfound belief, and the more I read, the more I understood and was convinced I had been led to Islam. Thanks to Allah and His love for me, Islam began to change my life and mold my character and behavior. I could have been the biggest alcoholic, dope fiend, or dead.

I wanted to have more information so that I could explain it better the next time we spoke. That was, if she'd talk to me.

لَآ إِكۡرَاہَ فِى ٱلدِّينِ

There is no compulsion in religion. Al Quran 2:256.

This means we cannot force anyone into our way of life, it is not permitted.

لَكُمۡ دِينُكُمۡ وَلِىَ دِينِ
And to you be religion and to me be mine. Al Quran 109:6

Now, if anyone wants more information, I've provided a means for you to look it up yourself. Allah guides whom He pleases, and who He chooses to guide is not for me to comment on. Most people who know very little about Islam judge it by the actions and cultures of others and not by the teachings of Allah in the Holy Quran or the example of our Holy Prophet Muhammad, who was instructed by Allah and did nothing on his own. We don't pray to Muhammad or any man. If those of us who believe in God, be you Muslim, Christian, or Jewish, if you were to pick your belief based on the actions of others who claim to believe as you do, who would want to follow any of it? I definitely wasn't a blind follower, in fact, I was asking Saud questions about why we were still doing certain things that we both knew were Haram (forbidden). The more I studied, the more I wanted to learn, and learn, I did.

With all of the new things happening in my life, the feelings of loneliness still overshadowed me. I missed my sisters and other family members. I wanted to show them that I was OK and being treated well. All I wanted was their approval. It would be years before I would stop feeling that need.

Desperately needing and seeking the approval of others dims your light and prevents you from doing extraordinary things.

It was my two grandmothers that told me that they were proud of me and for me to keep on doing good deeds.

"Khadijah," my Nana said into the phone. I was shocked that she referred to me as Khadijah.

"Yes ma'am," I responded.

"Let me ask you a question."

"Okaaay." *Here we go.*

 Do you believe in God?"

"Yes ma'am."

"And Jesus?"

"Yes ma'am, just not quite the same as you do. We Muslims have to believe in Jesus and his miraculous birth and all the miracles he performed with God's permission. We also have to believe in the original books which include the Bible and the Torah, and yes, we believe that Jesus is coming back and will fix this division between us all with God's Permission," I explained.

"That's all I needed to know," she said, "I believe we have some cousins in Pittsburgh, I'll send you their information. Look them up, they are on your grandfather's side of the family." I was now staring at the phone in disbelief and tears falling down my face. Allahu Akbar, (God is Great!) My Nana still loves me and accepts me, as a Nana would. A few weeks later, I got a call almost identical to Nana's from my Granny. Now, my granny had been the church secretary at St. James in Atlantic city on Baltic Ave for a million years. Every church service that there ever was, she was there.

"Let me ask you something," Granny said. That's how she started the conversation. Granny was a bit sterner than Nana. "Are you doing OK?" she asked.

"Yes ma'am," I said.

"Well, what have you been up to?" She went on in her questioning. I was not about to tell my Granny about no nightclub life.

"Granny, I am really OK, for real," I said.

"You believe in God?"

"Yes, I do. I'm not in a cult Granny. Mommy seems to think that I am. I don't hate white people and I believe in Jesus," I confessed

"OK," she said, "that's all I wanted to know."

That's it? No more questions? I had all this anxiety and that is the end of the questioning? Thank you, Allah.

In the years to come, Saud and I progressed as a family. I would ask him stories about his life as I continued to read everything that I could about Islam. The stories he told me were larger than life.

Only a few of my new friends were Muslim. I wondered why we didn't go to the masjid often, or at all in most cases. I found out later that Saud had a problem with the Imam (minister). But, I had hardly any Islamic identity outside of our home. There were always a lot of brothers around that came by to ask Saud for advice on Islamic topics, and he would answer them and then he would go on to provide them with evidence of his statements, often quoting the book, chapter, and page where the answer could be found. If he had a question, he'd call or write the author of the book. He was always there to help out a friend and we both loved to host guests. Saud was a very generous person; he often reminded me of the character Robinhood. I am not glorifying bad behavior or crime, but I never saw him do anything against anyone, that is, unless you crossed him; violating family, friends, or children.

When I wanted to know anything about a subject or a person, the most important thing I learned and learned well, was to go straight to the source if I could. Saud also taught me that when it came to Islam, our opinions didn't count. If Islamic information doesn't come from the Quran and/or the Sunnah (the way of life of our prophet, peace be upon him), then we don't add or take from it. Period.

Every night, I would hear another story about my husband's life before me.

"Saud," I asked, "just how many times were you in prison?" I seriously wanted to know.

"Before or after I ran away from bad boys' school?" he laughed, as he began to answer my questions.

"What the heck is a bad boys' school Saud?"

"Reform school," he said. "I was sent to Morganza Reform School for Boys when I was 17 years old, to this work camp. While I was there, they sent a baseball scout for the Pittsburgh Pirate Farm Club Organization. Me and some of the other guys were pretty good. I played shortstop for the Pony League while I was there. The other inmates and the warden got jealous when we kept winning every game. Our punishment for winning the games was that the warden wouldn't let us play. When the scout asked about us, the warden would give a phony reason why we couldn't play. Also, the points we were making as a team that made us qualified, were suddenly mysteriously missing."

Saud went on to tell me that when he got the chance, he just walked away from Morganza.

"I hitchhiked back to Detroit!" he said.

"Dang! Really!? Nobody ever caught you or looked for you?" I asked.

"Well, if they did, they didn't look in the right place," he said, as he pulled his newspaper back over his face.

"What about the bank robbery?" I asked, deep into his story.

"You awfully nosy," was his reply, with a grin. And with that, he turned his face back to his newspaper.

One thing Saud never did was give names; he would never say what anyone did except himself. But he'd prove to me what he was saying was true by the paperwork or old news articles. Before we got married, Saud told me that his rules were these; never bring pork or alcohol into the house, and under no condition, unless it was a 911 call for a medical condition, do we call the police. We still roll like that. But I would not fully understand that until much later either.

Saud also began to tell me about his life as a Muslim and being a Black Muslim in Detroit, New York, and in the American prison system. Saud had been gassed, put in solitary confinement, fed broken glass, and beaten, all while trying to get Muslim rights implemented; the same as Christians and Jews had while in federal and state custody. He helped stage a hunger strike trying to get halal foods in prisons, and it was successful. He also told me about the hit that was put out on his life, while in prison, and how they almost got away with it.

Saud won the decision, Walker vs. the State of Pennsylvania. When this happened, they really made it hard for him. The authorities kept Saud on parole for 25 years after serving his time, mainly because he never snitched about any money and because he became an infamous jewel thief; but also because of his affiliation with Malcolm X, Louis X, the sons of Elijah Muhammad, and the siblings of Malcolm. Now, none of these Muslims had any dealings with anything that Saud did back then. Just being Muslim was enough to get you followed by the feds and police.

Malcolm X was Saud's teacher while he lived in Detroit. According to Saud, Malcolm tried to guide him to do right. Being an old street hustler himself, game recognizes game. Saud told me that it was Malcolm who gave him his name. He originally met him at the Shabazz Restaurant in Detroit. The owners of that restaurant were the ones who introduced him to Islam and were a second family to him. I know that he loved all of them. He would talk about this family often. There was one sister, in particular, in that family he truly loved until the day he died! He loved her.

Saud was about 19 at the time and he told me about the lessons Malcolm taught him in and out of classes. Some were held at the temple, some were not. The last time he saw Malcolm, they were on the Brooklyn Bridge. Malcolm was going to teach a class and Saud was going to hit a bank. He regretted not listening to Brother Malcolm. I was learning more and more about Malcolm X. Of course, this gave me a sense of pride with my new surname, Shabazz. My whole new name was something to live up too.

Listening to these stories held some meaning for me, but as time went on my understanding became clearer. There were limited opportunities for Saud to 'go straight', trying to hold down a job with a criminal record, making pennies. Holding down a family today, still ain't easy. In all fairness, Saud did have a family, a well-to-do family. For some reason unknown to me, Saud tried to handle his business on his own.

Living up to family expectations isn't easy. When a man is not used to handouts or working for other people, this becomes a sore spot. If you feel like your family may suffer, it's only a matter of time before you seek to do something. You can have all the education you want and all of the street life you want. We all have a destiny to fulfill, with lessons to learn and teach. Some of us have to walk back and forth through the fire in order to come out whole, with a greater understanding.

Prophet Yusef (Joseph) was in prison for many years. He asked for help from a fellow prisoner before asking Allah to help him. I am not comparing Prophet Yusef to Saud, Prophet Yusef was innocent, but spent a great amount of time in prison. Saud, like a hella number of Black African American men, spend an unjust, ungodly amount of time on these legal plantations, innocent or guilty, so the stories are relatable. Saud would later in life confess to me how his last stay in prison prepared him for his inevitable journey.

Saud had Hassan with him the entire time we were together. After 35 years, I have yet to meet or speak to Hassan's birth mom. I have never spoken to her, I have never seen her, nor have I ever seen a picture of her. She dropped Hassan off with Saud and left, and never came back. But what she did, was collect her son's disability money for years, unbeknownst to us. To this day, I don't know if she is living or dead. Hassan also had two brothers by his biological mom that we have never seen. He may have more siblings. I don't know what Hassan can understand. I hope it's not too painful for him, if he can remember her.

Saud was having some sort of a disagreement with his family, and it came time for us to leave 3202 Iowa Street. He was also without a job. He had been fired from the family business because of a dispute. The dispute had nothing to do with money or anything underhanded. It was a family dispute.

***

With everything going on we had to move. We had just found a new home to rent, in Wilkinsburg, at 561 Peebles Street. With little or no money coming in, Reese was unbearable to deal with. I wasn't allowed to work unless it was some business that I could open. But he would not take any money from me, so even if I did make some ends, it was to be used for whatever I wanted or needed, not bills.

I don't know what he did, but whatever business dealings Reese came up with were productive because he came home one day smiling from ear to ear.

"What you smiling at?" I asked.

"The best wife in the world. Alhamdulillah, all praise is for God."

"What does that mean?" I asked, smiling too, because I knew I was about to get a big surprise. Plus, it was close to my birthday. We didn't really celebrate birthdays, but Reese had been hinting around that I had something coming.

***

This time in my life was new for me. I was slowing down with with all the clubbing and joining grassroots groups around Pittsburgh.

One day, Salina and I walked out of our home on Peebles Street down to Penn Ave. to join hands with the Hands Across America protest. Everywhere you looked, from one shoulder to the next, strangers held hands in solidarity with the poor and disenfranchised to combat hunger and homelessness in America. This was 1986 and the beginning of my formal activism.

Hands Across America Protest

In 2022, we still here, barely making a dent in hunger, homelessness, and the prisons of America.

Shame is something the greatest nation on earth should have a lot of. But instead it's arrogance that she definitely has. And that is in abundance.

Chapter 17: Cars, Furs, and JT?

I was making friends. Sandy had hooked me up with a few; Linda, Laura, Freckles, and Madelyn. Linda had a man named Bubbah who was a sadistic SOB. He was one of Reese's associates. I tried not to be around him too much because he liked to hit women. He probably hated his mom or something. Beating women seemed to be a favorite pastime in Pittsburgh. Soon, I would see another friend get beaten at the hands of her husband and it would change my world forever.

Reese was back to staying out at night, sometimes coming in days later. Money was not a problem, so I didn't understand why he was gone for so long.

"Look outside," he said to me, rushing into the house after being gone a few days. I looked up and down the street.

"What?" I asked, "Look where?"

"You don't see that big ass car?" he said.

"The one that's in front of the house?" I asked.

"Why would I be talking about any other one?" he asked.

"Yeah, I see it, what about it?" I said, with my smile turned upside down.

"You don't want it?" Reese shouted.

"It's for me?" I asked, "but you know I don't drive."

"That's your problem," he said, "the car is yours!"

So this was the big surprise he had hinted at before! I went outside to see the car. It was a 1982 Volvo; the car was only four years old. Inside on the backseat was a midi fox fur jacket.

"This mine too?!" I squealed, as I snatched it out of the car window. It was in May, and it was getting warm outside. I'm now trying to figure out how to wear fur when it's almost June. I grabbed my husband's neck, and he swung me around, as I expressed how much I loved my gifts.

"But I can't drive," I said.

"That's your problem. The car is paid for. Get one of your friends to teach you or go to driving school."

"You not gonna teach me?" I asked.

"Nope," was his response, and he didn't. I had not been going out much, just hanging with my friends and kids. I learned that Linda and Bubbah were meeting us later at this club in McKeesport. It was my birthday and Saud had planned a big party for me. It was the only birthday party that I had ever had. Sandy was nowhere to be found; she had fallen off the wagon and was heavy into her heroin addiction. When she was bad she would not come around.

My party was everything. I had on a midi sequined dress with matching shoes. I put in my contact lenses and had my makeup and hair done. In the 80s, the only people that did this were the rich and entertainers. (I thought I was both.) I didn't drive, however. Pittsburgh had a jitney service, something Cleveland didn't have. A jitney service was an old-fashioned cab, cheaper than a yellow cab. And this was way before Lyft and Uber. The drivers would sit around a station and wait for a call to come in over the phone that hung on the wall. They'd ask where you were located and come pick you up. I didn't ride the bus; this is how my bougie butt got around.

After spending a nice time out with my husband and friends, once again, I found myself drawn to the nightlife. I simply loved it, but this time it wasn't as appealing as it once was. I would still attend anywhere that had a gong show or talent show, or wherever they would let me sit in with the band.

Linda, or my other friend Laura, would drive to my house and then let me drive my car to wherever we were going, and I must say, all praises be to Allah that we survived that. I never had a car accident. It was Allah who was looking after this foolish fool, me! I would drive into the parking lot, jump out of the car, and ask somebody to park it for me. As long as the car was going in one straight line, we were good, just don't let me backup or park, you couldn't tell me nothing. I was 23/24 years old and brand new to everything. I had a bad understanding! My bad understanding, meaning my spoiled-rotten behind is what got me a car – so what I can't drive, but I'm driving it anyway.

I loved to be out with my friends any time of the day or night. I loved to spoil them with gifts. I wasn't showing off or looking for anything in return, I just loved the feeling of giving. But a few so-called friends over the years have tried to use my kindness as weakness. They would quickly find out that they were mistaken.

One of the first things I learned and or tried to embrace was, "Want for your sister what you want for yourself." I also learned, if my sister is in need and I have it and don't need it, then it's really not mine to keep. To this day it disturbs me to know that someone is in need and I can't help, or at least try to help. Also, the lesson that I learned years prior to this, the one about asking for material things stuck with me. The smell and what was in the trunk of that car came back to me and will live with me forever. So, I am grateful for everything, big and small.

The car was nice. The fur and jewelry were nice. I like nice things but have never been materialistic or designer-struck, and I am grateful for that.

I was still struggling with my driving. I could have gone to driving school, but all my friends said it wasn't a necessity, they could teach me for free. Car insurance wasn't a factor then, so I could keep my money for something else. My husband only said to me that if I tore it up, I wouldn't get another one. Winter was upon us, and I took every opportunity to drive, but most of my friends could not get out during the day because of work or household duties. Laura and I had made plans for an upcoming weekend, and I was ready to try my hand at driving in what may be snow. After dropping the kids off at Layne's house, I took a deep breath and began my drive to pick up Laura, then on to McKeesport to the club. After we arrived, she and I sat at the bar, me drinking a virgin non-alcoholic drink and Laura drinking whatever she was drinking. Suddenly, I heard a loud shout coming towards us.

"Get your ass up and out of here," he said. I did not move because I didn't know who was talking or who he was talking to. I zeroed in on who was talking. He had on a full-length, black diamond mink coat. He was over six feet tall, not bad looking, but that is all I could assess before he pushed past me. Before I could react, Laura was on the floor. He had slapped her down. She was screaming and yelling for anyone to help. I jumped up only to see that this maniac had a bottle in his hand. Just as he was about to hit me in the face, the owner, an older lady named Maureen, stepped in between me and the bottle. It caught her on the shoulder but didn't do much damage. She knew my husband well. She was renting the club out from the Walker family.

"John," she yelled over the jukebox music, "you don't want to do this. This is Reese Walker's wife."

"I don't give a fuck who this bitch is," he said, "she jumping in my business with my wife,"

"Wife! Who his wife?" I said as Laura got up off the floor and tried to get out of his swinging range.

"I am," she answered.

"I didn't even know you were married," I yelled back at her. I don't even know what was said or what happened after that. I was confused.

"I didn't know she was married," I said to Maureen.

"Yeah," Maureen said, "and to a fool at that."

I knew this wasn't going to be good. The first time I'm out by myself, and now this? I was feeling like a fish out of water as it was. The new things I was learning about Islam and believing, but not living, it was beginning to affect me. I felt like I was in the crowd, in the mix, but not yet a part of the crowd.

Anyway, Laura had left with her husband, which meant I had to drive back by myself. At least that time of night there was no traffic, and I wouldn't have to worry about backing up and parking. I picked up Salina and Hassan from my friend Layne's house and drove home, still in shock about what had just happened. I was worried that Laura wasn't OK and back then there were no telephones, no voicemails, and no text messages to see if she was.

I told Saud what happened and with his usual quiet self, he asked me if I got hurt or did Maureen, the owner get hurt. I told him I wasn't hurt and that I believed Maureen was OK as well. He went right back to reading, then looked up, and before he could say anything I said, "Yeah, I know I can't go back there without you." Nor did I want to.

"You need to find a driving school," he said, "before you tear up your ride because if you tear it up being hardheaded, then I'm not buying you another one," he said.

"OK," I said. But I never did.

I usually knew when Saud was planning to be away for a few days because bill money and pocket money would always be left on the dresser, but he'd never tell me about his comings and goings. So, he could have been around the corner or halfway around the world. I pretended that this didn't bother me, but of course it did. Not knowing what he was up to always worried me. I worried that one day he may not come back, and then what? I'm still in a city where I only know a handful of people.

Pittsburgh, with the exception of the folks mentioned and an older relative I encountered, was a cold place to live. It was the most racist place I had ever lived. I had never been called a nigger in my life, but I was called one by a group of white men hanging out of a car window on Penn Ave. in broad daylight. I was just crossing the street, when they rolled the window down and called me a nigger bitch, and that I had better hurry up and get out of the crosswalk. At that time, Pittsburgh had never had a Black elected anything. To me, it really had a small-town-good-ole-boy feeling.

I knew my husband was coming home soon because there was no money left out and groceries were low. Just like when my daddy was hurt in the car accident, I had a bad feeling. I went to bed feeling so uneasy, almost sick to the point of fainting. This time another kind of hurt was on the way.

My phone was ringing, and it woke me up. I must have fallen asleep not long before it started to ring but it scared me, nonetheless. The pit of my stomach was turning.

"Hello," I said.

"Are you awake?" It was Laura on the other end of the phone.

"I fell asleep," I said. "What's up?"

"Is your husband home?" she asked.

"No," I said as I sat straight up. Now noticing that her voice was funny, she sounded as if she were crying.

"What's the matter? I asked her.

"So, you haven't heard?" Laura asked me. Now she was crying hard.

"Heard what? I was asleep. What's going on?" I said, trying to shake off my sleepiness.

"John, my husband was shot and killed tonight, and they said Reese did it!"

I sat there in silence for I don't know how long. I don't even remember the rest of the conversation or even if we had one. From that day to this, I don't remember if Laura and I ever spoke again. Our little daughters were friends with each other and had play dates before all this happened. The phone was ringing again. I could hear it in the distance, or it just sounded like it was coming from a distance.

"As salaamu alaikum," I said.

"Wa alaikum salaam. So, I guess you heard," Saud was saying to me.

"Laura said that someone killed her husband. Until that incident in the club, I never knew she was married. She never mentioned him."

"Did you hear who they thought did it?" he asked. Silence. Then I said, "Yes, she did mention someone."

"Did you see the news?" he asked.

"It's on now," I said, "they are saying someone by the name of John Taylor was shot and killed by someone in the *Name of the Game*. Ain't that your dad's place?" I asked.

"Did they say it was self-defense?" Reese asked me, ignoring my question.

"They didn't, but Laura mentioned you. Are you asking me something or telling me something Reese?"

"Neither," Reese said, "you know I can't come home. I will call you."

Chapter 18: He Can't Come Home!

After a few weeks of not hearing anything from Saud, in the middle of the night came again the ringing of the phone.

"Open the back door and don't turn on the lights," a really faint voice came through the receiver, then silence.

I had moved since the incident in the bar. The Feds were following me everywhere, hoping I would lead them to my husband. I really didn't know where he was. Saud had always been on federal parole, and this is why the feds hounded me and him. They really could care less about a Black man killing another Black man. I had moved from the house on Pebbles Street, because they kept following me. I moved deeper into Wilkinsburg.

The North Avenue residence was a three-story walk-up. I would have to go down the back steps in the dark in order to open the door. It was about 2 AM. I hugged the wall as I went blindly down the steps, scared to death, not knowing if he would make it to the back door.

He must have used a payphone somewhere in the area and just took a chance to call me because no doubt my phone was tapped. We could always hear them listening to us. When he did call, all of my friends' lines were tapped. Elayne and I could always hear them sneezing or saying something in the background. As Allah would have it, not tonight, though. When I finally made it to the bottom of the steps, I could hear him outside of the door. He had parked a few streets over and walked to the apartment.

It had started to snow. Thank You Allah for the snow because it covered Saud's tracks.

We crept back up the stairs, praying that no one saw him. We had to be quiet, we couldn't trust the neighbors not to tell. When we finally made it back up and inside, I couldn't help but faint. All that emotion was too much for me. I came to rather quickly and Saud was just sitting with me, putting a cold towel on my face.

"Where have you been Saud?" I asked. Saud had been in touch with me through a few of his partners. They set me up to move and get out of the watchful eye of the Feds, who were looking for Saud for murder and a jewelry store robbery.

He stayed with us for a few days. We made plans for our next step, then he disappeared back into the night. Saud would remain on that federal parole until the day he died. Those dirty bastards even came to my home to find him and lock him up for that parole violation years later, after he had been dead a year!

Of course, the Feds followed me from Peebles Street to North Avenue. Everywhere I went, they would pop up. I would open up my bedroom curtains, only to see them with their binoculars watching me. They followed me to the store and to the laundromat. They would cough into the phone, so I would know they were listening. Finally, one day, they came to the door to question me

"You know he has another family in Detroit," the big ugly one said. "You are too young to throw your life away on a murdering lowlife like Maurice, you are going to get into trouble."

Now it was the handsome bad cop's turn.

"F*** her, we should lock her up and show this black bitch what she's really up against."

What I really wanted to do was spit on both of them. I was still stuck on him calling my husband a lowlife. As they got up to leave, the handsome asshole said, "Be careful driving at night by yourself."

The next day, I got up to go shopping and my car was gone. Somebody stole my dang car; damn, I can't call the police. Imma have to call one of Saud's partners and let them know that the Volvo is gone. The car was gone for about two days when miraculously it reappeared, parked in front of my house. Maybe Saud took it. Anyway, it was cold outside, and I gathered Salina up with Hassan and got the dog. We had a beautiful red Malamute named Sgt. York. It was a present we got for Salina.

"Let's go get in the car, y'all," I said, waving to them to follow me. I was still not good at driving, and I didn't go very far in the snow. I didn't want to get stuck anywhere. I put on my Anita Baker cassette tape, and we were out. The car was dirty and had black dust all over it. I wondered where Saud had taken it and why. There was black dust all over the inside as well.

Pittsburgh is very hilly, just like San Francisco; up one street and down the other. I went to visit my friend, got groceries, then headed home around 8 PM. I was slowing down to go down a very steep hill, plus it was snowing and getting slippery, too slippery for an unskilled driver. I thought I would just use my brakes, pumping them lightly until I could reach the bottom, but the car wouldn't slow down, and the brakes were not working. I couldn't slow the car down! I was about to be smack dab in the middle of ongoing traffic if I couldn't stop this car. *My God, it's sliding in the snow and ice.*

Nobody had on a seat belt, we didn't use them like that back then. We were heading straight for Penn Avenue, a major street. Salina, Hassan, and the dog were now in the front with me. How they got there, I don't know. To the right of me, just before I would be in oncoming traffic was a snowbank. The snowplow had made a huge mound, so I headed for it. I turned the car in its direction, and by Allah's permission it worked. Me and the kids were fine. People stopped to see if we were OK. There was a payphone nearby, so I got out and called our mechanic, Doug. He arrived with a tow truck and took the car to his shop. He called me two days later to say I could pick up the car, free of charge. When I arrived, Doug was at lunch, so I just took the car and left. I had such an uneasy feeling because the traffic was heavy, and I couldn't concentrate. The bottom line is, I was scared to drive. At the red light on Penn and Herron, I put the car in park, got out, walked to the pay phone, and called me a jitney.

When I got home, I called Doug to tell him that he could go get the car and I would tell him what to do with the car as soon as I heard from Reese. Doug told me that I should have waited for him because he wanted to tell me that my brake line had been cut deliberately, and that the black dirt was fingerprint powder! The Feds had taken my car hoping to kill Saud or us both. I can't tell you what happened to that car. I never went back to see it. I left it at the red light in the middle of the street. I grabbed Salina and went home.

"Saud," I muttered.

"Shhhhh, before someone hears you." Saud had managed to sneak back home to give me some money and to see his dad. We had made it inside. We began telling our stories of what had happened over the last few weeks, which had turned into almost a month.

"I was coming to get that car. Damn, I can't believe you left it in traffic though. I bet I won't be buying your ass another one," he joked.

"Why would the police do that?" I asked. "You don't understand why the police or the Feds cut the break line," he said, as if I was asking a stupid question.

"I thought you took the car, that's the only reason I even drove it."

"I have not been able to leave here. They are watching me everywhere."

Now truth be told, the police and the Feds could give two shits about John Taylor or Saud. It was Saud's connections and ties that sparked their interests. It was also a way to discredit his family as a prominent Black business, owned and operated.

Saud told me that he had been to New York, watched football games, visited old flames, you name it, and they were all so worried about him. I was glad to see my husband. He told me what happened that night at the **Name of the Game**, something that we hadn't had a chance to talk about, as it was not something to talk about over the phone. He told me that he was in the bar that night because he would be getting the change out of the jukeboxes that belonged to his dad.

This big dude in a full-length black diamond mink coat came in ranting and raving about someone slashing his car tires, cussing out everyone. Saud said he was comical in this big coat. He described the guy as being well over six feet tall, Saud was five foot eight. He went on to say the man began to approach him and he mumbled to himself that he hoped that fool was not coming over to him. But, too late.

"What the fuck you looking at?" the fool asked. Saud remained silent and watched as the man came closer to him.

"You must have done it," he said. "You standing over there with that smirk on your face."

Just as the man stepped towards him, Saud noticed the gun at his waist. As the man went for his gun, Saud intercepted and took it from him and laid him down. Saud shot the man several times with the guy's own gun and killed him. Saud then walked out of the bar.

"Wow," I said, "did you know that John Taylor was Laura's husband?"

"No, not at that time. I found out later who he was. Anyway, you don't pull a gun unless you're gonna use it. I took it from him and laid him down. I wasn't gonna play with him, he was much bigger than me," he explained. "Tomorrow I'm going to turn myself in."

"You what?" I replied.

"I have an attorney, and my dad has my bail. As soon as I turn myself in, they are gonna pay it," he comforted me from my state of shock.

"How much?" I asked.

"50,000 cash or property."

"So, how much of that will you need?" I asked, astonished at the monetary amount.

"$50,000 cash or property!" In the 80s, $50,000 was unheard of, but Saud's dad put the bail up for his son, and Saud turned himself in. He was released a few hours later and sent home to await trial.

Those few months were bittersweet. I was glad to have my husband home, but of course, we had to be careful. People were upset that he was free and jealous of him because of how he got free. Not a lot of Black folks have 50k lying around and are able to pay a full cash bail, plus property. And on top of that, another 50k for an attorney that secured his bail and represented him at trial.

People said that Saud's attorney was one of the best, but hell, I could have used that 50k and represented him myself! All of the questions I had asked were never asked. I felt they were important questions, like the fact that Saud was working in his family's business. John Taylor's family's attorney kept saying that Saud had been hanging around, not drinking, and had no business in the bar that night. Which was not true. He had every right to be there because he was working. Something that should have been addressed was the fact that he wasn't drinking because he didn't drink! He was trying to put the idea into the jury's minds that Saud had no good reason to be in the bar.

The prosecution kept emphasizing how John was shot and where. We all knew that Saud shot him and proving that Saud took the gun from John was easy, had they listened. They were describing how the incident could have happened, and I kept telling them how it didn't happen as they described, because Saud was left-handed! Every witness from the prosecution lied and said Saud pulled the gun out of his right side pocket! An important piece of information, right?

The pockets on the jacket Saud wore that night were too small to hold a gun and no gunpowder residue was found on the jacket. That jacket was identified by John Taylor's attorney and witness. I thought that was good, because now all Saud's attorney had to do was to prove it could not have happened as stated. It would have proved that John's witnesses were lying or mistaken. Me being younger and female, they dismissed what I was trying to say, that my husband killed a man in self-defense. He was found guilty of third-degree murder.

There are times in our lives when days of reckoning come. Sometimes we answer for past transgressions that we may have thought we'd gotten away with. But this reckoning comes around and we sometimes lose part of our lives, or it's at the expense of our own lives.

Chapter 19: Making Plans

"Khadijah," Saud shook me out of my daydream, "you know I'm not going to go walking into no prison cell. The catching comes before the hanging."

"Where will you go?" I asked.

"I'll let you know when I get there," he said, as tears welled in his eyes. I had only seen my husband cry three times in my life, when I took Shahadah, when we learned about Teddy, and when our friend, Boe, was killed by the police.

The judge said third-degree murder and released Saud on bail to settle his affairs and turn himself in. He was to return in three weeks for sentencing.

The judge looked over his bench at him.

"You aren't going to allow your family to lose all that money, are you Mr. Walker?"

"No," Saud said.

Salina walked into the room and climbed up on her daddy's lap, and Saud fell apart. I had never seen him like that before. Salina grabbed his face and asked him why he was crying. These gangsters and babies have a strange relationship. They would drown in their tears for them babies!

Little did I know; Saud was already packed, and the car gassed up to leave. There would be no returning.

I was on the outside of the circle, and I couldn't hear what was being said, most of our life was like that. It wasn't that he didn't trust me, he didn't want me involved so if I was ever sweated by the popo, I really wouldn't know anything about anything. I could pass a lie detector test.

I went home and collapsed into a chair. *What in the world am I going to do now?* Saud was gone and had two more weeks to turn himself in. I overheard a conversation between him and his dad about the bail. My father-in-law said something to this effect: *They are going to give you the same amount of time today or next week. Don't worry. The catching comes before the hanging.*

That would be the last in-person connection they would have for a very long time. Saud's attorney started in on me right away about the balance due him.

"We gave you over $15,000 cash money. You did not listen to one suggestion I had. You got him over 15 to 25 years so I am not paying you jack," and that was my last conversation with that attorney.

There was no one I could think of to talk about what had happened. I sat in the dark with Salina and Hassan for weeks, trying to pull it all together.

My son Ranel, for the most part, still stayed in Cleveland with Clara and his dad, visiting us occasionally. My phone had been ringing off and on for the past few days. I knew it wasn't Saud because we had our calls planned and because we knew that my phone was tapped. Saud had some favors out in the street, and he called them in, in order to help me and the kids. I was a housewife, so I did not have a job. My cooking had become well-known around the area, so I would cook and sell dinners on occasion. Saud's comrades would drop off groceries.

The apartment where I was staying belonged to a friend of his too, a sweet woman named Maria who didn't live far from us. She had large pit bulls who hated everybody but her. I remember ringing the doorbell one time and the dog came through the screen. Her son looked up just in time to stop the attack. I never rang that bell again before letting someone know that I was on my way.

Her home looked average from the outside, but once inside, it looked like something out of a magazine. She even had a jacuzzi in the middle of her bedroom. Everything was elegant. She offered me a job as her assistant in her decorating business. She was about to launch her new store and wanted to show me the ropes. I was known for being honest and fair in my dealings with people, especially in the few businesses I had tried to operate. She hired me to order the merchandise she wanted from various specialty shops around the country. I loved the position. I learned a lot from her about hustling as a female.

With this job, I didn't go to the clubs so much. I would go sometimes with new friends, but there was one friend missing that none of us had seen for a while – Sandy.

No one had seen her since before Saud's **Name of the Game** incident. I missed her. She was my lifeline to what was going on in the Pittsburgh nightlife. She had introduced me to most of the people I knew. After inquiring about her, the word had finally come, Sandy had died of a drug overdose. She was found dead, hiding in a closet, half-dressed. The other junkies that had shot up with her had made it to the hospital and lived.

We later found out that she had gotten some heroin that had been cut with rat poison. Word on the street was that the bad batch of drugs were sold to them by one of John Taylor's guys. I was enraged to find this out. This put a bigger gap between me and my friend Laura, who I didn't see anymore. I wanted to reach out to my friend, even though my husband was responsible for her husband's death. Some said he was responsible for his own death because of his actions. Reese's word was good enough for me. He had no reason to lie, and no reason to take a life. And if you knew him, you knew he was not one to just pull a gun on anyone for any ole reason.

I never got to talk to her about why she never told me she was married. My daughter would ask for her daughter; she wanted to play with her friend, and I couldn't explain why they could no longer play together.

Layne and I had decided to look after Sandy's only son, Tangy, for as long as we could. We wanted him to know about the good side of his mom. The ringing phone jogged me out of this memory.

"Hello," I said, annoyed.

"Hi. I'm coming to see you. I'll be there on Friday, on the Greyhound about 10 AM. Can you pick me up?"

"Yes ma'am," I said in disbelief. It was Mommy!

"OK," she said, and hung up.

I immediately called for the housekeeper to come and help me clean the house, get food, do my hair, and other miscellaneous stuff. This was Wednesday, she said she would be here at 10 AM on Friday. *Why?? Is someone dead? Naw, she would have said. Maybe she wants to disown me to my face, or maybe she wants to see Salina. Or maybe she heard about*

Reese. Who knows. What I did know is that my Mommy was coming to town.

I told you how Mom was a different kind of grandma. She wasn't the babysitting kind or the drop-by-my-house kind. We made appointments to come by. She would take all her grandkids over for a weekend, but one thing's for sure, you drop off and pick up on time. Be late and see if you get asked back. That's why it was so strange that a few years ago she would even talk to Saud about me and invite him in and call me on the phone.

I went to pick Mom up in a Jitney and I tried to look as good as I could. I was trying to imagine Mommy on a bus. Mommy did know how to drive and owned her own car. I had never known her to be on a bus of any kind. Mommy looked beautiful stepping off of that bus. Neither one of us were huggers, so we did our air hug and kiss thing. We made it back to the apartment and I was hoping that no Feds would show up while Mommy was here.

Or is that why mommy was here?!

I had the entire third floor of the building. I could see in all four directions, but I would also be seen in all four directions. We didn't talk a lot on the ride home, but I sure was glad to get into the house.

Mommy seemed happy to see Salina. The last time I saw any real concern for me from Mommy was when Curly died. She did show up for me, even though she didn't offer much by way of advice, but how could she? No one we knew had ever died! She still had both her parents and a great-grandmother on both sides of the family. As soon as she came in and sat down, I offered her Salina's room, but she said she would be fine with the couch. That shocked me!

She told me that she liked my home and thought that I was doing a good job with Salina. She didn't say much about Hassan. His demeanor frightens most people. He sits and stares at people and it can be very uncomfortable. At first glance, you wouldn't know that he was autistic. Back then the term was TMR, which stood for Trainable Mental Retardation. Hassan was only 12 years younger than me, and could have easily been my little brother, but here we are 40 years later. We have been through so much, me and Hassan.

Mommy looked over Hassan as if he didn't exist and continued to bounce Salina up and down and show her more affection than I had ever seen her show anyone. I cooked for her, and we talked about everything except why she was here. She never asked me about Saud, or becoming a Muslim, or nothing. The next day we went shopping and had lunch. I had never been shopping with Mommy as an adult or had lunch with her in a restaurant. I showed her *Windows and Willows,* where I worked, and I could see that it impressed her. I went with her back to the Greyhound station the next day.

Windows & Willows

She was so beautiful standing there, so elegant and poised. I was crying and so was she. Her perfectly made-up face would only show a glimpse of a tear.

"Are you OK?" she asked me.

"Yes Mommy," I answered. I really wanted her to hug me and say that everything would be OK or ask me to come home. I really wanted her to say that she loved me. As I waved goodbye to her as she boarded the bus, it would be almost 20 years before I understood that her coming to see me was her saying, I love you.

Chapter 20: It's Time to Go

It was springtime and the trees were amazing. Pennsylvania is a colorful and beautiful state in the fall. In the spring, its trees and mountainous farmlands are gorgeous. After Saud left on the run and didn't turn himself in, the Feds started to follow me again until it became an unbearable joke. I would pass them on my way to work and wave. In the evenings, when I went to find a payphone to call Saud, they would be sleeping in their car or gone for the day. So, all I had to do was watch them watch me.

They suspected Saud of a bank robbery and a jewelry store hold-up. One of our acquaintances had gotten killed in a robbery, which made Saud guilty by association. That was the rule of the day. The influence that my husband held in the community was dangerous to them. Saud had been able to get the State to rule in his favor about the Muslim diet in prison, and they were threatened by whatever ties they believed he had to organized crime and Black Muslims. He had also survived death attempts made on his life while he was held at the Federal Plantation.

I was also planning my escape from Pennsylvania and the watchful eyes of the Feds.

It's Showtime!

I had submitted a tape of myself to *Showtime at the Apollo* in New York and I had a callback. *My dream is about to blow up.* Kiki Shepard and Sinbad were the show hosts, and I just knew I would be hobnobbing with them. I was leaving all this madness behind me, or so I thought. Now, all I have to do is win the contest and go be famous. Easy peasy, right?

I loved New York and I also had family there. But once again, going against the grain, I had decided that everyone was against my going there, everyone except me, that is. Daydreaming about my new life, I couldn't bring myself to leave Saud. I also couldn't see myself back in the clubs and that lifestyle. Or was it that I was afraid that I wasn't good enough? Whatever the reason or excuse, I chose what I had been learning about being a Muslim. What I was starting to believe, and who I used to be, weren't adding up to the person that I now saw myself as.

I didn't have much money, and everyone was against me leaving Pittsburgh, and frankly, leaving was not a good idea. Still, I chose meet up with Saud who was on the run and tried to talk me out of coming. He wanted me to pursue my dream of singing.

Nonetheless, I was determined to get out of Pittsburgh. I would usually go to the laundromat once a week. Without a car, I'd push my laundry down the street in a grocery cart. I had really gone down in rank from being driven around everywhere to pushing a cart down the street (and in broad daylight mind you).

It was either that or wash the clothes in my bathtub and hang them up around the house. This was an all-time low for me, and my understanding of this situation was bad. I started saving cereal box tops that had a coupon for reduced airfare. I don't remember how many I saved. I also started to send my things to my friend Layne for safekeeping. Layne thought I was going back to Ohio.

After putting together what I wanted to take with me, I started the process. I actually sent Salina ahead. I had a friend pick her up on a fake playdate, but she was actually going on the second airplane ride of her life. We tagged her on a plane and sent her on her way.

A week later, it was time to go.

I had done my usual thing of pushing the cart to the laundromat. But once inside, I wentinto the bathroom, took off my glasses, put in my contacts, put on a wig, and placed a pillow in my pants after changing clothes. Then, I went out the back door, took a bus to the greyhound station, and shipped a few of my things off to my real next destination – California.

I don't know if I was followed that day or not, but if I was, I gave them the slip.

A friend picked Hassan up from his school program and met me at the airport.

They had dressed Hassan up to look homeless, with sunglasses and a hat. We all met up at the ticket booth.

I had all my important papers and an old Quran. I don't even know if I fully knew or understood the consequences of my actions. I just wanted to be left alone with my new family. My old family in Ohio showed little or no interest in me at the time.

Leaving old drama for new drama

I had actually flown out to California before to see the lay of the land and if Cali had anything to offer me. But this time, my anxiety was so high getting off that plane, I felt ill about the decision I had made. I was second guessing myself.

After meeting up with Saud and Salina, we took a tour of Los Angeles, the City of Angels. So many devils would be my companions on this journey. I lost a lot to gain so much. Learning about Islam and implementing it in my daily life would take on a new meaning. The setbacks started almost immediately,

"Where is the bag with the Quran?" Saud asked me.

"I have it," I said. Saud had a very old Quran that was handwritten in Arabic on onion skin paper. I was told to guard it with my life and to carry it on the plane with me, all of which I did, or thought I did.

"Well, where is it?" Saud asked me again, as we began to put things into the back of the BMW that he had gotten on loan from a friend.

I don't know.

"Oh my God, I must have left it on the plane."

"You did what?" Saud yelled at me. I could see the anger in his eyes. He was so mad he just stopped talking, which totally ruined our drive. That's when I noticed that we had been driving for a while.

"I'm sorry," I said, "I don't know how I could have left that bag on the plane. I was so scared I was being followed. I guess I got careless."

Saud was still silent but his facial expression said 'that's not a good sign'.

"We are going to Las Vegas."

"For what?" I asked.

"The cost of living is cheaper there," he said.

I admired the ride all the way, and we occasionally stopped so that the children could eat and use the restrooms. I had brought along Salina's two pet turtles. I had even sneaked them onto the plane. The steward thought they were rocks, and nobody said anything to us about them. I had never been to Vegas before and was excited to go. I was getting a taste of the difference in the heat, though. Heat like I could have never imagined.

Chapter 21: Vegas

We arrived in Vegas late on a Friday night. The only room we could find was downtown. Everything else was over our budget. I began to get the kids ready to see the lights on the strip and to get some real food. We had not eaten since we left Pittsburgh.

"I'll be back," Saud said, as he left the room.

"OK, we will be ready when you get back."

Saud didn't return for several hours. I wanted to see Vegas but from the look of things, when I opened the door to our motel room, we were not in an area to go roaming about. The children were hungry, so I went to the office of the motel and asked them if they knew of a pizza place. Before I reached the office I noticed that Saud had pulled into our parking stall. The look on his face was dire.

"What is the matter now?" I asked.

"I lost it all," he said.

"Lost what?"

"The money."

"What money? How did you lose all of our money??? Are you kidding me, we have no money? Wait," I said, "are you telling me that we have no money at all?

"Yes I'm saying that we have no money at all, we are going to have to check out of this motel at noon, then find a phone so we can call my dad. But first, let me get in touch with a few people on this end."

"So, technically, we out here, don't know nobody, and all the money's gone. I really don't expect you to stay now," he said, "I knew when you lost the Quran that things were about to go way wrong."

"So, it's my fault now?" I asked

"No, it's not your fault, but when we could not find that Quran, I knew we were in for it."

"You still didn't tell me how you lost the money," I said. He never answered me. I had about $1000 on me out of my stash money, but that was what it was supposed to be MY stash money. Omg, maybe this would hold us over till we reached somebody. Only thing is, we couldn't call anyone except for a precious few. Nobody could know where we were.

We began looking for housing only to find out that everywhere in Vegas did a background check, and that you needed a health card and a Sheriff's card in order to work there. Needless to say, that $1000 didn't last long.

Saud finally got in touch with his dad, who rightfully told him, "I just spent $50,000 on you. You on your own. You can either turn yourself in or deal with your decision – you figure it out."

"But I have my family here," Saud told his father, "and your grandson is here." "Well," my father-in-law said, "Nobody told her to go anywhere. She has to deal with her decision, just like you. I've got no more property and money. I probably won't get my bail money back, so you can come back or stay gone, but I'm not helping." I learned years later that he did get his bail money back, but it wasn't easy.

I've been homeless over the years on more than one occasion. I thank Allah for each time, because when you talk about being bougie and homeless, that was me. That combination doesn't mix, but that was me.

We were in a BMW with all our jewelry and personal things that we packed in the car. We headed out to find a pawn shop. Vegas was full of pawn shops. We couldn't go too far because of gas. We spent the night in the car, changing our clothes in hotel bathrooms. We got free coupons from the vendors on the strip. Thank God they were passing them out to everybody. We got a free hotdog here and a drink there, until we'd collected enough to make a meal. Saud and I wouldn't eat, so that Salina and Hassan had enough to eat, and having friends in Los Angeles didn't help much because everyone was out of town.

We decided to go to the county office to see if they had any help for stranded visitors. I walked my silly self in there, dressed like I had a million dollars, and the lady didn't believe a word I said. I felt bad looking around the room, seeing all those people who were really down on their luck. Social services had advised us to go to the Salvation Army, that they would have beds for families, but we would have to split up. When we located the place, we were greeted by some very nice people, but the rules let us know that we wouldn't be there long. In order to get a meal and bed, you had to shower and listen to a Bible story. What they didn't tell you was that it was a community shower, with all the women showering together with their small kids. The men were on the other side. When I requested to shower alone, they almost got us kicked out.

"Well, I am a Muslim, and we don't do that."

What did I say that for? Now all eyes are on me. I'm not dressed like they think a Muslim should be dressed, but now here come the soul savers. I showered in my underwear and dressed quickly only to find out that they had Spam for dinner. I can't make this stuff up!

After listening to how we were all going to hell, I learned that we had to be out of there by 10 AM so that they could clean the place up after our filthy selves. We were served oatmeal and orange juice for breakfast; we appreciated that meal.

Outside, we noticed the police were all over the place, asking questions to everyone. "Where do you live?" "How long have you been in Vegas?" These were some of the questions being asked. The cops told us that we all had till noon to find a place to be and that we couldn't hang out in front of the shelter.

Vegas was its hottest at noon. For those of us with children, the heat would be too much for them. The cops said that they would be back at noon with social services because it was abusive to have small children in that hot Nevada Sun. And they were right, it was. But couldn't they try to help without the threat of jail and taking your kids?

OK, well that did it for us.

We went to the nearest pawn shop, pawned all the rest of our stuff, the jewelry, the furs and the TVs. We got gas, and went back to the Salvation Army. There were two ladies with three children still there, one could hardly speak English. We piled them in the car and drove them across town. One went to the social services office, the other, to an address she gave us. We thought that we would try our luck one more time at the social services office. The lady who we had talked to when we first got there a few days before helped the women that we had driven there. She told the worker that we had helped her get there and had fed them. The social worker asked what kind of car we had. When I said BMW, she not only came outside to see for herself, but she also said we would have to sell the car in order to get services, and since we had money enough to help others eat, that we probably didn't need their help.

She was right up to a point, with her evil ass. I say that because her comment to us was, "I don't even have a car and y'all out here helping people in a BMW."

She was half right, but her jealousy of our car kept her from doing her job. After all, I had kids too. She never asked about them or our situation. It was really hard on Salina and Ranel, who stayed with us a short time before returning to Cleveland. Salina's beloved turtle had died before leaving the social services grounds. We buried the turtle at the welfare office. We had a proper service for the little guy.

We had enough money from our pawned things to try and head back to Los Angeles. We barely made it to Barstow, California, then we got a tire blowout on the freeway. Thank God it happened next to a gas station truck stop. We managed to pull over into the service station, while Saud went to check to see how much a tire would cost. I went inside the little convenience store to make some phone calls of my own.

I couldn't believe that everyone was out of town on both sides of the family. We were down to our last $20, but if we could just get back to LA ,a job was waiting on Saud and so was a place for all of us to live. The bad part was that we had to have money sent to us through Western Union. There was no Cash App back then.

Saud had a cousin who had offered him a job. He was out of town as well and wouldn't be back for two days. And so we sat at that truck stop gas station for two nights, at least. We were able to use the truck stop bathroom, and we tried to spend our last $20 wisely. The people at the rest stop were very friendly towards us, but we didn't risk getting too friendly or ask for anything. We told them we were waiting on a Western Union deposit. Finally on the second day, someone answered the phone. Saud had the biggest smile on his face. I was trying to read his lips from the car window.

"Man, we didn't want to bother anybody." – I made out some of the words. – "Naw man, we were going to stay in Vegas. I didn't do any homework, shuddah known it was a police state. OK, I'll see you tomorrow."

Saud walked over towards the Western Union inside the 7-Eleven at the truck stop. I said a prayer and prayed that it would be answered.

Chapter 22: Finally, LA

As soon as we rolled into LA and Saud stopped that car in the driveway, I for real jumped out and kissed the ground. We pulled in behind a car which had plates that read PGH BEY. PGH BEY was one of Saud's lifelong friends, and he offered us the downstairs duplex of his home in Mid City, LA. These were the rules: Don't offer any info about home. Don't assume people know your business, and if they think they know, still keep your mouth closed.

I didn't have a habit of talking to men who were not my family in the first place, and I didn't have any friends in LA, so that wouldn't be a problem.

The house was a nice three-bedroom with one and a half bathrooms, a large living room and dining room, nice sized kitchen, and a nice yard for the kids to play in. The neighborhood wasn't bad. We were between Washington and Venice, a few streets from La Brea, not far from St. Elmo Village. After we settled in, Saud asked me if I wanted to go with him to his job, since it was within walking distance.

"Sure hon, can the kids come too?"

"Yep," he said. "I will be working for relatives."

"Relatives? I didn't know you had relatives here." Saud just gave that wink that he used to give when he was being mysterious.

"I didn't know either until Herb, my new boss, and I got to talking. Our grandmothers are both Davidsons on one side of my family, which makes us cousins." Herb Hudson left Pittsburgh, went to New York hustling and whatever else people do before making it, and at some point moved to Los Angeles and opened the first Roscoe's Chicken 'n Waffles. He opened his first restaurant in Hollywood, near Gower and Paramount studios.

Black Stars and the Hollywood elite would come and support Roscoe's, a Black-owned business in Hollywood, plus it served soul food! The Roscoe's on Washington and La Brea, where we were, was actually his second store.

It was around 4 PM when we got there. In the front of the place was a bar with a restaurant in the back. I don't like waffles, so I was not feeling the idea of waffles and chicken. I tried it.

It was my first time eating sweet, savory, and salty, at the same time. I got what the hype was about. My favorite on the menu was the number nine; three wings and a waffle. I substituted my waffle for greens and potato salad. The number nine eventually became the Obama Special. After a visit to Los Angeles, in later years, President Obama stopped by Roscoe's and ordered a number nine. Roscoe's then changed the item number on the menu to the Obama Special.

We walked in and were seated in the back of the restaurant, when its cast of characters greeted us. Jean, Alma, and Momma were some of the names of the waitresses. Some of them had food items named after them. They were friends and had come up with some of the recipes.

They all knew Salina because she had visited earlier and had made quite a name for herself. Every time she walked in, she walked out with no less than $200. The waitresses would give her tip money for helping to put a napkin on the table.

I wasn't used to seeing so many famous people at one time, but I have never been starstruck or thought that anyone's get-down was brighter than mine. I have always respected people for their knowledge and behavior, their kindness and generosity, and to this day, I have not met people kinder than quote, unquote street people, as long as you don't cross them, that is. Junkies too. You just can't trust them, but they are as sweet as they can be.

I have seen waitresses come out of Roscoe's, able to buy cars with cash saved from tip money. I have seen them able to put down payments on new homes. I've seen dishwashers who worked at Roscoe's, not from this country, buy property, farms with cattle, and beautiful homes by doing the jobs we, as African Americans would not do, like cleaning bathrooms and garbage, etc. They laughed at some of us, all the way to the bank. If it wasn't for these workers, who went out of their way to make your business look good, you would not have a business.

There would be a small music trio in the bar part sometimes, and I loved to sit in on a song or two. It wasn't the same though. I didn't know anybody. Saud and I used to go down to the old Wick Stand on Slauson. Now it's called Simply Wholesome, a health food store and restaurant, but it was once a jazz club.

Saud managed Roscoe's at night, and by day we managed a motel on La Brea, The Edmar Motel. When I tell you that LA had something to show a little square girl from Cleveland. I mean this little fleabag of a motel by most standards had too much going on. I learned the day-to-day operations of running a motel. Our shift would start when a very nice older lady, Ms. Simson's shift was over.

We would see rock stars, gospel singers, and R&B singers. They would come in there to get high or to get their freak on. It was one gospel legend, who is no longer with us, that I could not stomach. This pedophile would hide young boys he picked up on Hollywood Blvd in the trunk of his car. He would back the car up to the door, then open his trunk, and the young boys who were hiding in the trunk would rush to the room. The room would always be a disgusting mess, and the smell would kill a maggot. In the morning, we'd see young teenage boys in the parking lot. We could not figure out at first which room they were leaving from. When Saud asked one of the boys how old he really was, he told him he was 16 and had run away from home. Learning that these children were being exploited made us so sick. I thought I was going to pass out.

We couldn't have any law enforcement interactions, plus policemen were people we did not call. So, we had a really nice talk with Mr. Gospel Singer, grammy-winner, and pedophile, about how many different ways and color shades he'd be if he showed up there again. He didn't come back around anymore, well, at least not around us anyway. He has since died and hopefully made his peace with his Maker.

We went on like this for a few years, changing our names so much that I almost forgot mine. Saud really didn't like me working in that hotel environment.

He had made two more decisions, and, they were not all that good, either. The decision was to open up his own after-hour spot with a woman who already had one up and running, but had no muscle to back her up. Despite all that we knew morally and Islamically, and our need to stay under the radar, we kept getting caught up in the traps of shaytan.

Being threatened with poverty will make some deviate from the path.

We left the hotel after a short stay and after making enough money to pay our own way. We decided to move. Saud had found us a place in Palmdale, California. Palmdale was on the rise because of Edwards Air Force base. We moved into a very nice apartment on 11th Street East. It was a brand-new building that no one had ever lived in before. It was nice, quiet, clean, and boring. There was no Muslim community that we could find, and just a sprinkle of Black folks. No one I could relate to until much later. It wasn't long before the gifts and the services that I was used to resumed, however, I absolutely wasn't allowed in the after-hours bar or nightclubs.

Saud would be home during the week but gone from Friday to Monday morning. He was getting more and more arrogant by the day. He had informed me that some family from back home were coming to LA. I advised him not to see them, but he didn't listen to his wife.

"Nope! You can't take them out," I tried to reason with him. "You are generous to a fault, but right now, you downright showing off, they are not used to this lifestyle," I told him. Our after-hour club was one of, if not *the* best in LA. We had a limo service to pick you up, a valet service to park and watch your car, and a babysitting service with licensed childcare if you needed a sitter in order to come out. We had private rooms for celebrities. We'd put you in a cab if you were too high or drunk to drive home, plus we ran it in a quiet community under everyone's noses and never told on a soul living or dead. We had live entertainment, a chef, waiters and waitresses in uniform, and security who you didn't want to mess with. You had to come through the door well-dressed, sober, chic, and classy.

Faces of our After-Hours Bar

Saud's people arrived and of course they were mesmerized by what they saw. It had been three years since we left Pittsburgh. Saud was now acting like old Reese. He should have let Reese stay gone.

He took his people out that night and rode them all around Los Angeles in a limo. The limo belonged to a friend of ours who had a partnership with Roscoe's. The limos were the only cars he drove. In later years, they became my only transportation, which gave people a different understanding of me. People assumed that I had more going on for me than I actually had. When my daughter, Salina, attended Sr. Clara Muhammad School on Central Avenue, sometimes she was dropped off in a limo. When I needed a ride to the grocery store, that's how I got there. Anyway, Saud showed his so-called friends and family such a good time that they couldn't wait to get back to Pittsburgh and sing like birds about the good times they'd had in Los Angeles.

I told you!!

One of the worst things that can happen to a person is the inability to move forward, and to change the way one sees things.

Allah will continue to test us with a lesson until we learn it. And shaytan will continue to whisper in your ear until you say 'enough', and mean it.

Some of us learn fast, some slow, some not at all. Hopefully, we will not be charged in life for our innocence, for what we truly did not know or understand. But we absolutely must be and will be charged for what we *do* know, especially when we know the difference between right and wrong. Oftentimes, we like to stay in the blurred areas because they can be quite comfortable.

Chapter 23: Palmdale and Pittsburgh

In the late 80s, when Palmdale was on the rise, the homes were mostly new. They were building up in that area of California. Palmdale is about an hour from Los Angeles, in the Mojave Desert. It was also located near Edwards Air Force Base, which was a source of income for the area. Otherwise Palmdale, Lancaster, which is still part of LA county, was desert land, hot land. If hell is hotter than this, then I need to act right! The area also had farmland, ranches with horses, and no sidewalks. A lot of Black folks started to migrate that way because housing was cheaper, or they, too, were trying to stay under the radar of law enforcement. Dang, who wasn't? Was Palmdale, California the 'go and hide out' city?

Palmdale had a bus system that would remind you of the 50s. One driver would call the next and say things like, "I have a lady with a kid on the corner of Ave. H and L." They would report to each other back and forth.

"How much longer 'till you get here?" the bus driver would ask the other bus driver, using a walkie-talkie to communicate.

"10 minutes," was the answer.

"Hey lady, your bus will be here shortly. Wait right there and don't lose that transfer," he said.

"Thank you," I said.

I waited patiently. I could not wait to get home. I was burning up. We had just moved from 11th East across the street into a townhome. The BMW that Saud had borrowed had been returned to its rightful owner and so I was stuck in the desert. The Greyhound bus only went into LA once a day and returned once a day. So, if you missed it, you were messed up.

Saud's cousin, Herb had just come a couple of weeks prior, to get his car that was parked in our garage. He had a nice Rolls Royce. We kept it under lock and key until he'd found a suitable place for it. I didn't understand why we kept it. Surely he could afford to pay storage for it? Anyway, it wasn't my business and I never asked. Herb and one of his managers, Cash, came to pick up the car. That car would cause such a disturbance. Little did I know, visiting a prison in a Rolls wasn't the best of ideas. But I'm getting a little ahead of myself.

Remember, I said my memories are all over the place, you gotta keep up!

Finally, the bus came, and we were on our way. I had Hassan with me, but Salina was with her dad. When I got off of the bus, I got physically ill. The house was only a few steps away, but my legs felt like I was walking through mud and sand. I just wanted to lie down.

"Omg, Hassan! Mommy sick," I said.

"Mommy sick?" Hassan repeated.

"Yes, give me your hand. We are almost home."

When we got to the front of the house, we could see Salina in the window with the curtains opened behind her. She was crying.

"Oh my God, what's happening?" I said to Hassan. We made our way into the house and I began shouting for Saud.

"What's wrong with Lina Baby? What's wrong?" I asked my child.

"They beat up daddy. They got my daddy," she said frantically.

"Who?" I asked.

"They put him in a truck," Salina said, trying to explain the best she could.

"In a truck?! Who put your dad in the truck?" I questioned her, struggling hard to make sense of it all. Salina was crying too hard to answer me.

"Did they come in here?"

"No," she said. Then it sank in. They got him, after almost 4 years, they got him.

Saud (Third Husband)

The Feds never returned to my home, although I got out of there quickly. It was all over the Pittsburgh news, more so than here in Los Angeles. The newspapers read:

'Most wanted' fugitive arrested at Palmdale home

PALMDALE (UPI) — A "most wanted" federal fugitive, sought by three states on suspicion of murder and armed robbery, was arrested here Thursday as he sauntered out of his girlfriend's house, authorities said.

Maurice Walker, 50, was arrested as he left the house on 11th Street East wearing bermuda shorts, wraparound sunglasses and a baseball cap, detective John Petievich said.

Walker, who was on the U.S. marshal's list of 15 most wanted fugitives, was living in the house with his girlfriend under an assumed name, Petievich said, adding that the fugitive has used seven aliases.

Law enforcement officials in Massachusetts, Virginia and Pennsylvania had sought Walker

for more than two years for murder, armed robbery and parole violation on a bank robbery conviction, said Petievich, of the Los Angeles Police Department's fugitive section.

Walker was held at the federal Metropolitan Detention Center in Los Angeles pending arraignment and extradition to the East Coast for trial.

Walker is wanted in an armed robbery and murder in Allegheny, Pa., on Oct. 5, 1986.

Officials in Palmer, Mass., also were seeking him in the $50,000 armed robbery of a jewelry store.

He is wanted in Virginia on a parole violation.

Walker's girlfriend, whose name was not released, was not arrested.

I didn't get how Allah had blessed and protected me once again, despite my being oblivious to what my decisions could have brought down on me and mine. They could have come into the house, taken my child, or arrested me for that matter.

Reflection Time!

We sometimes know the why of our stories immediately. But sometimes, we don't get to understand the why until much later. We often use clichés and catchphrases because they sound good, we also take parts of the Bible and Quran and use the parts we like and dismiss the rest, when it doesn't serve us.

Only God can judge me!

This overused phrase makes me cringe every time I hear it. Well, didn't He give us guidelines in which to live by? Didn't He leave us instructions, teaching us right from wrong? Are there not punishments for these misdeeds? If you abuse drugs and can't stop, are you not a drug addict? If you sell them, are you not a dealer?

No, we cannot judge your heart, only Allah (God) can do that, but we can absolutely judge your actions.
If you did it, you did it. Sometimes the end justifies the means, and sometimes they do not. So, let us not use our ungodly conduct as a means to justify our wrongs. But also know, that what may seem wrong to you, may make perfect sense to someone else.

A few lessons that I learned in this part of my life didn't come easy at all. I was very trusting and forgiving. I didn't have a middle; meaning I either loved you, or you were just someone that I knew. I still don't have much of a middle. But I am much better at handling my feelings than I once was. All of the memories that have come crashing back down on me came with a lesson. Some lessons I am still learning. I pray that I never stop learning.

Chapter 24: In Charge

The after-hours club was still doing well. I had met some of the people who worked with Saud. I really had to get used to the Cali-phony people, or should I say, the ones who were in that Hollywood state of mind. I am so grateful that I was and still am adaptable. I can do a limo one minute, and stanky, nasty bus the next.

There was a time when people would laugh at me when I tried to cuss, I didn't use bad language. If I called you sweetie or baby doll, that was venom out of my mouth. The one thing I had never done to any of my husbands, was cuss them out, nor did any of them call me out of my name. Bitch, Hoe, MF were words we did not say to each other (at least out loud). Getting ready to take on my new role as 'boss lady' required me to get into a character that I was uncomfortable with. All this switching back and forth wasn't good for me. It would be only a matter of time before I would have to decide where I wanted my life to go.

Gary, Hassan, Karen, and I were left to run the after-hours operation. We also had Big Ed, Melvin El, and Tracy Mayberry. I was really only a figurehead, because without this crew helping, I would have gotten run straight over. Since we now had two Hassans, Gary became Big Hassan. Big Hassan, Melvin, Tracy, and I all called ourselves Muslims. Tracy and Melvin were originally from Chicago and were former members of the Blackstone Rangers, a dangerous gang. Right or wrong, they protected me with their lives. This made Karen uneasy because her role had shifted. The original club was Karen's, then Saud had joined in. But that Muslim crew was no joke. These brothers would protect me with their lives, as they would also protect Tiny and Thai, who weren't Muslim, but were women whom I had befriended and had formed a bond of kinship.

Big Hassan

I had no knowledge of the infamous Black P. Stone Rangers, or who had taken a liking to me as their 'little sis'. The group went into action, as instructed by Saud. Hassan not only looked after the club, which everyone knew as Karen's place, but after me, Salina, and Little Hassan as well.

Saud was able to call me from the new federal jail in downtown LA. He had gotten Hassan and Tracy to move me from Palmdale back to LA. Tracy was a big hulk of a man, who often did personal bodyguard jobs for prizefighters and security for celebrities, or whoever was gonna pay him.

Saud would call home almost every time they would let him near a phone.

Operator: "You have a collect call from a federal correctional facility, will you accept the charges?"

Today was no different – around 2 PM daily, my call would come in.

"Khadijah," Saud said from his end of the phone line, "you know all of these calls are monitored, so just remember what not to say."

"OK, Maurice," I said to Saud over the phone, "I guess that means we talk about the kids, since I don't know what's correct and what's not."

"That's right," he said, "same goes for when you come see me. They listen in on those calls, too."

Really, except for the club, I didn't know anything to tell or talk about. I never did. The federal hold would eventually land him in Lewisburg, PA. The Federal Prison of Lewisburg was about three to four hours from Pittsburgh, near State College, Pennsylvania. It was close to Penn State University. I often wondered why they put these plantations (prisons) in these sleepy, creepy towns near colleges.

On one of my visits to Lewisburg from Los Angeles, I got a hotel room at the Wyndham and had forgotten my toothbrush. The front desk didn't have any, so I was prepared to walk a few blocks down the street to the 7-Eleven.

"Where are you going?" the bellman asked me.

"To that 7-Eleven that I saw down the street."

"Oh, so you speak English?" he said.

"Yes, I speak English." It was then that I realized I was dressed in my African garb and was covered up.

"Well, if I was you, I wouldn't go walking around here," he advised.

"Why? Because I'm Muslim?" I snorted at him.

"Gawd dang, a Mooslim too? Naw, I was saying 'cause you a black girl up here by herself. If I was you, I'd stay in that room." Needless to say, he didn't have to tell me twice. I took my black ass in that room, stinky breath and all, until the *Friends Outside* people picked me up and took me to the prison the next morning.

Friends Outside is a national nonprofit group that gives families support while they are visiting an incarcerated loved one. This group of *Friends Outside* were Mennonite; a division of the Amish people. When I told them that I was Muslim and my ordeal the night before at the hotel, they invited me to stay with them free of charge. All they wanted was for me to talk about being 'Mooslem'. Was I a Black Mooslem who hated white people?

"No," I said, "I don't hate white people. There are white Muslims, Chinese Muslims, you name it, and you will find a Muslim anywhere."

This family lived on a farm. It was the first time I had ever been on a farm where they had hogs and chickens. I never realized how big a hog could get until I saw those ugly, smelly things up close. This family dealt mostly with chickens. They had chickens for their egg business and told me that when the chickens got too old to lay eggs, they then sold the birds to soup companies to make chicken stock.

It was also my first time eating butter that had just been churned and milk a few hours old from a cow. The wife showed me my room and the bathroom. Then, she showed me their money drawer and told me if I needed any of it to please use what I needed. I was so shocked by that gesture that I didn't know what to say. I didn't need any money, and if I did, I would not have asked or taken any from them.

The whole family helped in preparing the family meal while we told stories of our lives. The next few days, they drove me to and from the prison, then to the Greyhound station where I would take a bus to the airport.

Williamsport was also a place where families who had caged loved ones would stay. They had a nice *Friends Outside* group. But this family of Mennonite people were hands down some of, if not *the* nicest group of sincere people I have ever met in my life. May God guide them, aameen.

What I took from them that day was their kindness. I wanted all people to remember me fondly and to think of me in a pleasant way. It was a nice feeling, leaving them. I had vowed to come back, but I lost contact with them. Throughout my life, I have tried to live up to the example they showed me.

But, getting back to the trip into Lewisburg.

That visit was straight out of a Hollywood set. I saw a group of white male inmates having a meeting with their visitors, who were other white men. They sat in a circle with each other while their women and kids were on the other side, talking among themselves, playing with the children, and serving food they'd cooked and brought into the prison!

We (meaning Black people) had to sit across from each other. I don't know which mob boss that was, but the guards were kissing their butts, and ignoring ours.

I was able to visit three days in a row and stay all day because I was traveling from California. It was called a special visit. If I wanted to talk privately to Saud, I had to fly to Pennsylvania. When the Feds were done with him, he was transferred to

Graterford State Penitentiary, where he served most of his time. He also served part of his time in California at San Luis Obispo, and Lompoc.

He made a name for himself in every prison he was ever in. He helped to raise money for a single mom with AIDS. He did it in Teddy's memory. Sister Yvonne Ali, a teacher at Sr. Clara Muhammad School, was the Muslim chaplain in Los Angeles, California. She told me about a young, sick sister who had AIDS. She was dying and wanted to get her children somewhere safe. Saud and his comrades inside raised about $1500 among themselves and sent it to me to give to her.

He went on to teach the high school program while locked up and helped quite a few to earn their GED. He corresponded with some major Sheikhs and Imams worldwide, seeking firsthand information and sharing it with his Muslim brothers inside and out. Saud also kept busy writing poetry and had some of his work published in a few magazines.

May Allah reward him and make his grave comfortable, aameen. But, you know, no matter what good you try to do, the authorities continue to mess with you, as they continued to mess with him. They were still mad about him being able to walk away and stay away that long. He had not gotten into any trouble the whole time he was on the run.

It didn't help his situation any when we rode up to see him in Lompoc in the Rolls Royce that Herb had stored in our garage. Pulling up to the prison grounds in a Rolls Royce surely raised eyebrows; raised them enough for them to want to search the car.

"Whose car is this?" the guard said. Herb ignored him.

"Who are you here to see?" another stupid question the parking lot guard asked. Again, Herb ignored him. "Whose car is this?" the guard asked a little louder.

"Oh, are you talkin' to me?" Herb asked. We had not even gotten out of the car, but as we were beginning to walk toward the line where the visitors stood, the guard kept harassing us.

"Why? You want one?" was Herb's reply to the nosey, nasty-acting parking lot guard. The guard was a Black man. The look on his face was priceless! I only mention the fact that he was Black because there is nothing worse than an Uncle Tom with a badge and a gun. His little ass needed to move out of the way and let us pass, but instead, he kept asking questions until they found out that Herb owned Roscoe's Chicken and Waffles. Then 'Tom Guard' got all friendly and asked if he could get something free if he came to LA.

"Herb," I said, "you handled that well." I was still in my non-cussing stage when this incident occurred. Lawd, what I could have said! What I did say with my fake smile was, "Of course Honey," which translated into, *you big son of a b****!*

We were the talk of the visiting room. Saud was happy to see his family. We spent our time trying to prepare ourselves for the move that would separate us for a long time to come, and just what were we going to do about it.

Herb and Saud

Chapter 25: Back in LA and It's All The Way Live

Hassan had a large apartment. It took up an entire floor. The kids and I stayed on one side and Hassan stayed on the other. He even had a bar door that separated one side of his apt. from the other. We stayed there after leaving Palmdale until we found a place, but in the meantime, the place was jumping. We had a really nice layout going on. Right smack dab in the middle of Mid City. I must say, a lot of what I learned to do in these places helped me a lot with my organization skills. Besides Hassan, Tracy, and Karen showing me the ropes, there was also Tina and Thai. Tina and Thai became closer than sisters to me and kept a careful lookout; they had my back.

Tina was tall, always dressed sharp, and was loud, crazy, and fun. Thai was always a little more laid back. She was always a lady, her demeanor commanded respect, and she had a watchful eye over everything. Being an ex-entertainer herself, she had political influences and was well-connected in the entertainment industry. Thai also managed an apartment complex not far from the after-hours club we ran.

At the club, my new role was to oversee everybody's job and collect the money. I was also the hospitality go-to person. If you needed anything—food, drink, a ride, a babysitter—I was your person. We also kept up with what everyone did for a living and used each other's services as needed. I began to see some familiar faces among our clients, and when we locked eyeballs, we would look away and pretend that we didn't know each other. I would usually see these faces on Fridays at the masjid!

The After-Hour Club, FROM THE INSIDE,
LA California

I would sometimes jump into character and sing a few songs. I was always ready to do that. What made our club unique was its members. You had to be a businessperson of sorts and we didn't admit anyone under 25. Everyone that worked there was in uniform. We had a valet service, because we operated out of a private home. We didn't want all the cars in the neighborhood to cause a problem for the residents. So, we hired someone to park and watch the cars. We had licensed babysitters (not on site) in case you wanted to come out and couldn't find one. We had a chef and private rooms for conversations only. If you could not drive yourself home, we would call you a cab and send you home, on us. If you drove, we would make sure that your car was safe. We even paid some of the neighbors who may have been inconvenienced.

I sat in the back room of the club most nights, half asleep. When the waitress, waiters, and other staff made their money drops, I would have a total recall of what was handed to me in my sleep. I can't find my glasses on top of my head today, but back then, I would remember every nickel handed to me.

Every Sunday morning after closing up, I would ride with Hassan while he picked up his mom, Ms. Myra, for church. We were already dressed from the night before. Hassan stayed in a suit; I can hardly remember seeing him without one. His mom would fuss all the way to church,

"Khadijah, make sure he stays awake."

"Yes ma'am," I'd say. We would either take her to breakfast or home to eat some of her food. Ms. Myra taught me how to make old-fashioned banana pudding from scratch, this also helped sharpen my cooking skills.

After leaving the club on Monday morning, we'd pile Salina into a cab or sometimes the limo. Bro. Melvin El would escort Salina on the bus sometimes, so she did have some balance and security. Her destination: Sr. Clara Muhammad School, 4016 S Central Ave.

"Mommy."

"Yes Salina," I answered.

"Do you want to hear my Arabic?" she asked.

"You know Arabic?" I'd tease her.

"Bismillah Allah Ar Rahman Ar Rahim."

"What did you say?

"Bismillah," she started to repeat, "Mommy, why are you crying?"

I had not realized that I was, but at this moment, more of the funny words that her daddy Albert used to say, came flooding back to me. I just smiled at my baby, and I was so proud of her. I enrolled her in the school and started going to Jummah (Friday prayer). The school and the masjid were located in the same place. We had become more and more involved in the Muslim community in Los Angeles.

As time went on, Big Hassan would introduce me to some of the believers and we would spend most of our Fridays there. Since everyone calls each other brother and sister, some people assumed that Big Hassan was my big brother, and he really was.

He looked out for us as best he could. Salina really loved him as her Uncle Hassan.

Ramadan came and we fasted all day and ran the club all night. Ya Allah, I was going through a change that only Allah could get me through in one piece. I would come out of my office and talk to the people at the after-hours club. Our clientele were athletes, some celebrities like those from the TV show *227* and the movies *Friday* and *Friday After Next*, before these movies actually came out.

A lot of comedians dropped by. All were nice people and caused no problems. I was the problem. I started talking about the fast of Ramadan from sun up to sun down, and how they should not be drinking and smoking and other activities. I still smoked cigarettes, but I didn't do other activities. My not engaging in other activities, made me feel like I had a little superiority over people. They did the bad stuff, I didn't! I had been known to suck up little piles of white power with my dust vac while trying to talk about Ramadan. Lawd help me.

"Little Sis," Hassan would say, "you're gonna get us killed. You can't be sucking up they blow. Do you know how much that shit cost?"

"No," I said, and I didn't. And I still don't know to this day. But what straightened up my attitude of thinking that I was somehow better than I was, is when I learned God's punishment for participating in someone else's addiction or use. I never sold no drugs, but I cannot say I never benefited from someone else's buying and selling.

I was beginning to dread coming into the club. Karen had fallen out with Saud and Big Hassan, and the damage was unrepairable; a couple of rowdies had gotten in one night and started making trouble for us all, threatening to come in and take over the operations, which made everyone uneasy. In other words it just got dangerous.

I couldn't wait for Friday, even though I really didn't know anyone or have any friends at the masjid, I just loved being around the Muslim community. Salina really liked her teachers and was doing well. We were semi-stable in our dysfunctional little group.

Back in Cleveland, my sisters were doing well. Denise would call me every once in a while and she would catch me up on the Cleveland News and who was doing what on 109th street. Denise had married Edmond Kavanaugh years ago. They were so young, but they are still married today, and it's been over 40 years.

Layne would update me on the Pittsburgh happenings. She was like a big sis to me. She'd tell it to me straight. We had gotten so close when I lived in Pittsburgh. Whenever Layne and I talked, I enjoyed all of our catch-up conversations. I remember on December 18, 1985, the movie, *The Color Purple* had just hit the city, and Layne and I went to see it. There was not a dry eye in the house. Seeing this movie together was one of the last adventures she and I had together. We are only blessed with a few friends in life, some you keep for a lifetime. This was Layne and me. Pittsburgh is a place I have no desire to visit again, but I left a piece of my heart there with Layne and her daughters, Lyssa and Marketa. I was Lyssa's baby's G mom. Her baby was beautiful, her name was Shalonda. She died of SIDS a few months after she was born. This broke all of our hearts.

I have been back to Cleveland a few times. My brother Shawn joined the Navy and was stationed in San Diego, but I had not seen him since moving to California. I missed Freckles from Pittsburgh the most, though. She was my sister from another mister, my Muslim ride or die, and we almost did die on several occasions, like when we rode around town, and she didn't have her glasses on. She was my "frying-chicken-at-midnight-when-we-can't-sleep" buddy. She would call me up at night, she in Pittsburgh, me in Cali. We would eat and catch up, way before there was Facetime or Zoom.

My Mom was enjoying Shaker Heights, a nice section of Cleveland where the Black folk in that community usually had a stuffiness about themselves, and so it goes without saying that it was a good fit for Mommy. Auntie Olga and I never really lost touch; however, I stayed in the background as much as I possibly could. None of this lifestyle was anything like I had ever experienced. In some ways I was self-sufficient and in others, I was totally dependent on my environment.

Sometimes when we don't get the lesson we keep getting that same lesson back-to-back in a different form, but the same lesson.

The more I read, I was beginning to realize that my participation in the operations of the club and the benefits that I received as a direct owner of the business, made what I did worse. I was much worse than the recipients and the consumers. I was benefiting off people's addictions and habits that Allah absolutely forbade. I had everything I needed financially, but I was at my lowest. I was lonely and embarrassed. It crossed my mind again that I might need to go home to Cleveland. Plus I'd be closer to Saud and could visit him more often. It was hard for me. When you have thousands of dollars a day and have to go back to finding money for a cup of noodles to feed your kids, it takes faith that Allah has your back.

It is a hard test when you have to let go and let God, as they say, and very scary. I was soon able to let go of the thread that held me connected to nightlife. The one that could have landed me in a place I didn't want to be, but let's just say I had to be pushed a bit harder to make the clean break from this lifestyle.

Chapter 26: The Masjid and The Old Ladies

It seemed like the only time I was happy and smiling was when I was at the masjid or studying somewhere quietly. The police seemed to be following Hassan. I knew that feeling all too well. Hassan was flamboyant, always in a suit and tie. He was definitely a ladies' man. I had to always explain to somebody that I was his sister, not his wife nor a girlfriend, and I never was.

Hassan was known for his Cadillacs and vintage cars. One day, while riding through the hood showing off one of his cars, a 1935 two-seater Roadster, the bumper fell off! I was the one who had to jump out and pick it up in the middle of the street. We made jokes about that for years.

After Jummah, while waiting on Hassan to finish talking, one of the older teachers, Sr. Yvonne, came over to me.

"Khadijah, can I tell you something?" she said.

"Yes, ma'am," I responded.

"Khadijah, you ain't foolin' nobody ova here," she said. And when she said that my heart just dropped.

"We see you, you ain't fooling nobody." After saying that to me she just walked away. My heart dropped to my feet.

"Come on, let's go, Khadijah," I heard Hassan say.

"Go get Salina, Hassan," I said, "they know."

"They know what?" he asked me.

"They know about the club. I guess someone came back and reported to them about the club. I'm done. You know we see some of these people there. Maybe they mentioned it, but I can't have that sweet old lady looking at me like that," I said, quivering on the inside.

"I don't know how they got something to say when they were in there theyself," Hassan said.

"I'm gonna have to tell Saud I don't want to do this anymore. Y'all can do what you want. But I can't do this anymore," I said, remorsefully.

We had a rival club that had just threatened us with violence if we didn't cut them in, so all these signs were signs for me to exit. I was done.

My Saturday morning call from Saud came through as expected.

Operator: You have a call from a correctional facility in Lewisburg. Do you accept the charges?

God how I hate that woman's voice.

"As salaamu alaikum, honey. I have something to tell you," I said.

"Well, let me talk first," Saud said, "just in case we get cut off. I want you to close the club down. You and Big Hassan close it down as soon as possible. We don't need to be involved in this business at all. I can no longer put you in any kind of danger, plus Allah will not bless us in this. However, if you choose to continue, I'll let you go without a fight, but I'm done, and I can't have a wife of mine involved in anything like this. It's been eating me up all along. Is Hassan there?" he asked. "Put Hassan on the phone."

I went over to Hassan's section of the house and called out to him.

"Saud wants you on the phone," I said. All I could hear were his responses. I had just found out about the rival club. They were supposed to hit us soon. When we got off the phone with Saud, I didn't get a chance to tell him how I felt about the situation. I didn't get the chance to say that we were on the same page. Hassan and I planned to close up and move out, putting everything in storage and moving on with our lives, whatever that looked like. When Hassan and I got to the club to start the moving process, we noticed most of Karen's personal things were already gone, and so was Karen. Her intent was to leave us high and dry. Well, that was OK. We were done. I never saw Karen again.

All praises be to Allah, we had been put on the same path, both wanting to get out of that ungodly business. We packed and closed up shop within a day. The next Jummah, I couldn't wait to see Sr. Yvonne. I was also amazed at some of the people at the masjid that we saw in our club. We kept recognizing each other, but Oh, how they would turn their whole body when they saw us coming.

"Sr. Yvonne, can I talk to you?" I asked.

"Yes," she said, "what can I do for you, Sister?"

"We closed the club down," I said.

"What club?" she asked.

"You know, the club, the after-hour club." I was getting confused by her responses.

"You said 'we all know what you do. We see you.'"

Sr. Yvonne gave me the strangest look.

"Girl, I don't know what you're talking about."

"You don't?!" I said, "Sr, Yvonne, I really am confused. You said, 'we all know what you be doin'.' If you were not talking about the club, then what were you talking about?" I asked her. Sr. Yvonne started to laugh.

"I was talking about you and smoking cigarettes," she said, "we see you walk across the street and light your cigarette, you trying to hide smoking it, but we can see you and I thought that you should know. So, you're the one with the nightclub," she laughed.

"I'm so embarrassed," I said, "but yes, we were the ones but when I thought that you knew I couldn't hold up my head." Sr. Yvonne just laughed.

"Girl, I could tell you a few stories." She said.

Look at Allah, how that whole situation turned out. I never felt as free as I did in that moment. We still hadmore things to clean up and disassociate ourselves from. As we began that journey, another punch in the gut was on the way.

Chapter 27: Jail? Not Again! And Tracy

In the next few weeks, Hassan would be arrested. While I was watching TV one afternoon, he came through the door with 5-8 police officers.

"What's going on?" I asked as I jumped up. My son, Hassan, jumped up too. Big Hassan shouted, "He's special. He don't understand anything. I told y'all about him. Please, don't shoot him," Big Hassan yelled.

"Don't shoot him," I screamed, "shoot him for what? What's happening?"

The cops began to ransack the house.

"Why is this bar door in the middle of the room?" Cop #1 asked.

"We share this space," Hassan said to the cops, which was true.

"What's your name?" Cop #2 asked me.

"Khadijah Shabazz," I said.

"What is the name your momma gave you?" he asked.

"What's the name my momma gave me?" I repeated.

"The one on your birth certificate." Now I'm mad at this disrespectful MF. He had sent me to another mental zone.

"Excuse me?" I said, annoyed and trying to compose myself.

"Let's see some identification," he grunted back.

"I told y'all, she ain't got nothin' to do with anything," Hassan said.

"Shut the fuck up before I arrest her ass too," Cop #3 said.

After tearing up the house, they finally left and took Big Hassan with them, leaving me and Salina in Big Hassan's big torn-up space. I didn't know that Hassan had a warrant, but I suspected the cops had been watching him. I began my duty of packing up all of Hassan's things to put into storage. My new apartment was going to be ready for me to move into on the first of the month. Thai had rented me a unit on the property she managed. Whatever the cops were looking for, they didn't find it, but I sure did!

Thank you Allah for not letting them find those drugs and cash or my story would have been altogether different. My mind was made up that I wasn't going backwards. The items had cash value but were of no value to me. There was also cash hidden right in plain sight. Guess where it was? Aha, I'll never tell.

Hassan's best friend, Tracy, had come to help me again with my moving rescue. This time we were not coming from Palmdale. I was to stay with Tracy and his girl, Madelyn, until my apartment was ready on Norton, the building that Thai managed.

I would visit Big Hassan in LA Men's Central Jail once a week for a few weeks. The shame that they put the families and friends through let me know that it was designed for you to never want to come back as a visitor. The way they spoke to the elders and the kids was disgraceful. On the other hand, I was seeing young people half-dressed and high out of their minds, standing in the line with little regard for their own self-respect.

My dad and stepmom, Brenda, were due in town to see me and to visit with my dad's cousin, Dr. Russell Jackson, an anesthesiologist. And Brenda, my stepmom, had a cousin, Gabe, who owned a farm out in Lancaster. Thank God they didn't want to stay with me. And thank God things were as normal as normal could be when they showed up. My friends and new family had my back. We showed them around LA. My dad was able to spend time with his cousins and see the sights and we all got to enjoy the farm in Lancaster. Daddy asked why I hadn't been in touch with any LA family since I moved to Los Angeles.

"Well, first of all, Daddy, I didn't realize I had family here. Secondly, nobody reached out to me either." Shortly after, I was able to meet two more cousins, Jonae and Wanda. It was so nice to meet them. We began a cousin relationship, and we always have each other's backs.

***

I took Daddy and Momma Brenda to the masjid with me that Friday. They had a ball. Daddy couldn't sit on the floor, so they got him a chair and got momma Brenda one, too. After the service, we ate fish sandwiches and bean pies, and honey punch.

They loved the food. We took them around Leimert Park. Leimert Park is an Afrocentric section of LA off Crenshaw in Degnan. It was full of African and African American shops, food, and fanfare. They vowed to come back and stay longer. They were amazed at the hospitality shown to them by the Muslim community. Daddy talked about the hospitality for years. I was always so thankful for that.

Our stay with Tracy wasn't long; the environment was not appropriate for a young Muslimah, or anyone else for that matter, but we had nowhere to go. I would keep Salina as close to me as I could. We would often hear yelling and fighting from our room and were told to stay in and not come out. This happened a lot. I was determined to get moved quickly and was excited about being in my own space. Only a few more weeks until the first.

One great thing I can remember about Tracy is that he taught me how to make turkey wings on top of the stove. Tracy could cook up a storm. You wouldn't think so, but these gangsters had soft spots for kids and cooking.

"This will be the first time I will be on my own ever!" I said to Thai. I was so grateful to her. She became Aunt Thai to Salina and Hassan, and a big sister to me. Thai loved to do something I hated, shopping! Salina and Thai would go for hours, and they would have the best time.

"Khadijah," I heard Thai's voice on the end of the phone.

"How long y'all gon' be? I'm leaving Thai, right now," I said. Thai had shown me how to catch the bus in Los Angeles, and although I had ridden a bus before, it was nothing like this hot mess that I was now subject to. I was in for a shock. For the most part, it wasn't too bad, depending on what side of town you were going to.

Tracy and Madelyn, Tracy's girlfriend, lived in Hollywood, not far from Melrose, off Bronson and Norton (by Paramount Studios near Gower, close to the original Roscoe's). Back then, that area was not a bad place to live.

I was surrounded by old-school gangsters most of my adult life. However, I had no knowledge of street gangs. In the 1990s, gang action was popping up all over South Central Los Angeles.

For the most part, I had always lived west of La Brea, and by that time I was in Hollywood.

I moved to Thai's complex, which was located in Crenshaw, another area of South Los Angeles. The year was 1991. I was on my way to see Tracy because Madelyn had called me frantically.

"What's wrong, Madelyn ?" I asked.

"Tracy is on something," she said, "and he is not listening to me."

"On something? Like he took something?" I asked.

"Yes," she said.

"OK, sis. I'm on my way." Tracy had a fear of upsetting me for some reason. I was his Muslim sister. He didn't want me to see the out-of-control side of him. I don't know why, but it shamed him, and he would straighten up right away if I saw him acting out. He never smoked or drank in front of me. As I said before, Tracy was a big guy, but a gentle giant who looked up to Hassan. They were almost the same size, in fact, Tracy started to wear some of Hassan's suits, and driving his car while Hassan was locked up. Hassan didn't like that at all.

By the time I reached the corner of Tracy's street, I could see the ambulance pull off and the whole street in an uproar.

"He said he couldn't breathe," one neighbor kept yelling. "They stomped him to death," yelled another.

"What happened? Who y'all talking about?" I asked the neighbor lady and Madelyn who was staring at me blankly.

"Tracy," she said.

"What about Tracy? Where is he?" I questioned.

"They killed your brother," one neighbor lady said to me so matter-of-factly.

"What the hell you mean they killed my brother? Who did?" I screamed out.

"The police," someone said.

"The police!!!!" I said, "Why? What did he do?" I screamed and questioned over again.

"He didn't do nothing. He was scared, running back and forth up the street, having some kind of mental breakdown, and they started beating him. They broke two billy clubs on him. They put him in handcuffs behind his back, and hog-tied him while he laid on the ground. But they still hit and kicked him. He was saying please stop hitting me," the neighbor said. "He kept saying he couldn't breathe, and they still didn't stop. Girl they took him in the ambulance but he dead." I went to try and console Madelyn. I was messed up myself.

"Madelyn, what happened?" I asked her, trying to hold myself together. Madelyn was in shock like the rest of us.

Tracy was an only child. His parents had adopted him, and he had no siblings. His parents lived in Chicago and were elderly. He had told his parents about me, and that he considered me his little sister. He also told his parents that he considered me and Tina from the club as his family.

Tracy's parents asked me to go ID him.

"Yes ma'am, I can do that for you," I said, not really wanting to do it. I wasn't ready for what I was about to see. I went to see Tracy with one of his friends from Chicago, Kevin Tolbert. Kevin was involved in one of the biggest American criminal cases ever. His mom, Marie Tolbert, wrote a book about her son who was doing life and how he got out of prison. They were known as the Pontiac 7. Her book is called Pontiac.

In Ms. Tolbert's book, she spoke about one of the witnesses that had helped to get her son exonerated. His name was Daniel Henderson, also known as Sheikh Shafiq. Sheikh was a beloved member of our Muslim community here in Los Angeles, may Allah elevate him as well, aameen.

Ms. Tolbert was a classy lady determined to clear her son's name and she did just that.

Never underestimate a determined mom.

Kevin and I arrived at the coroner's office together. Tina came too. We went into the building and followed the directions that led us down a hallway and into a room with a window. You could see the covered-up body of an overly large person. When the sheet was removed, I almost passed out. If you want to get a visual of how bad Tracy looked, think of Emmitt Till or a little closer in our time, Rodney King. But Rodney didn't look half as bad as Tracy did, and Rodney survived. Tracy was bloated and both eyes were swollen, one eye was out of its socket, and the other one was swollen shut. Tracy was a medium-toned tan Black man, but he was beaten so badly, we could hardly recognize him; his face was black.

I didn't have a cell phone in 1991; the cell phones back then were as big as a book. As soon as I could manage to get to a pay phone to call Mrs. Mayberry, the sicker I became. I pulled myself together in order to make the call. I had to fight off the screams wanting to blurt out from my core, and the tears that threatened to roll down my face. I didn't want to make this news more difficult than it already was. I didn't know how she would take it. Needless to say, the city was able to sweep it under the rug. Most people didn't hear about this incident. Los Angeles has a long history of killing Black and brown folks and then paying off or scaring families off from telling our stories.

Mr. and Mrs. Mayberry did get a sizable settlement from the City of Unholy Angels, otherwise known as Los Angeles. After receiving their settlement, they disappeared. I never heard from her again. She changed her number and never called me again. At one time, I thought I had done something to offend her, but now that I know how these devils operate, it was probably part of their settlement agreement, not to disclose any information, including telling me and Tina, because we would have surely told the world about what they had done.

Another memory tucked away and blocked out. I remembered Tracy, but my mind and my heart would not allow me to remember what happened to him. This memory would later come flooding back to me on the day I heard the horrible news about my ex-son-in-law, Malik.

Tracy Mayberry died twice: first at the feet of some half-dozen Los Angeles police officers at about 8:30 a.m. last Nov. 3; second, four months later in the minds of his neighbors on the 400 block of North Norton Street as they watched the home video of Rodney King taking his beating on March 3. One of them remembers, "My stomach started grinding and I said, 'My God, it's the same.'"

In the arc lights of the King case they relive the moment when they knew that after minutes of relentless beating, during which people screamed at police to stop, Tracy Mayberry died.

Tracy Mayberry and Prizefighter, Marvin Hagler

Chapter 28: What Riot?

There was so much madness going on; the continuous untold stories of violence at the hands of the LAPD and LASD, along with the Rodney King verdict, all led up to what they called the 1992 riots.

THE RIOTS, the moment when the streets of South Central Los Angeles vomited up its misery. *I personally* called it a rebellion. The safest place was in the streets! What I saw was unbelievable. People were helping themselves to the property of anyone who wasn't Black. People were driving people home with their stolen items and helping each other push carts of stolen goods. People were having cookouts in their yards, watching the mayhem, or selling what they had stolen. We saw Korean shop owners on top of their stores with shotguns, ready to fire at anyone coming to harm them or the store. I ain't mad at them for that. I would be on a rooftop, too, trying to protect what was mine. I respected the fact that they fought back, even though they needed to get their disrespectful, overpriced asses, and their businesses out of our neighborhood. White and Jewish shop owners just left.

Black shop owners stayed and put 'Black-owned' signs on their businesses' windows. Some were robbed, most were not. The foolish, tired, and mad, half-crazed community started to burn down everything that Blacks didn't own (which was damn near everything), all under the watchful eye of the LAPD. It lasted as long as it did because nobody tried to stop it. The law only got involved to stop the looting and the fires when the mob got too close to Beverly Hills and the West LA areas. That was the cutoff point. Now, if you intended to go into West LA with that madness, then you intended to get your ass whipped and arrested. The law had something for you at that point.

Thai had instructed her kids not to loot our neighborhood market. The family that owned the corner store had been very good to the community, and for the short period of time that I was there, they were good to me.

I know this might seem off, but through the riots, I saw unity (in a mixed-up, crazy sort of way).

During this time, I was becoming a regular at all the masjids, meeting people, and continuing my Islamic studies. Sister Sharon and Brother Herbert from the Felix Bilal community would pick up Salina and get her to school for me. Sr. Sharon, at one time, was the school's principal. Salina loved her teachers, Sr. Yvonne and Sr. Ummil Khair. She was doing well with her schoolwork. I had put Hassan into a special-ed school, and he was doing well also.

During one of my visits to see Saud, when he was still in California, I stayed at the home of the Imam (minister) who was also the chaplain at Lompoc Prison. The nicest families that you would ever want to meet were there to help me with my every need.

One family had a lot of children; the sister ran the home like a drill sergeant, but in a nice way.

"You have such control, and your children are so well-mannered," I remarked to her. "The children I usually see in large families are always running around, totally out of order. How do you do it?" Sr. Bahiyah told me that she was a foster parent, and that she took care of these children until she could return them to their parents.

"I took a lot of parenting classes," she told me. "And passed a background test."

"What are they looking for in a background test?" I asked.

"Drugs, jail, abuse," she went on to say, "also drunk driving, things like that."

"You have well-behaved kids, Sister," I said to her again.

"Khadijah, why don't you consider it?

"Consider what? Babysitting? Girl, I got a house full now," I laughed. "Somebody must have put an 'open house' sign on my door, because many sisters with their kids come in and out of my house," I joked. "Plus I have never babysat in my life."

"You would be helping children that cannot help themselves. Think about it, sis," she said. "You can make a little money, not a lot, but it's halal and will keep you home."

Home is where I wanted to be.

Since moving on my own and leaving all nightlife alone, I had been working the night shift at Roscoe's on Manchester and

Main. Thai would keep an eye on my apartment and the kids while I was gone. We lived in a row of houses that she managed. Some of the residents were her family members, who became my family. Her daughter, Telesha. and her kids lived there, and her niece, Día. Both of them and their children are part of my heart.

The row of houses where we all lived was packed so close together that you could hear what was going on next door. I had a unit in the back which wasn't attached to the other apts. Mine was one of two that had an upstairs. The neighbors to my left were drug addicts and drug dealers. They presented a danger to our little community. Thai was only so effective at trying to keep the activities of those neighbors under control. She tried everything she could, without calling the police, because that is what we don't do!

Top: The apartment on Norton
Bottom: Debra, Thai, Me

I worked at Roscoe's on the night shift, which was way on the other side of town. This made me afraid to leave Salina and Hassan alone. Crackheads started knocking on my door at night, mistaking my house for the drug house. I needed help. I told Saud about the problem, and he instructed me to tell the brothers at the masjid. The next Jummah Friday, I did just that. I asked for help. I had asked them for help previously when they had put Saud in the hole (solitary confinement) for not cleaning the pork pots and pans. I didn't get help then, and didn't think I was getting any this time. I remembered the conversation that we had.

"Hey, Khadijah."

"Hey, Saud," I said in the phone, "As salaamu alaikum."

"Wa alaikum salaam," he responded, "I'm gonna be put in the hole if I don't get a letter from an Imam saying we are not allowed to handle pork. I need you to ask the Imam for a letter or phone call. That's the only thing they will accept."

"OK," I said, "but what happened to the Imam there?"

"He is out of town for a month," Saud said.

The community that I was becoming a part of still did not know me very well. They were not the friendliest, and needless to say, I didn't get a letter. As a result, Saud did two months in the hole. He was there until we were able to get the letter, but it didn't come from that masjid. I believe Sheikh Shuaib from Masjid Salaam gave me the letter. Sheikh Tajuddin Shuaib later became a good friend of my family and my children's Islamic Studies teacher. The Sheikh was from Ghana, and he had written several books on Islam, a popular one was *The Prescribed Prayer Made Simple*. His family and mine would become good friends.

Saud had told me the story of how he almost lost his life in a Pennsylvania State Pen fighting for the rights of Muslims. This was the lawsuit he started and won, a lawsuit to be able to have Halal food in prison. Remembering the broken glass that was put in his food by the guards and the beatings, having survived all this only to be told he had to wash pork pans, was too much. Even some Muslims told him that he should just wash them. Well, for everyone who said that, they really didn't know who they were dealing with. Saud would gladly rather clean toilets than be made to do something that he had fought so hard for.

He had so many young people who looked up to him that backing down was not an option. The same fury that Saud had put into his street life, he had put into implementing Islam, which indeed made him dangerous to many. Any time you have someone not afraid to die for their beliefs, that's a person to watch. His fear was not pleasing Allah and leaving this life without forgiveness from Him. He was always fighting for anything and everything that went against Islam. Not standing up was not an option for him.

Not being able to find help with the drug situation was a big disappointment for me and Thai. Back in The Courts (we called where we lived The Courts) meant that we had to come up with a plan that would give safety to my kids and to the others that lived there, for that matter. Thai and I got so tired of the junkies' and the drug dealers' traffic coming back and forth that one day we just snapped.

"Khadijah," Thai said, "they are all laid up there high as hell, and they keep walking back and forth."

"Laid up where Thai?"

"Back there in their house. The door was not closed all the way, so I looked in," she said. "We can't even sit out here and enjoy the fresh air."

"Yeah girl, it's like watching a bunch of zombie roaches," I said.

"Come on," Thai said to me, "we have to do something."

"What are we gonna do Thai?" I asked, as she grabbed her bat. Thai always had a bat close at hand. Aww shucks, they pissed her off and now we about to get into a fight. I followed Thai 'till we reached the door of the house right next door to mine. Thai yelled inside.

"You m***** f***ers gonna stop all this shit today."

That is when she noticed that the door was still ajar. She pushed the door open with the end of the bat and we could see them all laid out not paying us no mind.

"Hold that door open Khadijah," she commanded.

"What are you 'bout to do?" I asked her again.

"Don't worry about it, just open that door and watch my back."

"Aww sh*t, sis, I ain't got no pistol on me," I yelled.

"You don't need one," she said back to me. Thai grabbed the garden hose, turned it on full force, and went inside. She wet up the zombie junkies and the drugs, the furniture, whatever was in sight. They didn't know what was happening. The cold water woke them up and messed up their high. Talk about mad! The Zombie Junkies called us every name in the book.

"Oh my God Thai. We messed up all they shit." I laughed so hard, but then reality set in. "Now you know we got to do something about security because I got to go to work. I can't leave the kids here alone."

I had been given a tip earlier that day on who to call for help and support. I made a call to Brother L, who was in the Nation of Islam. They sent somebody right away. Two FOI (Fruit of Islam) brothers showed up at my door and posted up for about three days, not letting any junkies in the court or by my door, while I was gone. I had never experienced this before. This experience taught me more about security and how to watch my own back. Something I needed to know, since all my adult male family was gone. Not coming into Islam through the Nation, I didn't know much about how disciplined they were. I was so grateful and impressed by the security and the assistance, that when Herb and J Rich, the night manager of Roscoe's, asked me to help them get security at night for my shift, I called Brother L again, who sent more brothers to secure the store. They would wait until I left at closing before they would leave.

Mr. Robinson would often take me home. He owned a limo company and was Herb's right-hand man at one time. We called him Pops. I learned so much from this old head. Pops treated me like a daughter. While working at Roscoe's, I met Brother Cecil. Cecil was the night shift head cook. He would whip up something from the leftovers that should have been on the menu. He was soft-hearted and also Muslim. But as a friend, he was loyal to a fault. He'd bring groceries to my house and just leave them at the doorstep, knowing that I was a single mom. Cecil also was a firearm expert. We would buy our firearms from Cecil. He always gave us free lessons on how to handle a gun and got us (meaning

Debra and a few of the female workers at Roscoe's) registered with a few of them.

I would drag Cecil and Thai to all of my get-rich-quick seminars. Everything that came on TV talking about how to make money, I dragged these two along with me. They would tease me.

"Hey Thai," Cecil would laugh, "what she got us into now?"

Thai would crack up and say, "Hold on to your wallet. Whatever Khadijah got us doing, it's crazy."

Cecil died at a Roscoe's Xmas party, after years of service to that place.

My second sister was Debra, a short, brown-skinned, pretty Black woman. Everyone loved and respected her from the hood where Roscoe's was located. I always thought that Cecil had a secret crush on Deb. Even though Deb wasn't Muslim, and neither was Thai, they were my sisters in the sense that I could be myself, and she could be herself as well. We were thick as thieves and had kids to raise. Quenda, Debra's daughter and Salina were about 15, and best friends. They talked on the phone almost all day every day while Deb and I were at work. They kept each other's secrets, so of course this meant boys.

Everyone was teaching me the street life in LA and basically keeping me from getting into trouble. I wasn't into gangs, nor did I know who was who in the streets. I had a mouth on me, so I needed to be reminded from time to time what was appropriate and what was not. For the most part, I am and have always been respectful towards elders, people in authority, and everyone that showed me respect.

***

I remember the day Jesse Jackson came into the restaurant. Mr. Jackson, as I called him, because he was my elder, would walk into the restaurant and around the tables, shaking hands with everyone, and would steal a piece of chicken off the customer's plates while he waited for his order.

Me and Jesse Jackson

"You can't be sticking your hands in people's food," we would shout at him.

"Oh, you mean I can't have this piece of chicken?" he would playfully say to the customer.

"Hell naw," someone would yell back at him. We all would laugh and then fix his order and give the customer another piece of chicken. Mr. Jackson came in a lot when he was in town. In the 90s, Roscoe's was a fun place to work. We loved coming to work just to laugh at the people that made up the neighborhood. We were in the middle of two rival gangs, but Roscoe's was a neutral place where people from the hood could come. We had very few problems. Politicians and celebrities all mingled together. Even during the so-called riot, we came to work and watched chaos all around us. We were untouched.

Chapter 29: Life at Roscoe's

Taking Bahiyah's advice, I began taking classes and training on how to become a foster parent. I learned so much about the plight of these children that it began to concern me deeply. Our little Black babies were going into the homes of people who could not relate to them or accept the parents of these children. People, who were much like the people I was coming into contact with every day at Roscoe's and from the hood. It was weighing me down. Some of these children were born drug addicted and labeled from the start; this was bad.

During my foster care training, I didn't see anyone that looked like me, i.e. Muslim and Black. At the training, I was watched closely. I knew I would be. I was always mistaken for a member of the Nation of Islam because of my name, which put people on alert. Black and white, all wanted to see where I stood. That seemed to always creep into a conversation or interview. Or it would switch to a conversation about the Taliban. I guess because I'd started wearing the hijab every day. Did I hate white people? Did I think that they were the devil?

The devil, no; devilish, hell yeah! As a Muslim I am not taught to hate. I am taught to stand up for what is right, even if it goes against my own self. The Truth is the Truth!

"Hey, Dee," Deb was calling me from Roscoe's door. (Dee is what some of the people called me, those who had a hard time saying KHA DEE JAH.) "Girl, come look at this. Maria and Carl are out there fighting on the lot."

"I can't leave the cash register. Deb, what's going on?" I asked. Maria was a young Hispanic girl in her 20s on drugs and a prostitute. Carl was a man about 60. Maria had a baby boy named Jorge and claimed it was Carl's baby. Well of course, Carl's old ass wanted to be the daddy, and so we minded our own business, but laughed under our breath. They were always fighting. This was nothing new except this time someone called the cops. It was never a dull moment on this corner. The police showed up and took them both to jail. We went back to work. About 30 minutes later, some customers came in all excited saying there was a baby crawling down the street!

"What the hell?" Deb and I went outside to see little Jorge crawling down the street. Maria and Carl lived in the apartment right next door to Roscoe's. Debra picked up the baby and we went next door to knock and see who was home. When we didn't get an answer, we tried calling the police back to tell them they had left Maria's baby when they arrested her.

"What you mean it will take hours before you can get somebody out here to get this baby?" Deb asked on the phone. The baby was hungry and cold.

"We are working," we tried to explain to the cops. All of the employees took turns watching the baby while Deb and I went next door and broke in to get Jorge some clothes and a bottle.

"Hey Deb, it's almost time to go home and the police have not called back. I think I should call the agency where I am taking my classes and ask them what I should do.

"I'm scared to take him home and have someone say we kidnapped him," I said nervously. I called West Side Children's, the agency where I was taking my training, and told them what was happening. They told me to take him home and that they would send a social worker and meet me there.

"Deb, they told me to take him home, can you believe that?"

The police never did come back. Jorge stayed with me until they found a Spanish-speaking family for him, even though his mother from jail requested that I keep him, since she knew me.

Their Secret

Salina and Quenda were about the same age, they got along well and shared each other's secrets. Neither one of them was old enough to have a boyfriend at 15-16 years old. Deb and I didn't play. We noticed that Salina had been acting out. For a while, it went unnoticed by me because of my work schedule and me trying to figure out our new life.

We would visit Saud as often as I could get away. It helped because Salina loved her daddy, and she didn't want him to know anything bad that she may have done. She had even run away once. I was so scared that she was kidnapped because I just couldn't conceive of her running away from me. I found her at a friend's house. She had actually been hiding from house to house. Her friends didn't turn her in. I was glad she had a friend she felt safe enough to talk to, but how could I possibly be a good mom to others when I failed my own child so miserably?

Salina and Quenda were making plans to finally tell me and Debra their secrets. Apparently Quenda had a boyfriend, Shawn, that she wasn't supposed to have, and Salina had her own secret I would soon come to know.

While the girls talked, Shawn showed up at Quenda's door. Salina told Quenda to not let him in because they were already going to be in enough trouble.

Quenda went to the door to tell Shawn to go away, and something went terribly wrong. Through the door, Shawn shot Quenda. He shot her, and killed her!

Debra got a call while working her shift at Roscoe's to get to the hospital right away. Her teenager daughter had just been shot.

I had to stay behind and work. I couldn't leave the store. I didn't know what was going on.

My sister Deb died a little that day. I couldn't stand to see her in that much pain. We still don't understand it. I never knew the answer as to why he did it. What I also could not understand at that time, was why our girls were acting out.

Salina's attitude had changed so much towards me, yet still, she was a quiet unassuming person. I think I missed the transition, where she went from being my little girl to a teenager with teenage problems. This would be one of my most painful life lessons. I don't have too many regrets, but I still feel a little guilty that I didn't see that my baby needed me.

I had to go home and tell Salina what had happened to her friend, her sister. Salina just stared off into space and smacked her lips as she did right before she would have a fainting spell or seizure. When those spells returned after years of her not having any, they lasted for a longer period of time. Salina went deeper into herself and as much I would like to say I helped her through it all, I think I made it worse.

Shawn was caught, arrested, tried, convicted, and did some time for the murder of our baby girl.

With all of these terrible events, I knew that I had to find a way to get home and stay home. I needed to be able to support my family with a halal income. I needed to find a way to work from home. My child needed me, and I was not there. Other single moms seemed to be able to do it. Or at least it appeared as if they figured it out. I was trying to figure it out.

Roscoe's and the What-cha-ma-call-it Deli was coming to an end for me. The What-cha-ma-call-it deli was a deli located on Roscoe's lot. Hassan and I had started it when he was released. 'We sold sammaches' was our slogan, we did ok for a while, but still I needed to look after my children, and with my own child acting out, how could I possibly foster someone else's?

The What-cha-ma-call-it Deli

Mentally and physically, I was feeling the pressure take its toll on me. I needed to see a doctor, but I wasn't looking for a conventional doctor. Sis. Bassemah Muhammad, who was making my teas and herbal supplements, suggested two remedies for me. One was to eat right for my blood type and the other was Dr. Manuel Colin. Dr. Manuel is a Mexican-Jewish man who was once a surgeon but had turned to eastern medicine. He'd look at your tongue and then diagnose you. I wouldn't tell my regular doctor what Dr. Manuel said and vice versa. Dr. Manuel didn't have a regular office. He would make house calls or rent out a room in someone's home to treat his patients. He treated us with herbs and acupuncture. His treatments allowed me to bypass a few surgeries and regain my health. He is still my doctor today.

Chapter 30: Dana Malik

I was so excited. Freckles, my old friend, had agreed to come and visit me. I wanted to show her Cali and was hoping that she would stay. She was too wishy-washy for me, never making up her mind and so in order to get her here, I sent for her baby daughter, Madinah. Madinah showed up with my dad who'd come to visit his cousins, and they dropped her off with me.

Madinah was about eight when she became a part of my heart. She was only supposed to stay a few weeks. We took her to see all the kiddie highlights of Los Angeles. She loved Roscoe's food so much. She was even featured in Roscoe's very first TV commercial, which did not go down well with Salina, who had been the baby princess, and now this bad little snot shows up. Salina treated her like a bratty little sister, but they loved each other.

Our life on Norton was coming to an end. I wanted to move. I would be getting my foster care license soon, and there was not enough space. We had outgrown Norton Ave. Freckles and her other two kids, Mecca and Hakeem, had come for a visit and to retrieve Madinah who I had refused to send home. Mecca and Salina were also thick as thieves, and I was happy that Salina had someone she could relate to.

Hakeem was about seven years old, a boy's boy. He stayed into everything. I wasn't used to having a boy around. Ranel spent most of his time with his dad, and Little Hassan would only sit in one spot. Hakeem went from door to door in the court, karate kicking them, causing damage and hostility in the courts, but the mean old lady Ms.Forbes lovvvved him. She didn't like anybody but Hakeem. Hakeem could do no wrong in her eyes.

Hakeem would watch over me and his mom very closely. We had a pint-sized bodyguard. Being a Muslim and knowing what

Muslim women should wear, he'd cry if his mom or I were not covered properly before leaving the house.

"Your khimar (scarf) isn't on right Mommy." He would literally stand by the door and cry! In the Courts, Freckles had stopped being Freckles and became Sakinah! It was wonderful having Muslim family that knew me from way back when. Oh the stories we have!

There was always music in The Courts. Everyone had some sort of history with the music industry, either themselves or their family. Thai was once a background singer for Diana Ross, and her daughter, Telesha, sang as well.

Día, who lived in the first apartment with her grandma, was Thai's niece, who Día called Momma. Día's parents were once a part of *Ike and Tina Turner's Revue*. Her mother, Lejune, was a background singer and dancer, an Ikette, and her father, the infamous Soko, was the drummer for Ike and Tina for years.

Freckles' (aka Kim aka Sakinah) sister was Phyllis Hyman, to name drop a few. But yes, The Courts were a musical bunch. Somebody always had the music blaring.

I started to revive more of my political awareness there, also. Thai, being part of the old US organization, and me being around Black Panthers and NOI, put us up on the current situation in Los Angeles.

Thai introduced me to Emmett Cash. Emmitt had a voice like Johnny Mathis and was once a music producer. Emmitt, now into politics, had an office down on Crenshaw next to Church's Chicken in Leimert Park. I would help Thai with whatever task Emmett had for her. I was like Thai's assistant. Thai and I worked on Senator Diane Watson's campaign. We also hosted Celeste King's (a local bail bondsman in the area) black tie cocktail party, and other meetings for the local politicians Emmett was associated with. Who would figure that in the years to come, I would be fighting to shut down bail bondsmen and their unfair practices that hurt our community?

Thai would also produce and MC comedy shows in the West Hollywood area. We would see Chris Tucker, Jamie Foxx, DL Hughley, Mike Epps, Robin Harris, Dave Chappelle, and Eddie Griffin. We were all in for a change. Sadly, our happy little lives in The Courts would soon end and scatter us all west of La Brea.

Back to the Secret

Debra was slowly working through the loss of Quenda and so was Salina in her own way. Salina's secret was that she wanted to get married.

"I want to get married, Mom."

"What Salina? What are you talking about? Married to who?" I kinda laughed at her. My 15-year-old daughter is talking about getting married, and in my mind she was just now finding out the difference between boys and girls!

"To whom and why?" I asked her. Salina said to me, "You said Muslims don't date, so we can't have boyfriends."

"So, what does that have to do with you? Salina you got a boyfriend?"

Salina continued to look at her feet, "You can meet him if you want."

"If I want to! Your daddy's gonna hit the roof," I warned her.

When Saud called later that day, I told him what Salina said.

"Put her on the phone," he barked at me.

"Salina, your dad wants to talk to you." Salina picked up the phone and of course the water works started. She wasn't doing all that crying when she was talking to me. In fact, her voice was quiet, always respectful, yet forceful when talking to me. Through her sniffs, I could hear her, "Hum, hum, OK, yes Daddy. As salaamu alaikum."

"Here Mommy, he wants to talk to you."

Saud was talking really low. I could hardly hear him saying, "That nigga comin' over tomorrow around this time. When he get there, hold him there until I call."

"What are we getting ready to do?" I asked, almost afraid to hear the answer.

"She wants to get married," he said.

"I know but, why?" I asked.

He said, ask her. Well, I didn't ask. I kept avoiding the question that needed to be asked and chose to go another route.

"So, Salina," I asked, "is this someone I know?"

"No mom."

"Is he a Muslim?"

"No, mom?"

Now, I am really trying to hold back tears and anger. Anger at her and myself.

"And if we say no that you can't get married, are you going to keep seeing him?"

"Yes," Salina said flat out.

Saud had two friends here in California that had visited him while he was incarcerated at Lompoc. One brother was a Muslim chaplain, the other, a brother he had met. Their names were Muhammad Abdullah and Abdul Latif. These two brothers showed up at my house at the same time Salina's friend did. I invited them all in and about 10 minutes into the visit, Saud called.

"Yes Saud, all three of them are here," I said, "Ok. Muhammad, Saud wants to talk to you." I handed Muhammad the phone. "And Latif, you can use the phone in the kitchen." The two brothers went into the other room to talk and left me sitting in my living room with Salina and her friend.

"So, Salina," I said, "what's your friend's name?"

"Dana," Salina said.

"So, Dana, why do you want to marry my daughter?" Before he could answer that question, Muhammad and Latif returned from the kitchen.

"Yeah man, let me holla at you," Latif said to Dana. The three men stood up and walked out of my front door. Salina just sat there crying. When the trio came back about 30 minutes later, to my surprise, Dana apologized to me for sneaking out with Salina. He said that he really did want to marry her. He went on and recited the shahada better than me!

"Wait a minute," I said out of concern, "Oh, so he Muslim now just like that? Oh no, y'all can't force nobody into no Shahadah. We not doing that. Oh, heck naw. Listen Dana, there is no compulsion in this religion. We cannot force our girls into marriage or slavery. Did y'all scare him?" I asked them both, who were looking off into space.

Just as I asked that question the phone rang again. **You have a call from Saud who is calling from a correctional facility.** (*God how I hate this woman's voice.*) **Do you accept the charges? This call may be monitored.**

"Saud, why you got him taking Shahadah? You can't..."

"Khadijah, put Dana on the phone," Saud interrupted.

"Here Dana, Salina's daddy wants to talk to you."

"Yes," Dana said into the phone, "OK. Yes. Yes, I like it. Naw for real I do."

"For real you like what?" I asked Dana. He handed me back the phone.

"Saud," I said as he cut me off again.

"Put my brothers back on the phone," he demanded.

"He wants to talk to y'all."

Muhammad and Latif got back on the phone, said a few words and gave me the salaams and they left.

"Oh, by the way," Latif said to me, "Dana took the name Malik."

"He took the name Malik?! Y'all are doing too much. Dana, you cannot be no Muslim unless you really believe that there is only One God who has no children and no partners, and that Muhammad, peace be upon him, was the last of the Holy prophets sent by God over 1400 years ago."

"I do believe that," he said, "some of my best friends are Muslim. Salina is not the only Muslim I been around. In fact, you know one of my best friend's parents. Her name is Sister Iskoke."

"Yes I do know her," I said, "still we can't force or make someone take Shahadah or marry."

A few weeks passed until I finally said to Dana and Salina that if I agree to this marriage, then some rules were about to be put into place.

"I don't know you and I'm not turning my daughter over to someone I don't know. First of all, Salina cannot leave my house until she finishes school, period. Secondly, that means you live here, but you can only stay here if you are working and paying bills. Salina, you can't go anywhere unless your husband or I say it's OK, which means if he is not with you, you ain't going."

This would go sour fast, but these were my conditions as part of the marriage contract.

"She is too young to get married," I heard from everyone.

"True," I said.

"Why are you going to let her?" was the response from my family. "See, y'all religion is crazy." While I was trying not to go off on anyone in my family, because I really don't care what other people thought about it, I was trying to make the best decision for her. Either one of them could have changed their minds at any time.

"Look, Mom, Salina told me that she loved him enough to run off with him. In case you didn't know, having sex without marriage is a sin. Being married cannot clean up a sin, but it can help prevent continuous sin in the future. Allah forgives and understands far more than I ever will. She won't be the first 16-year-old bride."

I didn't know if this marriage was gonna work out or not, but at least she can say she had a husband and not a boyfriend, or some baby daddy. Some folks ain't never been married, so what have y'all been doing all these years? With ya good Bible-thumping, Quran-reciting, no-husband-having selves? And to some of you brothers, the same thing; dropping babies everywhere and running off scot-free, leaving the sisters to hold the shame and the blame. My daughter and new son were not forced into anything.

"Let's plan a wedding, Salina. If you change your mind, let me know. Malik, if you change your mind, let me know. But for now, son, let's you and I discuss a dowry and your rights and hers."

Chapter 31: Lessons in Abundance

After a few weeks, I learned that a few of my new so-called friends had known about Salina and Dana and had kept it from me. I was so upset and felt so betrayed. Sabrina was someone whom I had befriended. She and I were so close, or so I thought. She taught me a lesson that I would soon forget. A lesson I learned the hard way, since I didn't get it the first time. I received it over and over again through my lifetime.

Sabrina was so close to my heart. All she had to do was ask. If I had it, she did too. In my Islamic lessons, I learned that faith is not complete until you want for your sisters what you want for yourself, that if your sister is in need and you have it or if you can help, then that's what you do. You share with someone in need. I couldn't have my bills paid and my sister needed something, or my family have food and my sisters were hungry.

Sabrina would go to my house to get whatever she needed. I would say to her, "I'm at work, y'all need food, come get it." Sometimes people will take your kindness for weakness. I loved being kind to people and still do.

One day, I heard Sabrina talk about me like a dog in a three-way conversation, but she didn't know I was listening in on it. I was crushed. She called me a bitch and a fool and how I was stupid for staying married to someone in prison. She went on to say to the other sister on the phone, "Watch me ask her for something and watch her dumb ass go get it for me."

I went through a grieving period. I was so hurt by her betrayal.

"Saud, I thought she was my friend," I cried, as if I had been kicked in the stomach.

"Why did you think that Khadijah?" he said. "You said you were her friend. Did she ever tell you that you were hers? What I am saying to you Khadijah is this," Saud said to me, "just because you were her friend, that didn't make her yours or make her friendship on the same level as yours to her."

Imma let that advice sink in a bit right here: Just because you say you are someone's friend, that doesn't mean they consider you a friend.

"She knew that our daughter was doing something wrong, and she didn't check her or tell you, that's not a friend. She always has a money problem and keeps coming to you, that's not a friend." Saud said.

"No, it's not," I said to Saud.

My feelings had me back on that balcony porch after Albert died, but this time, I didn't feel the rage or urge to kill something, I felt like someone I loved had just died. It was the death of a friendship that just turned my blood cold. It would be 20 years before I spoke to her again. And because of her, everyone I have met since then was given the side eye. I distrusted most women. My male friends have never let me down, well at least never let me down by lying to me, and if some of them did, I never knew of it. I also stopped talking so much about helping the incarcerated people, and I really didn't understand why. I learned that if you told people about yourself they would hold it against you.

I also learned in that lesson, that when we help and give, we should do it for the pleasure of Allah, not looking for anything in return from any human being. The reward comes from Him, and with that lesson I learned my heart never hurts from giving and so, as for learning that lesson, I believe I owe her. Thank you Sabrina.

This reminds me of a verse in the Quran from Suratul Insaan:

$$\text{إِنَّمَا نُطْعِمُكُمْ لِوَجْهِ اللَّهِ لَا نُرِيدُ مِنكُمْ جَزَاءً وَلَا شُكُورًا}$$
$$\text{إِنَّا نَخَافُ مِن رَّبِّنَا يَوْمًا عَبُوسًا قَمْطَرِيرًا}$$

[Saying], "We feed you only for the face [i.e. approval] of Allah. We wish not from you reward or gratitude. Indeed, we

fear from our Lord a Day austere and distressful."
Al Quran 76: 9-10

There was one friend I could always depend on no matter what, and that was my girl Sakinah aka Freckles.

"Khadijah, I'm sending Madinah back out there for half the summer and you must send her back."

"OK," I said, "what's going on?"

"Nothing. She just needs to go with you for a while." After Sakinah and her children left California for the first time, they were always there in my time of need. However, Madinah came back and forth more than the others. She would sometimes be picked up from my place by her Aunt Phyllis. Madinah would spend some of the time on tour with her aunty. Phyllis was Sakinah's sister, who took her own life on June 16, 1995, and this would impact Madinah and the rest of her family forever. This news devastated their whole family and the world. Sakinah spoke at her sister's funeral and her commentary about her sister appeared in Jet Magazine. We all miss her voice; she will be remembered always as the beautiful, sultry songstress, Phyllis Hyman.

A new home

We moved off Norton and settled into our home, almost back to where we started, in the same location as the after-hours club. But now it was our home. I started to have Friday night get-togethers with the Nation of Islam, Sunni Muslims, Black Panthers, some local activists, and some people from the old US Organization. The Panthers and the US Organization were at odds with each other back in the day. The founder, Ron Karenga, came up with what we now call, Kwanzaa. A lot of African American and African American Muslims celebrate this festive man-made holiday, but I have always been OK with the two Eids, the Muslim holidays; one is celebrated after the fast of the month of Ramadan, and the other commemorates the sacrifice our of Prophet Abraham, peace be upon him, during the month of Dhul Hijja, when the pilgrims who are performing Hajj descend Mt. Arafat.

I enjoyed these meetings while they lasted, because they gave me a sense of belonging and it allowed me to ask questions about the community I had joined. On Friday nights I would serve food and play host. I was interested in finding out what divided us and how we could possibly come together. As I learned, I tried to use my newfound understanding and also tried to show my children by way of example.

Salina and Malik were married at my house.

There was a young couple a little older than they were, Ebony and Zahhir, and they became close friends. I was glad they had someone to relate to. Ebony and her children would become forever a part of our extended family.

Our good friend and Sheikh, Said Tahir from Ghana, was a very soft-spoken, kind, but firm man. Said was also the Muslim chaplain at the Youth Authority where Malik and I would get better acquainted, unfortunately. Malik committed a crime and was convicted while married to Salina. We would go from mother-in-law and son-in-law to mother and son. Over the course of the next 18 years, I became his second mom.

In 1995, not long after the two were married, my first grandchild was born. Now, I could relate to what my mom felt. My mom didn't look like a Big Momma and neither did I.

It's a boy, right?

When I heard that Salina was in labor I got to the hospital as soon as I could. Her doctor was a family friend, Khadijah Lang. Dr. Khadijah said to me, "Salina is doing fine, and so is the baby."

"Thank you, Sister," I said.

Malik and I took turns tending to Salina, who acted an entire fool. She spit venom left and right. She didn't want to walk or do a back rub and didn't want to talk. In fact, if I remember correctly she told me to shut up! She only got away with that because she housed my grandbaby in her belly.

"You know what Malik?" I said, "I don't have to take this abuse." I went over to the table and chair that Salina had in her hospital room and went to sleep. When I woke up, Malik was on the other side of the table knocked out.

"Boy wake up," I said, "you can't leave your wife over there suffering like that."

"Ma, she cussed me out and told me to get away from her," he said pitifully.

"Cussed you out," I giggled. I have never heard my child say a bad word in my life, and I didn't know she knew the meaning of the words she said. Nevertheless, if she knew the meaning or not, she called him everything in the book plus some.

Malik was so excited waiting for his son to be born. After a few more pushes, out popped a little red squiggly thing.

"Let me hold my boy," Malik was crying and laughing at the same time.

"I can't," said Dr. Lang.

"Huh," Malik said, "Why can't I hold him?"

"Because it's a girl!"

"A girl? Y'all said she was having a boy."

"Well OK, but Allah said it's a girl," I said, laughing out loud.

"Well, can I hold my daughter then?" Malik asked Dr. Lang.

"Just a minute, let's get her weighed."

After getting her cleaned up, the baby girl was handed to her daddy, then to me. They had decided on naming her Niani, which I thought was cute. But they both had other names they were considering. Salina wanted to name her after her best friend, Quenda, who she was still mourning, and Malik wanted to name her after his sister, PomPom, whose name is Octavia. They also wanted an Islamic name, Ayesha. My grandbaby got all the names.

Niani started looking a little strange to Dr. Lang. She was yellowish and had a fever, and so did Salina. I had left to go home and change and get something to eat, but as soon as I got in the door, the phone was ringing. Malik was screaming into the phone.

"Ma!"

"Yes, what is it?"

"They said something was wrong with the baby and Salina got a high fever. I don't know what to do."

I got myself together and rushed back to the hospital. When I reached Salina's room, pissed off was the nicest thing I could say. My daughter was still in the gowns that she gave birth in, and the same bed I had left her in. I had gone home, changed, ate, and came back, and she was still in the same condition? I called Dr.

Lang, who sprang into action immediately. I had so many nurses in that room, you'd think it was a convention.

But, it was too late, I'm mad as hell now.

"Gimmie the dang sheets. I'll wash my child myself. Malik, you go to the nursery and watch your child, and I'll stay here and see to Salina." Salina's fever would not break, and it had been two days. Niani was doing better and was due to be discharged. Malik came into the room all excited, saying to Salina that the baby could go home with him.

"What?!" Salina said, "Oh no, Mom I don't want my baby to leave without me," she cried.

"Me and my grandma, Helen, can take care of her 'till you get out."

"Nooooo," Salina was frantic. "Mom, don't let them take my baby." Another quick call to Dr. Lang, and she handled the problem, but Salina didn't seem to be getting any better.

People were calling, asking how the little family was making out. When Sheikh Said heard how sick Salina was, he began to pray for her and instructed me to rub her belly and forehead and repeat as salaam, as salaam, as salaam, which means God's peace, Allah's Peace. After about an hour, I was blessed to witness another miracle. Salina's fever broke, her blood count came back to normal, and she was allowed to leave the hospital with her child. I refused to go to California Hospital for a bug bite after that ordeal. And because of this, I would never again leave a loved one alone in a hospital unattended. Even if I had to sleep in the hallway or ER, I am not leaving. This stubbornness of mine would come in handy when I started advocating for family members being mistreated during hospital stays.

Chapter 32: Anna Jean

Nunu

Remembering Niani's birth reminded me of Anna Jean, and my Nunu. It was October 1993. I remember this day like it was yesterday.

"Ain't you the one that keeps kids?"

"Who you asking?" Deb asked this very pregnant lady who had come through Roscoe's door, being very loud.

"That Mooslem lady, don't you take kids?"

"Why?" I asked.

"'Cause you can have this one," she said. "Ya'll got some leftover chicken?"

"Naw, we ain't got no leftover nothing', come back at the end of the night. Dang, ever since that incident with Jorge, all kinds of strange people have been coming in here," I said.

Me and Deb just laughed and went on with our work. Debra was doing the best that she could, dealing with the murder of her daughter and knowing the one who killed her made it even worse.

A few weeks later, while working, I got a call from Harbor General Hospital.

"Khadijah, phone," the cashier said while standing behind the counter.`

"Who's sick?" she asked. "The hospital has been calling here all day."

"I don't know. Now I'm scared to answer it."

I took a deep breath before I answered, "Hello, how can I help you? Yes, this is Khadijah..... She did what? Are you serious?... No, I am not a relative.... Yes, I do have a license." I hung up the phone and just stared into space.

"Deb," I said, "was that pregnant girl that comes in here named Anna Jean?"

"Yeah, why?" Deb asked.

"'Cause she really did leave her baby to me. That is why the hospital called me before they had to call someone else. They saying the baby is sick and that I need to come and sign the paperwork in order to get her. She had a girl."

"Oh wow, Dee," Debra said, "are you going to get her?"

"I don't know. Let me call Westside Children's Agency and see if it's OK." After talking to my social worker, Cheryl Newton, I was able to call the hospital back and confirm that I could take her.

The following day, I went to see Anna Jean's baby. She was in the neonatal ICU. I had never been in that part of a hospital. It was as cheerful as a kids' hospital ward could be. The walls were painted with Disney characters and bright colors were everywhere. It looked like a massive playroom.

The nurse led me to where Babygirl Clark was lying. I broke down into tears as soon as I saw her. The baby had tubes going everywhere, from the top of her head to her nose and mouth, and she was no bigger than the palm of my hand.

"What's wrong with her?" I asked. The nurse picked up her chart and began to explain the baby's ailments.

"The baby is not a preemie," the nurse said, "but she has a lot of detoxing to do, plus we did what was called a blood wash, because the mom had an infection that compromised the baby. But she is doing better and can go home in a few days."

"My goodness," I said, "and the mom asked for me?"

"Yes," the nurse said, "but if it's too much, then we can find another home."

"No," I said, "I'll see what I can do. I have already called the agency and I've taken classes on how to care for babies in this condition. I just can't believe that her mom left her here."

A few days later, Anna Jean showed up at Roscoe's to ask me if I had gotten her baby.

"Girl, what's wrong with you?" I asked her. "The people at the agency asking me all kinds of questions about you, they asked me if I knew you."

"Well, I ain't got nobody to keep her," Anna Jean said.

"Where is her daddy?" I asked, "or grandparents?"

"She ain't got no grandparents," Anna Jean said, "and her daddy family already got two of 'em."

"What you mean her daddy's people got two of them? How many kids do you have?"

"Well, she was number 16," she said. I must have stared at her for I don't know how long.

"Did you say number 16?" I asked in astonishment.

"Yes," she said, "I had 16 kids. I don't believe in abortion."

On that note, I had to go sit down.

This woman was my age, in fact, she had two years on me!

"Well," I said to her, "they want you to start a reunification program to get the baby back."

"I ain't doin' that shit," Anna Jean said.

"Huh? Whatchu you mean, not doin' it?"

"Naw," Anna Jean said, "I said you can keep her. I just want to see her from time to time."

"I don't get it," I said, "you don't want your baby?"

"It's not that I don't want her, I know I can't do right for long, and I can't stop using. I get clean for a short time, then I'm back out there and my kids get taken. The others who ain't grown, end up going from place to place. I know how you Mooslems do, and I want her to at least have a chance."

I took her baby girl, Blade, home and introduced her to her new family. Dayshawn, was my only foster child at the time. She had come to me at about 5 years old and boy did she give me a run for my money, always getting into something. Her mom was in jail and Dayshawn had no family that could take her in. Salina treated her like a little sister. Dayshawn stayed with us until her mom's release and fulfilled the necessary requirement of classes, and the judge's orders to finally reclaim her daughter. Yes, a Black woman was knocked down, but she rose back up in the end. Another case where if her mom would have gotten adequate help she would not have had to be traumatized with jail. Dayshawn made up a song about the new baby who was just two weeks old. That name stuck with her, and 27 years later, we still call her Nunu.

When I told Saud of the situation, he was as joyful as any new father would be. I sent her pictures to him. It sent him to the moon! As soon as I could get permission for her to travel, I took her to meet her new dad. He named her Najalah, the one with the big wide eyes. It took two years to finalize the adoption, and Anna Jean was there every step of the way. She became part of the family and my housekeeper.

Fajr Morning Prayer

We had all just prayed and gone back to bed. It had been unusually warm the last few days for January, even in Los Angeles. Out of nowhere, we heard a rumbling like a train coming down the street. Then, we felt it. At first, it felt like we were on an amusement park ride. It was as if two pairs of very large hands had grabbed both sides of the house and started a tug of war, everything was swaying back and forth. I tried to jump up out of the bed, but the force threw me back down. "Maaaaaaa, Auntyyyyy," was all I heard. I was so scared, but I knew what it was.

"EARTHQUAKE," I yelled, "get under something."

Nunu was sleeping with Salina and Salina had just grabbed her foot before she went flying off the bed. Furniture, that was at one time against the wall, was now in the center of the floor. Dishes were breaking as they hit the kitchen floor. We could hear Uncle Bay, who lived upstairs, and his family scurrying around.

"Is everyone OK?" we were all shouting at the same time. Just as we were able to calm down and regroup, the first aftershock hit almost as hard as the quake itself. Our area of Mid City, Los Angeles suffered some damage, but not as bad as other areas. We marked ourselves safe from the Northridge Earthquake of 1994.

Nunu always knew who Anna Jean was and loved her to death; my rules for Anna Jean were; don't come to my house high, don't bring drugs to my house, don't bring anyone to my house, and never steal anything from me. I let her know if she did any of these things, she would not be welcomed back.

Anna Jean would sometimes fall off the wagon. Those times she would just stay away for long periods of time, then show up straight and always happy. Anna Jean was the fried chicken queen and made the best potato salad! She would clean the house like nobody's business and tell us stories of street life, stories most people would never hear.

After about three years, she came to me.

"I'm ready."

"Ready for what?" I asked.

"OK, Imma be a Mooslem."

"Anna Jean, you just don't be no Muslim. I never said you had to become a Muslim."

"I know," she said.

"Well, you know we don't celebrate Christmas and Easter or eat pork? We don't drink or do drugs."

"Well, imma work on that one," she said.

"I don't celebrate Christmas or Easter and stopped eating pork." I said. "We don't have boyfriends either." I added.

Anna Jean got really quiet on that one.

"But the main thing is we believe in One God with no partners and that Muhammad who died 1400 years ago was the seal of the Holy Prophets, and we believe in all of the Prophets, but they are not gods or helpers. We believe in angels and jinn, and the Quran being the final revelation."

"I know," she said.

"Well, how you know?" I asked her.

"Whatchu think I been doin' here when these kids have Quran class? I hear all that y'all say. I see you and Teacher (Teacher was my friend and business partner, Ummil Khair

Elamin) and how y'all act. I believe all that," she said. "I'm reading the lessons the same as the kids. Are you saying I can't be no Moooslem?"

"Girl, if you don't stop saying Moooslem, Imma choke you. It's not my place to say who is Muslim and who ain't," I said to her. I called Sheikh Shuaib and told him that I had a sister who wanted to take Shahadah.

"Can it be done over the phone or what should I do?" I asked him. We decided that we would wait 'till the next day when we could bring her to see him. Usually giving the Shahadah is not delayed but I wanted to make sure she was in her right mind and knew what she was saying and doing.

The next day, we all went to the King Fahad Masjid, and not only did Anna Jean take Shahadah but two other sisters that had become a part of our household joined her that day taking the Shahadatain! Alhamdulillah, praise God!

Anna Jean spent the next two Eids (Islamic Holy Holidays) before her addiction problem took over her again, which ultimately killed her. May Allah elevate her good deeds and reward her with whatever was promised to her. She was the most unselfish person I have ever met, giving up a child and placing her where she believed she'd be loved and cared for. Allah blessed me to receive this gift, this beautiful daughter who has the soul of her beautiful, unselfish mom. People say Nunu is like me, but I cannot take credit for what Allah gave her through her DNA. When we see Nunu's kind heart, we see Anna Jean.

Chapter 33: Baby Two

During the time we were going through the adoption process of Nunu, I had another little boy in my care, Gregory. We loved that little boy, but he wasn't ours to keep. After being in our care, his grandmother was granted guardianship of him, but she lived in Philly. Yeah Philly, where my peeps Sakinah and her kids now live, close to Delaware.

"Yes, I'll take him there," I'd said to Cheryl Newton, the social worker. We were the only family Gregory knew, he was still a baby, and even though she was his grandma, he didn't know her. So, the plan was for me to stay a few days, to avoid causing him too much trauma. After a few days of being in Philly, I got a call from the agency.

"Can you leave and come back now?" the case worker asked.

"Why what's wrong?"

"We want to place a child with you."

"OK, but can it wait 'till I get back? What happened?"

The baby had been placed with two other foster homes before me. She had stopped breathing twice and both foster moms were afraid of getting her back.

"OK, well where is she?" I asked.

"Cedar Sinai," the social worker said. I got back on the plane. I must say, it was the most enjoyable ride. They were so happy that I said yes that they got me a first-class ticket. You know being in first class and being Black is always an opening for some racist remark. If you are not a known entertainer or into sports, frankly, they want to know how your Black ass got the seat, or if it's really your seat. After all of the questions and eye rolling, I settled back into my comfortable seat and watched as people passed me by, wondering what famous person I was.

I was still into wearing my African garbs back then; beautiful head wraps, and colorful flowing dresses. So, of course I stood out. The Teacher and I had an African dress shop next door to Harold and Belles on Jefferson in Los Angeles called *My Sisters' Place*. We sold African fabrics and clothes, and we had several businesses up and down Jefferson over the years. But selling African fabrics always gave us clothing, and we would style ourselves to fit our personalities. It confused people as to our ethnicity. In Los Angeles, you never knew who was who, or where someone came from. I would sometimes pretend that I didn't understand English, just so that I could see and hear what people said about me. I got that habit from Saud who could 'pass' for Egyptian, Arab, or anyone from the Middle East. He taught me this, you would be surprised at what you would learn pretending that you don't understand English.

When the plane landed at LAX, I went straight to Cedars to find out what was going on with baby girl Brianna. One look at her and I was sprung. She was adorable, a chocolate, fat little thing with hazel brown eyes. She looked up at me and smiled.

"What do you mean, you stopped breathing, young lady?" I asked the smiling baby looking at me.

"Allah didn't decree that for you yet. Do you want to go home with me?" I said to her playfully. Of course, she couldn't answer me because she was only three months old. I called the house and told them to prepare the baby bed where Gregory had slept. Salina had just gotten comfortable at home with Niani. Nunu liked playing the part of the big three-year-old Aunty to Niani, now she could be a big sister, too. All I know is that Nunu really understood that she was older and in charge.

"Saud, guess what? I got another baby and I think she'll be with us for a while. They are saying that she may need a permanent home. She has an older sister, Golda, who may need a place. Golda and Salina are the same age."

The phone went silent. *Did he hang up on me or did they disconnect the phone?*

The next day I got my phone call right on time.

"Khadijah," Saud said in a very low voice, almost scary, "I know you like helping the kids, and may Allah reward you, but you have started taking in the kids and not asking me anything. I asked you not to take any more for adoption but you told the people that you would if she needed it, plus she has a sister. What about our plans for my release? We not even supposed to be staying in the States. Now, you have created this whole tribe of kids. How are we supposed to move around like that? I guess I will be traveling alone. As salaamu alaikum Khadijah."

I just sat there holding the phone, and he was right, I had not asked him anything, nor did I even consider the fact that our plans were to move out of the States with all its ugly history and unfairness. But moving into the unknown with all these kids with ailments was something I had not thought about. I felt bad for moving so swiftly, but it had felt right at the time.

I sent Saud an apology letter and a picture of Brianna because he had never seen her before. A few weeks later, after receiving the letter and the photo, Saud called me. It had been a hectic day running a daycare and trying to homeschool.

"As salaamu alaikum, Saud," I said into the phone, "did you get my letter?"

"Wa alaikum salaam. Yeah, I got it," he said.

"Brianna is cute huh," I stated.

"Yeah, she cute, but stop calling her Brianna. Our daughter's new name is Niemah."

"Niemah, are you serious?"

"Yeah, I'm serious, that's why you sent that picture. You knew good and well if I saw her, I couldn't say no. Niemah, her name means present, blessing, " he said.

"You mean we can keep her?" I had gotten all excited because it had just been revealed to me that she too would become a permanent Shabazz.

"Well, I want to name her Sakinah, I said. "Sakinah means peace and tranquility. I want to name her after my sister, Sakinah, who was anything but tranquil. This child is so loud and uneasy. In sha'Allah (God willing) maybe her name will calm her down."

"Yes! We can keep her," Saud said.

I decided to take all the children to Pennsylvania, so that Saud could meet his new daughter, Niemah. With Niemah came an older sister, Golda. Golda was the same age as Salina and was just maxing out of her foster care placement. We kept Golda and her situation under wraps until we could find the right moment to tell Saud about her. That right moment never really came, but he loved his baby girl, Niemah. He would sing to her over the phone, some song about a brown-eyed girl. Anyway, whenever he could call she would hear his voice and calm down. My phone bill was stupid crazy.

Niemah Shabazz

One of the tricks we used before this new prison telephone system was to have multiple lines in your home. They would be set up like you had a rooming house. We did this just in case the phone bill got too big to pay. If Ma Bell (the phone company) turned you off, you'd already have another phone in the house to use, without trying to explain a new service where there was a previous bill. This went on for years until the phone company and the prison system figured out a new way to rob families. Some families had to do this using the names of their children. They would receive a lot of criticism over the years for messing up their children's name with utility companies, however in some cases that was the only way to stay connected to a loved one in prison. I didn't have to do this, but I certainly understood the sisters who did. Those phone bills could be well over $500 a month, sometimes more than your rent!

Salina and Malik were married for only a short time before Malik was sent to prison himself. He was accused of one the vilest of crimes, and I was beyond any type of understanding.

"Ma, it's police all outside the house," my son Ranel informed me, "I don't know who they are looking for, but they are coming this way."

"Oh, Lawd have mercy," I said. "OK, when they come in can y'all please just shut up and not say nothing, and somebody take the little ones to the back and don't come up here unless I say so."

About 10 minutes earlier, I'd received a call from a friend at Roscoe's, telling me that the police had been there looking for Malik but didn't say why. Malik had just left work and wasn't there. The fact that the cops showed up at his job gave me anxiety. I have a genuine dislike and distrust of law enforcement, Black or white. But for me a Black cop was always the worst, always trying to prove something. A Black cop would always treat you worse than their counterparts.

I could never hide how I was feeling. It always showed on my face. If something was contemptible, you saw it on my face immediately, and it made them treat me horribly. But I got my face together, I truly didn't know what Malik was being accused of.

There goes that threatening 'let's tear their damn door down' banging at the door.

"Yes?" I said, as I answered the door. "What's the problem, officer?" I asked as they pushed past me.

"We are looking for Dana. We know he lives here. Is he here?"

"Well, it's no secret that he lives here, but no he's not."

"When was the last time you saw him?" The ugly-acting Black ass cop asked me.

"Right before he went to work," I replied, in my most fake pleasant voice, which was the truth.

"Why are you looking for him?" I asked.

"Where is your daughter? We want to ask her," one of the cops asked.

"My daughter is with the children. I will call her, but I have a house full of kids, you don't have a search warrant, and..." Before I could say another word, stank-ass Black cop with the attitude said, "We looking for Dana for rape and attempted murder. Now Imma ask you again, have you seen Dana?"

All of my cool and quick comebacks left my body. *No, he didn't say rape.* I was stuck right there. Honestly, I recall very little of the rest of the conversation. A few days later, Dana was captured and caged, begging for forgiveness, but denying the charges.

"Hell naw, I am not trying to get no bail money. What I look like? I allowed you to marry my baby and your trifling ass do what?" I yelled.

"Ma, I didn't do all that they said."

Well, you did something," I said to him, "what did you do?" He went on to describe what took place as a consensual relationship with a woman who had just found out he was married, so he said.

"You don't believe me?" he cried into the phone.

"Nope, I don't. I don't have sympathy for no rapist or child molesters, and you border on the line of both. If I had my way, I would throw gasoline on a rapist and then light the match. That's how much I hate rapists and child molesters, and the same shit goes for you," I said, as I slammed the phone down only to turn around to look at Salina's face.

She looked as if she was about to faint. Her broken heart showed up all over her face, but she couldn't express how she felt to me. She just kind of shut down. She did have her sister, Ebony, to talk to. Ebony stayed very close to her, advising her over the years.

I immediately turned on my fix-it mode. What I didn't understand at the time was just how much my daughter needed me. She needed me more than she could say, and I didn't know how to help her through her emotions, nor did I realize that she needed support in understanding her feelings.

"Get ready Salina," I said, "we are going to every court appearance, because if he did this, you ain't staying with no rapist." We went to the trial out of embarrassment and anger. We listened to the witness and the victim and the story that was unfolding wasn't at all what I was expecting. It sounded like Malik was telling us the truth, that it wasn't rape, but he did have a side woman who was not his wife. He'd had an affair, it was consensual, they got into an argument and a fight, and he had put his hands on this young woman. *OK, now it made sense.*

Coming out of the bathroom at the courthouse after them finding him guilty, we ran into the victim who told us, "Naw, he didn't rape me, but I bet he won't put his hands on nobody else."

Omg this girl just told us she lied on him. Not only did she say this to us, but she went down to his job and told some of them that he had not raped her. But he will spend the next 18 years wishing that he'd kept his pants up and temper in check. He did beat her, and he beat her bad, but because he didn't lie to me, I told him, "Malik I'm so sorry son. You gonna have to beg Allah to show you how to do this one."

Saud was upset, but his hands were tied.

Salina just looked so outdone. I could hardly stand to look at her. But to be honest, I couldn't tell if it was relief, grief, or both.

"You ain't even 18 years old, Salina. You are too young to carry that weight, but I'm not goin' to tell you to divorce him. I will say, stay until you can't do it anymore or don't want to do it, period. Just don't be deceitful in your decision. I'll take the baby to see her dad if you cannot do it."

"Ma, he has another daughter, Tajanique. She's four or five years old."

"Really?" I said. "Do you and her mom get along?"

"Yes, we kinda do," Salina said.

"Well, I don't have a problem taking the girls in to see Malik." And for the next 18 years, I did. Since Malik told me the truth, I couldn't just throw him into the belly of the beast. He needed help as well, and Allah knows Best.

Chapter 34: Who Will Speak for Them?

The 90s had a lot going on, and trying to support three Black men in prison was a task. The only financial support I gave was to Malik. Big Hassan never asked for anything, and Saud really didn't need me to give him any money. I just spent a lot of money going back and forth with all the kids about twice a month to visit him.

My dad and stepmom, Brenda, would visit every few years and Los Angeles did not disappoint! They were here during the OJ Simpson trial of the century. We couldn't leave the house until Mom Brenda got her fill of the case, watching it on TV. She was the OJ expert. What you had better not do was talk bad about OJ in front of her.

"We all know he didn't do it," Mom Brenda would say. "These white folks are gonna railroad him like they always do us," she went on saying, "I hope he gets off."

"Yeah, well it's not likely," Daddy said back to her.

"Can we just go?" I asked, annoyed and acting bratty. After all, my daddy was here and that meant I could get stuff. Shopping has never been my thing. Most of my shopping has always been from the back of a car, but I have a love for household gadgets, home improvement projects, and one-of-a-kind things that are usually found in specialty shops.

We were going to pick up Thai. She was going to show Daddy all the shops she knew about in Leimert Park, then we would head down the Pacific Coast Highway for beach shops and dinner. We were all seafood lovers, and we knew just where to eat – Gladstones. Gladstones was Daddy's favorite beach place back then. Gladstones was an indoor/outdoor seafood house, right off of the 101. You could eat crab and lobster 'till it came out of your ears. It had a comfortable ambiance with wooden tables and stools. There was sand on the floor and sitting right on the beach you could almost grab your meal right out of the water!

Daddy loved to travel. He would show up everywhere, but when he came to California, he would bring his new toy; either a camera or his maps. His visits to California were before we had GPS, so he always had an AAA map. Those maps worked my nerves because I was the one who had to read them! Every time Daddy came, we would throw a big BBQ or do something special. We'd have live entertainment with clean comedy and some sort of music with a live band, right in my backyard. Everyone waited on them hand and foot, from the time they came 'til the time they left, but what we never did was talk.

Daddy never mentioned Saud or how much time he had. He never asked me how I was doing, but I guess he figured I was OK, with everything he saw. I didn't have to ask my dad for much over the years. He accepted my new family and lifestyle, my kids were his new grandchildren, my new sisters and nieces and nephews were now his as well. No matter how many I took home to Cleveland, Daddy welcomed them into his home and made them feel welcomed. Even when Big Hassan was released we flew home to Cleveland with all the kids. We rented a van so that we could take a road trip to Atlantic City while we were there.

I Introduced Big Hassan to my family as another big brother to me and the children's uncle. We drove all over the East Coast, so the children could see real snow. Living in Los Angeles, they had never seen snow except on TV.

From Cleveland, we drove to Atlantic City so I could show them the Famous Atlantic City Boardwalk. My Aunt Audrey let us use her timeshare while we were there. I was so disappointed, it was ruined! The boardwalk of my childhood was gone, it had given way to a new one with casinos. The city itself looked ravished. I was so hurt and disappointed that I couldn't wait to get home.

On our way back, we stopped by to see my sister, Sakinah, who was living in Wilmington, Delaware. I was so happy to see my sister.

"GURLLLLLLL!" we screamed when we saw each other. Out the van window we shouted, "As salaamu alaikum!" I jumped out and ran towards her, as she jumped off her porch to hug me.

"How are you traveling with all of them kids?" Sakinah asked.

"Yeah, I know chile. They ain't stopped talking for almost four hours straight."

"Dang, they still talking. I know they will be going to sleep in a minute. A couple of them are coughing, so I'm giving them some cough meds that will knock them out."

"That ain't no cough medicine," Sakinah said, "that's Nyquil and that's too strong for them."

"No, it's not. I just give them a lower dose. It will stop the coughing and the talking," I joked. "Well, the joke was on me, not reading the instructions properly. The bottle also said it may cause excitability in children, and that's just what we got; five overstimulated girls.

Sakinah and I vowed to see each other soon. After a short and sweet visit in Delaware, we got back in the van and started for Cleveland to prepare for our plane ride home. We made one more stop in Pennsylvania to see Saud.

Visiting a correctional facility is always bitter sweet. You get to see your loved one, but then the reality of leaving always looms overhead. The children seemed bothered. They asked questions that brought tears to my eyes: "Daddy do you work here?" Nunu asked. "Why do those police have guns and be so mean?"

"They are guards, Nunu," Saud told her.

"Oh," said Nunu, "to watch out for the bad guy?"

Saud and I just looked at each other. It was hard to tell her that her dad was considered one of the bad guys. It was also hard to sit and watch as grown men, having to go to the bathroom, weren't able to go without raising their hands like children.

The United States has always had punishment and control down pat, but lacks in the rehabilitation part of one's incarceration. This is my snappy comeback to some people's philosophy that incarceration is needed to produce better citizens. Then why does America lead the world in incarcerating citizens? If we claim to be the most civilized in the world, why does America lead the world for the most violent of crimes?

Niani and Taj were little, but they always seemed to enjoy visits with their dad. They got to play with him and eat that horrible food. It was no different with the rest of the children going to see Saud, going back and forth to those cancer-riddled vending machines. The food was so bad and expensive, we often came home sick and broke. The so-called fresh fruit had so much wax on it that you could use one to polish your furniture. But like most junk food, the kids liked it, and even the captured inhabitants of the prison seemed to enjoy the food.

Once while visiting Saud in Lompoc, my rings came up missing. My favorite emerald ring set in 22 karat gold came up missing. Did I say the ring was missing? What I meant was that it was stolen. After coming through the metal detectors and explaining that I was Muslim and didn't have to remove my headpiece, I was waiting to go in the back and be checked by a female guard. They sent a large, burly, intimidating female who said that it was my turn and she needed to see under my scarf before going into the visiting room. I had no problem with that. I expected it. She was a nasty hateful so and so. "OK she's cleared," the large, buff officer said.

"Where is my jewelry?" I asked

"What jewelry? the sergeant asked.

"The jewelry I came in here with!" I snapped. "Where are my rings and necklace?"

"I haven't seen any jewelry," the guard said. "Y'all seen any jewelry?"

"Nope," was the reply. Needless to say, I never got my things back. I never wore jewelry to visit anyone again. That was an expensive lesson learned. You see, if I had bucked up too much, they would have stopped my visits and would have started harassing my husband. Sometimes you have to pick your battles.

Always remember, your behavior on the outside, can negatively impact your loved one's life on the inside.

By the late 90s, I was established in the community as a daycare owner, The Shabazz Family Daycare. We were right across the street from Ms. Myles Daycare. Sister Elamin and I decided to join forces in order to combine our talents. She was a teacher at Sister Clara Muhammad School and was also one of Salina's teachers. She loved to teach, and I didn't. I wasn't a teacher and had no desire to be one. Our main goal was to keep the Muslim children in an Islamic atmosphere. After the closing of the Muslim school on South Central Avenue, Sister Yvonne Ali would be a great help to me as well, as we transitioned from being a daycare to a school.

We loved the roles we played, providing Muslim children with an environment conducive to their Islam. We would give the children great Eid and Quran memorization parties. We would invite the children from the Myles Family Daycare, and everyone had a ball. We had petting zoos, African stilt walkers, and all kinds of activities for the kids that lasted all day, inside and outside of the house. The food was catered halal food. The children had so much fun. The Eid parties lasted for three days. They never missed Christmas, mainly because they never had one.

The children's commencements were just as fabulous, the girls dressed up in dresses that were meant for royalty. They could have anything they wanted. We would rent out a hall and hire waitresses and waiters. As they so proudly stood before their parents and recited Quran, they had Bro. Bilal's halal BBQ beef ribs, halal Chinese food, fish dishes, Mediterranean dishes, sweet potato pie, bean pies, and every cake they could think of. We rained on them gifts galore. There was nothing too good for our little Muslimas.

Al Hibah Shabazz Day Care Graduation

I was not, and I'm still not qualified to run a school, but Los Angeles made it easy. We enrolled the children into the City of Angels Independent Studies Program and they gave us the curriculum we needed. We added the Islamic curriculum by using some of our local brothers, Imam Omar Sheikh, Said Tahir, Sheikh Shuaib, and Brother Jamal Adeen, to name a few. All Islamic studies teachers were scholars. In order for the children to move up a grade, they had to take the same standard tests as the rest of LA's students. And that's how they were graded, through the LA Unified School District.

We didn't receive much community support because we didn't come from any particular masjid. I went to them all and still do. Well, most of them anyway. I was able to find the good in most of the masjids and the rest I'd leave alone. We also had enough learned scholars around us to ask what we didn't know.

UCLA's Muslim Students' Association helped us as well. All of the children graduated and most of them went on to college and have earned more degrees than a thermometer.

Between the school, kids, and jails, I was struggling to keep things moving smoothly, especially with so many people that had become dependent on me. So many people have lived with me over the years, I've lost count.

A young family had just enrolled their children at my daycare. A lot of people inquired about my services. My name was getting around the community as a Muslim daycare provider. Families were interviewing me to watch after their children, all the while I was feeling so hypocritical.

How can I share my story?

It wasn't that they were unfamiliar with people in jail or prison or had even been there themselves. But, the way you are looked at, people treat you differently if you are supporting someone behind bars. Some would treat you like you were the one who committed the crime. Some treat you as if you are contagious, then there are those who treat you as if you are stupid or crazy for the support that you give.

And if you are married, everyone always assumes that you are cheating on your spouse. Men are always in your face, trying to see if they can talk you out of your clothes. Others treat you as a project that needs saving. I found out that being a hijabi (one who dresses modestly) didn't make a difference, men would try you. It was early on in Saud's incarceration that Allah and I had a long talk about what was in store for me. I begged and cried for guidance, and I must say that when Allah chooses to guide you, your fate is out of your hands. Never ever did I want a house full of children, or people for that matter. But I got a kick out of being helpful.

I really loved being married. Never ever would I have found the strength, courage, and patience, had Allah not chosen this waiting time for me. One thing is for sure and two things are for certain, this was not the life I chose for myself, and little did I know it was about to change again.

Nope, I didn't sign up for this!

After seeing the conditions of our locked-up family members and realizing how they and other incarcerated people were really considered America's throwaway population, I have known the talent and the genius of so many. I've seen them get themselves together and struggle to make their lives right.

For example, watching Hassan and his transformation. He learned how to use computers and turned around and taught the children what he learned. I've also seen them feel so defeated, the ones who are truly innocent, and society not giving a damn about it.

The penal system strips them of any humanity they may have had and offers no real rehabilitation to help them be productive if they ever find their way home again. This system is purposely designed to do that. Did you know that this system counts how many children come to visit a parent in prison?

They are counting them to include them in the space needed to house future captives!

I realize that people commit crimes and should be held accountable for the decisions they make. However, I know firsthand that the prevention and rehabilitation programs we have in place are useless. If we had more help on the front end and stopped using the jail system as a mental health hospital, we would have more productive citizens.

Chapter 35: Shabazz Family Daycare

Kim and Danny showed up with their three children, looking for a Muslim daycare. We immediately hit it off, but I recognized something was not quite right.

"Are you OK Kim?" I asked. "You seem upset."

"Yes, well we don't have a place to stay," Kim said.

"You mean you are homeless? What happened?" Kim began to explain their circumstances and it really bothered me that they were in such dire straits. I was trying to decide as to whether to let them spend the night. After all, I had just met them, and we were strangers to each other. Kim was a tall, pretty, pleasant young woman. We took to each other almost immediately. I'm not old enough to be Kim's mom, but I would be the closest thing she had as a mother figure for years to come. We would settle on the title, Aunty, for me. Over the years, Kim would have so many challenges, but basically, as with many of the people I adopted into my life, she had a kind heart.

Thank God the heart is judged by Allah and not us.

Brother Danny was another Black man who Allah sent my way, so that we could be an aide to each other throughout the years. Danny worked his own business as a handyman contractor. His eye for design and coming up with unique ideas always amazed me and reminded me of the time I worked at Windows and Willows in Pittsburgh. Danny was also FOI and a martial arts instructor. He was the children's first teacher in the art of self-defense. We also fondly named him Captain Save a H**! His mom, Lera and I gave him that name because he was always coming to the aid of some sister in trouble. Most of the young women were wonderful young ladies that helped save him as well.

Danny was always serious and always willing to participate in a good conversation about Black folks. There would come a time when Kim became ill and couldn't parent her children. Bro. Dan stepped in and took his sons and raised them into fine young men. I was able to take the two girls and raise them with my children, so everyone was able to remain in touch. We made plenty of mistakes, like most people, but I can say that I am proud of them all.

Kim would stay with me off and on for years herself, and she had learned so much from Danny, watching him work, that sometimes we would call on her to help with small construction jobs.

"Kim."

"Yes Aunty."

"Something is wrong with the toilet, and I can't find Danny. Can you come check it out?"

"Yes ma'am. I'll be there soon," she'd say. Now one thing that we all knew to be true was that her 'be right there' meant sometime in the next few days!

Kim and Salina were like sisters, I'm sure they held each other's secrets. It must be nice to be able to tell secrets to a friend who would not expose you or hurt you.

A few times, I stepped out in faith with the hope that I had found a confidant, and each time I was betrayed, even though I held a lot of secrets for others. I learned not to trust my stories to fall onto the ears of those who were close to me. And I taught my girls to be distrustful of others, not realizing the message I was sending out.

"Salina," I'd say, "If you want to know who your friends are, make up a story about yourself and see who repeats it back. But now, if someone entrusts you with information that you swear not to repeat, you take that to the grave. Unless it was about hurting someone, you keep your word and do good, even if those around you are not."

"I don't talk to anyone Ma," was her constant reply, which was a good and a bad thing, 'cause I didn't mean that she couldn't talk to me, but my baby bottled up most of her pain just like her Momma, and like my Momma. Trauma! The way we handled it was to not handle it. It's often a learned behavior and we pass it down to our children.

Until we learn how to release the pain properly we will continue this cycle.

Out of my trauma came triumph. I had always relied on someone for my financial support but now I was showing myself what I was made of. I was showing myself what could happen if I only trusted in Allah to guide me, and to always try to do what's right. Awwww but the haters, what they hold in their hearts for you is disgraceful.

Betrayal was hard for me to deal with, so with what I call a healthy distrust, I'm the quiet one, always sitting alone in any situation, trying to stay under the radar. Even in the Muslim community, I didn't know who really cared for me or wanted something from me. I didn't realize that part of it was my aloofness that kept people from reaching out to me as well.

One of my so-called friends decided to use my daycare for her grandkids. She had four kids she wanted to enroll.

"So, Khadijah," Sabrina began the conversation, "what do you charge?"

"For the week or month?" I asked.

"Both."

"$125 a week per child and $500 a month per child. We can work out something if you have more than one child or if you don't have a childcare agency to help you foot the bill."

"Girl, I'm not about to give you no $2000 a month for keeping my kids. You're not even giving up no deals?"

"Wow," I said. "That is my price. If you have a program then that is not coming out of your pocket anyway."

"Yeah, that's right," she said, "so how many kids do you have now? So if you got 6 kids now, that's $3000 and with mine that's another $2000? I don't know about giving you all that."

I am now staring at the phone, realizing that my friend is not any friend of mine, once again. Not only did she not send her kids, she bad mouthed me to other potential clients. She knew that I took people into my home, and she began to attack my business using that information. What she didn't know was that everyone in my house that was an adult was live scanned, whether they worked for me or were just visiting me, including any quote, unquote street people.

Teacher and I looked regularly on the Megan Law site to see if anyone had gone under the radar that we may have missed. The whole community may have been surprised at what we uncovered. I am not taking in any child molesters or rapists. There was a convicted child molester in our community, even closer than that, one listed in our masjid. Because of my son-in-law, I knew that every conviction wasn't accurate, but for everyone's safety, we had to go with the site. This predator in our community would stop and harass my 13-year-old, Niemah while walking to the school we had set up on Jefferson. He would pull up on the corner and block the kids walking to the school. He would pull up on them as they tried to cross the street and tried to give Niemah his number. We would always see this brother and his name was on the Megan Law list. I told the local brothers and didn't get the response I wanted. They were talking about a meeting. I was talking about whooping some ass!

Coming out of Jummah Prayer one Friday, I spotted the brother, who also saw me and kind of smirked; I snapped. My understanding went straight to zero.

"EXCUSE ME!" I said, as I made it towards the brothers who were standing, "Imma say this once to you, don't say anything to my girls, don't give them the salaams, don't nod, don't say anything to them."

He still stood there looking smug.

"Oh, it's funny?" I said. Now I am seeing blood. I'm mad.

"Let me say again, so that you can understand me. Don't you say sh*t to my girls." I had a mugshot of the brother in my hands that I had taken off Megan's Law page.

"You see this? I got about 50 of them in my hand. I intend to put them on every storefront and telephone pole up and down Jefferson and Crenshaw, if you ever say anything to my kids again. I won't be using them to show that you are a child molester. They will be using them for you as a missing person."

"Sister," he said, still half laughing, "that sounded like a threat."

"It did?" I said. "Then I must not have gotten my point across to you. If you try to say something to any of them, I bet they will be looking for your ass at high noon with a flashlight."

I was trying to have respect for the masjid.

"I am not threatening you. I'm telling you and them and whoever is listening what my intentions are. Because I'm not close to bluffing or playing."

Needless to say, I never had a problem out of him again, but unfortunately someone else's daughter did. As far as I know he is still doing 25 years, and I hope that whatever he did to hurt that child, he gets back tenfold. I also hope that he has redeemed himself. I pray that whatever sickness he had or still has, is cleansed from him and Allah knows Best.

The business thrived nonetheless.

Chapter 36: The Year 2000 Was One for The Books

The year 2000 came in with a bang! We all survived the 1900s, just barely. The daycare had turned into a little school, Al Hibah, meaning for the pleasure of Allah. We had moved three different times since starting the school and daycare in my home. Finally, I was able to buy a house in Jefferson Park near Arlington. The neighborhood was in an area once occupied by well-to-do Black doctors and movie stars. Some of the people who lived in this neighborhood were Marvin Gaye's parents, Nat King Cole, and Hattie McDaniel.

Ms. McDaniel was an actress, who played the Black maid in the 1940 movie, *Gone with the Wind*. Her house was on Harvard Street in an area called West Adams. There was a section in West Adams that had mansions. In the 1940s some white residents of the neighborhood filed a lawsuit against Hattie McDaniel. They complained that a Black homeowner in their neighborhood was bringing the home value down. The case went to court and surprisingly, she won the case.

Hattie Mc Daniel's place was huge. I attended a friend's wedding held in this fabulous house. I remember thinking I was going crazy because I would look up and see someone standing by the wall, then I would turn away and they would be gone. It turns out, the house had false walls where the servants would stay until the family needed something. The false walls had a little space between the kitchen and the dining room. Back in the day, your servant would sit between the walls, and if you needed something they would appear from inside the service wall to serve you.

I loved it. Ray Charles and Little Richard lived in this section of town. But today, most of the houses are hidden away on side streets where you would not believe this type of home had been built. Now this area is a part of the hood. Some of the great houses were made into apartments, and some of the servants' quarters, like the room over the garage (which was once the chauffeur's quarters) are simply extra rental rooms for someone. This area, Baldwin hills and View Park, were all prime areas to live in back in the day. It has turned into a gang-infested area, but some of the nicer homes are still there.

As I became more active in the lives of my foster children, I began to see the need for more foster homes in our community. Being Black and Muslim, I didn't see many foster parents, but I saw many of our children being put into homes where the child was not going to be understood. I also saw the reluctance of some foster moms to take their foster children inside the prisons to visit their biological parents. There was such a large hole to be filled. We needed people like them, for them.

And the school also kept growing.

We outgrew the area we were in, but I was able to buy a house on 31st, off of Arlington, right around the corner from Ibadullah Masjid. It was a run-down dump of a place, but it was what I could afford. Saud had sent me $10,000 from prison and my dad gave me $5,000 for the down payment on the house. My dear friend, Nassim, worked on my paperwork until the numbers worked in my favor.

"Khadijah, I ran your name, and everything came back perfect this time," he said. "I don't know how you got approved but you did, and I've found you a lender! Alhamdulillah."

"Danny! I got the house, but it's a wreck. Can you come and see the wreck?" I said jokingly.

"OK, Sis, I'll be there around one."

In Danny time 1 PM actually meant 4 PM. Danny was very creative. He painted and fixed up the last house to make it look like a daycare, but this one was smaller, so I just focused on fixing it up as best I could. It was a dump, but it was mine, and I was blessed to have it. Owning a home in Los Angeles meant you could've bought two homes somewhere else and a nicer one in a better neighborhood.

Having 30 kids in and out of the house made life unbearable. I would wake up to six kids, and before 9 AM, 10 more sets of kids would leave, and another set would show up. Working from home was very stressful. Between cooking and feeding the children, cleaning, and parents who didn't want to go home at the end of the day, I had social workers, homework, and a husband, brothers, and son-in-law in prison. Phone calls, visits, requests, and attitudes from everybody! I was trying to balance it all, keeping bills paid and a marriage together.

Saud had on several occasions offered to release me from waiting for him. Sometimes we would argue, and his form of punishment was not to call. Well, first of all the phone bill was my largest bill, so I was not upset. I would just call the Muslim chaplain and he would check on him for me.

On one of these occasions, Saud was hinting that he wanted to marry another wife.

"Saud," I said, "you know as well as I do that you not in no position to take a wife."

"It was just something I was thinking through," he said.

"And do I know this sister?" I asked.

"She lives in Pittsburgh."

"Well, if she is in Pittsburgh, where are you going to live when you get out of there because I am not moving to no Pittsburgh, period. After all the work I've done here, I am not moving back to no Pittsburgh." Saud didn't know that the sister he was referring to and I had been in contact. She was much older than I and said she had known Saud for longer than I had known him. To be honest, I liked her, but she had no desire to move to California.

Saud had plenty of ways in which to earn a living. He was always a good provider, but I wasn't about to share my husband, who had been locked up for all these years, with nobody. He had to make a choice.

It would be years before his release, but it made no sense to waste anyone's time. I was no longer the naive Baby Sister. I had grown as a woman and in Islam, most of which he taught me or showed me how to get the information I needed. Saud always said if you can go straight to the source, then go straight to the source, and that's exactly what I did.

Sister Amira was kind to me. She met me and Nunu when we landed in Pittsburgh.

"As salaamu alaikum Sis."

"Wa alaikum as salaam," I answered back, "it's so nice to meet you."

"You as well. Does he know?" I asked her.

"Not unless you told him," she said.

"I ain't told him nothing. I am not letting him get off with nothing."

He taught me the game and I was a damn good student.

Sister Amira drove me around Pittsburgh so that I could reminisce about the bad old days. Layne and her family were the only ones that I was interested in seeing. Sakinah had already moved to Delaware. Nunu was doing what a two-year-old does, getting into everything. We spent the night and the next day we headed out for State College, Pennsylvania, where the prison was located. It was a long, quiet ride. We arrived at about 9 AM. We were both nervous, not knowing what to expect. One thing was for certain, and that was that Mr. Saud didn't expect us both at the same time.

I signed in and where it said relation to the inmate, I put wife. The sister signed in and where it said relationship, she put wife. As we went through the routine, we could see the guards laughing and whispering and pointing at us. We both played it off, but I had to ask, "Did y'all get married?" Before I could hear her answer, we saw Saud appear, then disappear back into the guards' office. Then we noticed that the room had filled up with guards.

"What's going on?" I asked Amira.

"Us," she said. "They think we are about to beat him up or fight each other." We both laughed at the joke, which was on them. Saud sauntered into the room with that walk he had. He didn't know what to make of the visit or even know if we were together. We almost fell to the floor trying to hold onto our straight faces, as we watched him trying to figure it out.

Nunu broke the awkwardness when she saw him. She ran, and he scooped her up, and held onto her for dear life.

"As salaamu alaikum, my sisters. What brings you here?" he said in his joking voice. "My don't you both look nice. Y'all met I see."

"Not only have we met, we have had long conversations."

"Conversations?" Saud questioned, "how long y'all been here?"

"We have been here for about an hour," I said.

"An hour," Saud said, as he began to nervously play with Nunu who was struggling to get down out of his lap and go play, but Saud was still holding on for dear life.

"I was referring to our conversations over the last month and the long one we had last night while I was at the sister's house."

"You stayed at the sister's house?"

"Look Reese," I said, calling him by his street name, as I often did when I was angry, "I came all the way here for one reason. I told you that I wasn't moving back to Pittsburgh for anybody, and the sister said she is not moving to California.

You can afford one family, maybe two if we were both in the same city, but we are not and we're not budging on that. You and Amira have known each other since I was a child, I get it. I like the sister, but you have to make a choice. I am not going to remain in a marriage like this after all these years of waiting. I am not doing it. Allah has shown me what I am capable of doing and in as much as I don't want another husband, this, I am not doing."

Saud finally put Nunu down and turned his back to me and started a conversation with the sister. I got up and went to play with Nunu. The guards crept closer and closer, trying hard to hear what we were saying. I was trying to read Saud and Amira's faces but couldn't. I couldn't take it anymore, so I moved back to where they were sitting. They were so quiet. I snatched up the coin purse and went to the vending machine where Nunu was standing and pointing to the treats that she wanted. After getting her chips and a hamburger, I walked back and sat down.

"Well," I said softly, "have you made a decision?"

"I am going home to California," he said just as softly. I looked in the sister's direction, and I could see the hurt on her face.

"Shameful," I whispered, "Let's go, Sis."

"Y'all leaving?" Saud asked.

"Yes, I got a plane to catch and a business to run, my dear. Come on Nunu, say goodbye to your daddy." Now Nunu was crying and reaching for her dad. I could see the sadness in his eyes as we turned to leave. Later that week, after returning home, I received a call from Saud who apologized to me.

"Did you apologize to the sister?" I asked him.

"Yes," he said.

"You really hurt her, she was crushed. Frankly, because of your long history, I didn't know what your decision would be. Have you spoken to her?"

"Yes, I have, and you are right, she is hurt."

"I don't know how your life is in there. I don't know how you feel or how you even manage day-to-day or why you thought that that was a good idea, but please don't do that again. What we go through out here is hell trying to defend our decisions to stay with someone incarcerated. We are always looked at as a joke or stupid or less than. You don't have to worry about me telling this story to anyone," I said to Saud, "because it is embarrassing."

However, a few people did know and thought it was funny and wished they could have been a fly on the wall.

Did You Ever Wonder?

I would often close my eyes and try to put myself behind the bars in that small space with only my thoughts. It was too frightening to stay there. I can hear you all saying, "well, then don't put yourself in that position to be sent there."

I daydream about alternatives that could have prevented so many of these bad decisions, all of the good intentions that went into these bad decisions. I think of all of the talent and wisdom that dies there, and it makes me want to reach my hand out to help. But at times, I just don't know how to help, and I ask my God, "Ya Allah, show me a way to make it better for those who You show Your Mercy too. Bless me to allow my blessings from You to help some child, some person. Let me be in competition with myself to enhance my good deeds. Keep me humble and honest, In sha' Allah.

Chapter 37: This House Is Too Small

Business was doing well, and we really needed to find a place outside of my house. So many close friends had become family that the house was always full. Stepping over people was an understatement. I didn't get to go home to Cleveland as often as I liked. My responsibilities had tripled over the years.

Día, my niece from Norton Street and The Courts, needed a daycare sitter for her two children, Christopher and Skylor. Día is a straightforward, don't-take-no-mess kinda girl who I had the unfortunate pleasure of spoiling. Día would show up with every body part showing, I would just put my head down as she attempted to hug some of the Muslim brothers that were dropping off their kids.

"Oh," Día would say, "I just saw yo ass at the club. Now you don't know me." We would all just look at our feet and pretend that we didn't hear her. "Put some clothes on next time you come over," I told her.

Día would pop up with everything popped out, sheesh! Christopher was her oldest. He was the cutest little man, always looking out for his mom and baby sister, Skylor, with her binkies. They were not Muslim, but they would sit in the Arabic and Islamic studies with the other children. It wasn't long before she, too, came to me and said she thought she wanted to be Muslim, but it was her children who convinced her. Although we lived right across the street from Masjid Ibadullah, we would also go to Culver City to the King Fahd Masjid. The Sheikh there was Tajuddin Shuaib, the same Sheikh that gave Anna Jean her Shahadah and the author of *The Prescribed Prayer Made Simple*. His children attended our little school. After taking her

Shahadah, Día would tell her story and her story reached the ears of the program, Frontline.

Frontline was doing a piece on Muslim converts after 911 and became interested in Día's story. They knew that her parents were once part of the Ike and Tina Turner Revue. Her mother was an Ikette and her father, Soko, was Tina and Ike's drummer. Tina is her g—mother. If you have ever watched LA Hair, you would see Día appear on that old reality show. She is a friend of Kim Kimble who does celebrity hair. Día had her hands in a lot.

Shortly after she took Shahadah, she married a brother named Ahmad. They stayed married for years. Frontline filmed part of the segment on Día, titled, *Muslims in My Home on 31st Street*.

That year, I became the Muslim women's chaplain in downtown LA. That position only lasted a month before the job was taken from me and given to my Muslim neighbor, Judy Musa, who lived across the street from me. Judy was a wonderful neighbor and a better choice. At first, I was upset, then Saud forbade me to go.

"What do you mean I can't go? That's dawah (teaching people about Islam), and a little change in our pockets," I said. But I understood after seeing how the women were all stacked in there, beds on top of beds, in a big dormitory-type space.

There were two shaded stalls in the middle of the room. As I looked down from the upstairs open room where the sheriff overlooked and watched the female inhabitants, you could see the silhouettes of the ladies as they relieved themselves. You could see them clean their butts, you could see them change their pads, and pull their clothes on and off. It was awful. The Muslim sisters walked around with towels on their heads. I was glad Saud told me I couldn't take on that job.

I was always invited to Chino Youth Authority during Eid. That was the facility where Malik was being held, and I would get to see for myself how he was doing. I would send in bean pies, halal lamb and chicken, prayer rugs, Qurans, and dhikr beads. These items would be Eid gifts from Al Hibah. I would get to speak to the young men about how it felt to have a male family member locked up and tell them about the pain of a mother.

"*As salaamu alaikum. My name is Khadijah Shabazz, and I just want to talk to you today about what your mom may not tell you. You see, I am your mom today. As a mom, to know that your innocent child is within reach, but noto being able to touch him or her is heartbreaking. That mom cries herself to sleep, if she does sleep. Most nights, she is awake because she is worried that her child is not OK. She wonders if he has eaten, if he was beaten today, or harmed in any way. Your mom is upset that she cannot afford the bail money. Your family and friends are talking to her like she's crazy because she is supporting you. They talk to her as if her child's life means nothing, and then part of her dies.*

*Then you have that mother who is crying her eyes out because she knows her child is guilty, he/she did it! The sense of failure and shame that she feels, and the embarrassment that follows. Some of these young men leave behind wives, girlfriends, and kids. The overwhelming feeling of guilt and shame consumes your momma, but she will play it off when she comes to visit this hell hole. It's one f***** up feeling that you carry in your gut for an innocent person, but it's more f***** up when you have to sit in the discomfort of knowing that your child is guilty.*

And now you want to call every 10 minutes making a bill so high that it is almost impossible for her to pay it. Yes son, I am speaking to you. I am your momma today. I got to come here and be talked to crazy, humiliated by these disrespectful guards, because your ass won't do right. I can't get your baby sister and brother anything special because all my money goes to you. Whatever nasty cup of noodles that they got you eating in here, we are eating it too.

Sometimes she will wish that she could just leave you in here 'till you decide to do better, so that your little brother and sister don't turn out like you. That's some of the sh*t she won't say to you when she is having a bad day. You don't hear that part of her truth.

You are her baby they got caged up in jail and she loves you. She knows that you are a really good person. She thinks to herself, I don't know how I failed as a parent. I wish my child were home, God please don't let anyone harm my child, help me withstand the torture.

You see my tears that I have for you, and I don't even know you. Now you think about your momma who loves you. And don't you dare say anything unkind or unloving to her, if she forgets something or is late with anything!"

The young men would all come over and want to hug me but that was not allowed. They thanked me for the books and prayer rugs. I stayed and listened to the live jazz band they had. I was impressed. I even got up and did a few of Aretha Franklin's tunes before leaving. I got to visit Malik a few more times behind the scenes before he was moved from the Youth Authority to a men's prison.

Meanwhile, at home, my daycare had become successful. Teacher and I had managed to rent several storefronts on Jefferson Blvd. trying to find the right fit for us both, not wanting to be too far from home or the masjid, 3202 West 31st was to be our home for the next several years.

"Bro. Dan, this place is not as large as our old place on Orange Dr. How can we modify it? Everything we have is not gonna fit." Danny just laughed and said, "I'll hook you up, Sis."

The house was a dump as I said before, but still it was ours and what I could afford.

We decided that we would enclose the front porch to try and make another room, and we turned the largest bedroom into two rooms. The electricity didn't work, nor did the gas heating system. I called in a few Muslim brothers to help me fix up the house. We started work as soon as I got the materials. I asked Bro. Abdul Latif, a plumber, to come over with his two-man crew. He had come recommended from the Muslim community.

"Where are your permits, Sis?"

"What permit?" I asked.

"Sister, you can't just start work on no house without any permits."

"Why not, it's mine."

"Look Sis, I'm telling you without a permit, the city can come in here and shut down your work."

Now you'd think I was smart enough to take that good advice but nooooo, not me. After about a month of the workmen tearing stuff out and down, working in the evening and the nosy neighbors spying and doing what nosy neighbors do, I realized that the work had gotten out of hand and most of the brothers had just left me high and dry with holes in the floor and holes in the walls.

The yard was big enough so we held some classes there. We did the best we could for a while, but finally we located a place within walking distance for Shabazz Family Daycare and Al Hibah, all praise is due to Allah.

The house was always full of people, from social workers to parents, kids of all ages, and the misplaced community. They knew that they could get a meal and conversation at the Shabazz house. My Los Angeles relatives, Jonae and Wanda, would become my lifeline at times when the rest of the world seemed to be unraveling. My little brother, Shawn, was a welcome visitor too. He was in the Navy and stationed in San Diego. Shawn was traveling the world. We always had great times together.

I still found the time to go home to Cleveland between all of the chaos. Big Hassan had gotten out of captivity and I would visit Malik as often as I could. Malik had developed health issues in his late 30s, He suffered a heart attack in prison and after that he started having seizures.

"This is a call from a correctional facility inmate, Brian Taylor." *Who is Brian Taylor?* I pushed the number five so that I could receive the call and find out who this person was.

"Hello," I said into the phone receiver.

"As salaamu alaikum. This is Bro. Amir. I am a friend of Malik's. I found your number in his things. You his mom right?"

"Wait, you are who? And what's wrong?"

"Malik had a heart attack playing basketball on the yard, and they took him to the hospital. We knew that they wasn't going to call you."

"What hospital? A heart attack! He is not old enough to have a heart attack. Somebody get me some water," I said,

"Is he alive?" I asked quietly.

"We don't know. They won't tell us nothin'. I went through his stuff to find your number. He kept falling out of bed. He got the top bunk, they won't let him sleep on the bottom for some reason."

Bro. Amir's voice was drifting off. He was still talking, but all I could think of was how was I going to tell the girls. But first, I needed to know if he was OK. So, I called the new Imam at the prison.

"As salaamu alaikum Bro. Imam. This is Khadijah Shabazz, Malik's mom."

"Malik Young Shabazz, ah yes, Sister, how can I help you?" he asked.

"They have taken my son to the hospital, and no one seems to know why or where he is. Can you tell me where he is or how he is doing?"

"No Sister," he said to my great surprise, "I can't lose my job. We can't tell you information like that."

"Information like what? All I want to know is if my son is dead or alive?"

"Sorry Sister. I cannot tell you."

"Well at least can you go see him and tell me how he is doing?"

"No, I don't think I can do that either."

"Really?" I said sarcastically. "I will not forget this Bro."

It would be weeks before any updates on Malik's condition. We fought the system every way we could think of, using Saud's advice, as to how to proceed. Saud was working on his own interstate transfer agreement, trying to get accepted into the California supervised program; this was a trip as well. Malik did recover, but he would be on seizure meds for life.

9/11

Then 9/11 came!

"I don't think I'll make parole."

"Why are you saying that?" I asked, half asleep. **You have 15 minutes,** the recording shouted out. *God, how I hate that recording.*

"Is something wrong? You sound funny."

Saud took a deep breath and told me to turn on the TV. Half asleep and confused, I reached for the remote, struggling to find it between my pj's and the blankets. Really annoyed by now and really wanting him to get to the point, "I ain't ready to hear that your parole has not been granted. Why do you think that they will deny you?" I asked, as I was trying to adjust my voice so that he would not hear how annoyed I really was.

"OK, I said, "I found the remote. What channel do I turn to?" I asked with my eyes closed.

"Any one of them," was his answer. I opened my eyes and turned to channel two just in time to see the second tower come down!

"What the hell did I just see? Ya Allah."

It was September 11, 2001.

Prior to the 9/11, in 1993 in New York, there was a bomb attack. It was a truck bomb that went off in the garage of the World Trade Center, killing about six people. Now, I am fully awake watching the towers come down like a pile of Junga blocks! This was bad!

Muslim women were being attacked all over the country by cowardly men. I remember Saud and others cautioning me to be careful since I was an identifiable Muslimah because of my hijab. Muslim women were being spit on, punched, pushed, and bullied by men who would not think of doing that to another man.

As for me, that day, I decided that I wasn't taking a darn thing off and in fact, I was trying to find a face covering! OK, maybe a half-face covering. I wanted people to see me as a peaceful Muslim, but I also wanted them to know that we would fight for our safety, and yours, if need be. I wanted people to recognize that I was truly not the one to try. I was turning no cheeks. I had no more cheeks to turn. I am not forgiving anything. My motto was spit on me, somebody going to hell, and somebody going to jail.

"Saud, what do the towers coming down have to do with you?"

"First of all, there is a standing order that if there were ever a war on US soil, the government would kill all of its inmates first."

Now I could never find any place that said to straight out kill them, but I believe it. I wrote a letter to the warden, asking him straight out if he felt that Saud was suitable for release and release to California. California eventually accepted him, but

Pennsylvania didn't want to release him. They thought California was too soft on the formerly incarcerated.

Taking care of business

I got a call from Brother Abdul Latif, telling me that he was my driver for the day.

"Driving me where?" I asked. "Who is going with us, you know I can't go by myself. Is your wife going, too? And how do you even know I need a driver?"

"Dang, Sister, you ask a lot of questions," he said jokingly.

"Well, the last time I rode with you, we almost got in trouble."

"Why you keep bringing up old stuff?" he laughed.

While working on my house I needed to replace three toilets, so I bought replacements from a private plumbing store off of Western. The store was owned by a white family that had been in the community for years. I told Saud that the man had beaten me out of my money, and he called Abdul Latif to help me straighten the matter out. Abdul's truck was full of plumbing supplies with a small space on the passenger side to sit. I sat as close to the door as I could. As we pulled up and parked, Abdul Latif said, "OK Sister, just point the man out then get behind me or get back in the truck."

"OK Brother."

I watched as Latif adjusted his socks and pulled a Derringer pistol out of his sock and put it in his pocket. Then he opened the glovebox and took out another one.

"Wait. What are we about to do?" I asked.

"We ain't about to do nothin'. My brother asked me to help you get your shit and that's what I'm about to do."

Now I am scared. "We 'bout to die over a toilet, brother?"

"Is that him, Sister?" he asked, ignoring my question.

"Yes," I said.

"Stay here or get in the truck."

I don't know what Abdul Latif said to the man, but the man's employees put five toilets on the truck, gave me a receipt, came to the truck, apologized for the misunderstanding, and said he'd come again!

"Bro. Latif, what did you say to that man?"

"None of your business, Sis. Ask Saud if you want to know anything."

When we got back to my house, Abdul Latif asked me where I wanted him to put the toilets until he could install them. I gave him the two that I didn't need and that was that. He would continue to do small plumbing jobs for me. He and Danny were part of the family and my go-to brothers whenever a sister had to show that she wasn't alone.

Chapter 38: Where Are We Going?

"Khadijah, come on," Abdul Latif said again.

"But I am asking again, where we are going and why?"

"OK," he said, "to the airport."

"Airport," I said, dumbfounded.

"Yep."

We rode in silence most of the ride.

"I got to get back to the school and help out. I need to tell Teacher what's going on."

He just looked at me and grinned.

"Oh, I know what's up. He's home, right?" Latif just laughed

"I ain't said nothing," Latif said, still laughing.

"Are you serious, for real?" I knew Saud was out, but he had to stay in Pittsburgh before coming to Cali and he had fooled me on the release date. Now I was ugly crying and had to try to straighten up. I noticed that walk. You saw Saud's swag before you saw him. *My bay bay is home!*

After my big surprise, we took Saud home to put his things away, then on to the school for him to surprise the kids. To my children, he was Daddy, to Niani, he was Poppie. He was everybody's Uncle Saud.

They were all so happy to see him. He was so proud of what Teacher and I had done, making something out of nothing, using our resources to try and keep the children in an Islamic environment. But the school needed a new location. We'd tried our best to fix up, but this place had leaky plumbing and a dog stayed there at night, making the whole place smell of dog. It didn't take long to find another location. It was a few blocks down on Jefferson. Almost all of our businesses were on Jefferson.

Saud wanted to launch his own business. He'd always dreamed of a bookstore, but he wanted a bookstore and coffee shop, a place where young poets could hang out. So, we set out to try and realize his dream. We had a great time. Saud was able to meet, in person, all of the people who had supported me and him through all those years. He had written a lot of poetry while he was enslaved, enough to fill a few books. We invited the community over every Friday after Jummah to have Friday supper with us, which was much like a Sunday dinner. He became a well-liked part of the community. Everyone loved him. Imam Sadiq of Masjid Ibadillah allowed him to teach a class on hadith at the masjid.

Saud had total recall when reading something. This was truly a gift. He could read something once and tell you where he read it, on which page, and what line it was on. This made me lazy because I relied on his brain when I was asked a question. He was voted into a position at the masjid. I can't remember which one.

We finally found a location for Saud's shop, a little further down the street. It was a storefront with four empty spaces big enough for Al Hibah and big enough for Saud's dream coffee shop.

"This is it, Khadijah," Saud said, "we can sell coffee and tea pastries and do spoken word." I really liked the idea, and this location wasn't far from the house.

Saud and Abdul Latif would go out at night around the Leimert Park area to the spoken word venues. He would get the lay of the land and see how other coffee shops operated that offered poetry. Saud would allow militant poetry, clean comedy, and also clean uplifting rap. The funny part was that all the coffee was free! He would not charge for coffee. He would sell candy, hotdogs, chicken wings, soda, and on Fridays he'd sell anything that I wanted to cook. One of the best sellers was the Al Madina dog.

Saud had named the place the **Almadinah Coffee Hut, the Mecca of Jefferson Park.** Madinah and Mecca were the names of our best and closest friends, Sakinah's two girls. He had named the place after them, but he put the shop in our daughter, Salina's name.

The parking lot where the businesses were had a life of its own. We had a masala where Muslims could stop and pray. Unity

2, a Muslim-run gang intervention organization was there, along with a Muslim tax business run by Bro. Zaffar.

We had our challenges like any other community, but life was good for a minute.

"Saud, Thai is on the phone, she wants to talk to you."

"Hey Thai," Saud said. I watched as a big smile came across his face, "Really, OK."

"What's she talking about?' I asked, with my nosey self. Saud had been home a few short years and already made a poetry CD. It was selling in the community like hotcakes. The coffee shop was a haven for poets. Some just hung out and some comedians like Stevie Mack and Omar Regan the stand-up comic and actor, who wrote and acted in his own movie American Sharia, would perform. He was also the son of Sheikh Luqman Abdullah whom the FBI murdered in the Detroit area in 2009. Amir Suliman, the poet, would perform. He had been a guest on BETs Poetry Jam. He would perform at Saud's place and of course he'd bring the house down with his *Dead Man Walking* poem, which was one of my favorites. Saud would let some of the local talent showcase their acts on certain nights. They would make a video and then shop the tape around LA, looking for gigs.

"What did Thai say?" I kept asking.

"She said she wanted me and her cousin, DA, to host a local talk show on cable called Poets Anonymous. DA was a sax player. He and Saud were to interview local poets and allow them to read their work on the show.

I was asked to do the Kraft services but for free. I demanded payment for my service. Laugh out loud! No, for real, I was paid a small stipend. After all, wasn't he the one who'd taught me to get something for my time? I learned over the years that you get better service if you don't give it all away for free.

The show aired on Spectrum. They featured a lot of local talent, but most of his days, he spent at the coffee shop teaching the children Islamic stories mixed with street.

Down the street from where we lived on 31st was a Belizean community. My granddaughter Laila's father, Jason, was from Belize and this community had meetings and parties a lot. He would bring us food and stories about what was happening. They would often get a guest that Saud was very interested in meeting, Malcolm X's daughter, Attila Shabazz. She was the Belizean

Ambassador, I believe, at the time. You would be surprised at what goes on in your own backyard.

We walked to the back of the house and the smell of the food let us know we were in the right place. They had spicy whole crab, fish, and goat, and there was always rice! Jason was a pretty good cook himself. The backyard had festive lights and outdoor tables. It was not a large crowd, just enough to make it comfortable. Sister Shabazz was a tall, beautiful woman. Her brown eyes grabbed you right away. I continued to look around my settings as we approached her. Saud has always been an aggressive type and I am not one to be starstruck or moved by status or title, but when I saw her, tears welled up in my eyes and I could not speak.

"As salaamu alaikum, Sister Attilah," I heard Saud say.

"Wa alaikum salaam," she replied back. I don't believe I said anything.

"My name is Saud Shabazz, and I knew your father," Saud said. "I was one of his students."

"Is that right?" she replied, as she kept walking to her spot in the yard.

"He actually gave me my name," Saud said, "and I am sometimes asked to speak about my friendship with your dad." After a few more exchanges, Sis. Attilah turned around and said, "You really did know my dad didn't you? I hear that all the time. Let's talk when I'm done."

They did have that brief sit down, but I wasn't a part of it. Saud was so happy to have that talk with Atilla. He would talk about it often. The next time we heard from Sister Attila was when my granddaughter, Laila, was born. She had called my second son-in-law, Jason, to congratulate him. Jason had an older son, Cory, who we all loved. We loved his child's mother, Corinne, too.

Salina would later marry one more time, and I was blessed with two more grandchildren, Lalia and Lavalle Aqueel Jr. This time around, Salina was an adult and a nurse and married to the best son-in-law ever, Lavelle Aqueel. This is how my little man LA got his name from his dad.

But back to what happened after the birth of Ladybug (Laila). It was around this time that Saud was doing his Poets Anonymous cable show. We were invited to dinner at this former rapper's home who lived out by Magic Mountain. By this time in my life, I didn't know any rappers' names or their music. Saud was still going out to poetry slams in and out of other coffee shops around LA. Día and her husband, Ahmad were there, along with some local Imams.

The brother and his family showed us such a nice time. He made us feel so welcome. The young brother had even invited us to stay the night, which was a nice gesture. We had fallen asleep in the middle of the conversation. We were all having such a good time.

Saud woke me up and said time to go. Some guests were still talking, some had nodded off as well. Saud and I made salat (prayed). His home had a nice quiet prayer room. Muslims are known for their hospitality. The young brother was Mutah, from the group, the Outlaws, and a dear close friend and family to Tupac Shakur. Can you believe I had never heard of Tupac?! Saud would just laugh and make fun of me, saying that when I decided to leave the music business alone, I really left it alone.

"Khadijah," Saud said, "how do you not know who Tupac is?" Truth is, I had not heard of Tupac until his death, then I remembered him because he appeared on my favorite show, A Different World. Mutah, would later attend Saud's janaza and help carry him to his final resting place. I must say, Mutah makes our community, me in particular, so proud. He now lives with his family in Saudi and has a few coffee shops called MJ café, along with other businesses. For his kindness may Allah continue to Bless him, and I will always be to him and his family, Aunty Khadijah.

Chapter 39: The Beginning of the End

"My breast hurts."

"What?" I asked.

"My breast hurt."

I laughed and turned around and stopped laughing when I looked into his face and saw that he was in pain.

"Hurts how?" I asked.

"They are very tender, even my shirt is aggravating it. I think I need to see a doctor." We went to see the doctor and Saud was given the diagnosis of having a hormone imbalance, probably caused by his age. They gave him some meds and the symptoms went away. So, life continued as usual.

We'd planned a trip to San Louis Obispo prison to see Malik. We would make those times as enjoyable as we could. He couldn't get in to see Malik, but me and the kids could. After the visitations, we would go see the sights of the city. We stayed in the hotels geared toward tourists when they visited. San Luis Obispo was a tourist city with a beach, whale watching, and swimming with dolphins, among other things. We enjoyed those trips together and Saud got a chance to see what it was like as a visitor going into a prison. Well, he never stepped foot into another prison, but he got to see how the preparations went, and I got a bigtime apology.

Saud really enjoyed his coffee shop. The brothers would gather there and play chess. Saud's first poetry CD wasstill popping off the shelves in our local bookstores and masjid gatherings. The children of Al Hibah were right next door from the coffee shop. They would come over on breaks to buy candy and hot dogs. Saud had his favorites, Khalilah and Skylor. They could do no wrong and if they did, his words were, leave them alone.

All the coffee was free in our coffee shop. We didn't make much money. Even if you didn't have money, Saud would feed you. Needless to say, the kids paid for candy and hot dogs when they felt like it.

Saud was still on parole, and he tried to stay out of the way of any law enforcement. After two years of supervised off-the-plantation parole, the state of California released him.

"I'm officially off parole. Y'all, we need to celebrate," Saud said as we drove down La Brea on our way to the Hawthorn Masjid. We would be passing by Día and her new Muslim husband's home. Her father, Soko, lent Saud his car so that he would be more mobile. Soko and Saud had become instant brothers.

Grinning to himself and flashing a smile at me, Saud pulls Soko's car onto a car lot, and we pulled out a moment later in a minivan. The car dealer drove Soko's car back to our house and parked it in the front. Saud was so proud to be a car owner again. It was a big relief for him to have his own car. The minivan had only five miles on it. It was a white Toyota. Saud had big plans for his new ride. We drove back to the coffee shop and just as we were pulling into the parking lot, all hell broke out.

"Get home quick," is what people were saying to us as we got out of the van.

Bro. Z, who owned the business next door, shouted, "you need to go home."

"Why?" Saud asked him.

"The US Marshals have the whole street blocked off, and they are in front of your house." We just stared at each other.

"Did you do something?" I asked under my breath.

"Naw, I ain't done nothing," he whispered back. "Maybe they came to take me back to Pennsylvania." The state of Pennsylvania was upset with Cali for taking Saud off of parole and had threatened to come and get him.

"You know I'm not going back, don't you?" My eyes filled up with tears and a knot formed in my gut.

"OK, let me go see what's happening," I said. "I'll just walk up and watch."

But there was no blending into a crowd when you are in a hijab.

Our home on 31st street was maybe five or six blocks from the coffee shop. I got there as quickly as I could. My front yard was full of marshals. I went up to the punk a** officers just in time to see the marshal step down on my son, Hassan's back.

"What in the hell is going on?" I screamed in sheer horror.

"We trying to tell these fools that he's autistic, but they slammed him on the ground anyway," my son Ranel said.

"Shut the f*** up," the marshal yelled back at Ranel, "before we arrest you." Instant hate had now entered almost my entire body. *I hope they just drop dead and die.*

"What are you doing? He has the mind of a five-year-old." I screamed into the punk a** marshal's face, but that's when I noticed more marshals coming out of my house, where my daycare was in business and operating with babies up to five years old.

"There are babies in there. What the hell are y'all doing?"

"All clear," said the marshal exiting my house, as they held up a photo of someone that resembled my son, but clearly wasn't him, *but I forgot, we all look alike don't we?*

"He identified himself as the person we are looking for," said the punk a** marshal.

"He says yes to everything," we all said at the same time.

"The neighbors are all out here telling you he's autistic and that there are children in there. I understand you doing your job but there are babies in there."

God please just let one choke to death right here on the spot. They had their AK47s or whatever kind of rifle weapon pointed at my assistant, who was holding a baby.

"Do you know this person?" The Marshal exiting my house asked, holding up a photo. *Hell, naw you punk a** mother f*****. No, I don't, you have the wrong man, a defenseless man at that, on the ground with your foot on his back you cowardly piece of shit.* I was cussing him out really good in my head. I even had a few choice words for his momma, but I kept my mouth shut out of fear that they would find a reason to shoot my son.

"He's crying," came a shoutout from one of the neighbors.

"Hassan don't move baby. It's OK," I lied. *How in the entire hell is this ok?* The punk a** marshal finally let Hassan up, uncuffed him, and they went to talk among themselves. I called Saud to tell him what was going on.

The phones were tapped, but they always have been, so I don't know why they thought my son was the person they were looking for.

"I am on my way," Saud said. This was the third time law enforcement had Hassan on the ground or up against the wall for simply being Black and mentally challenged. Holding our breath while they held a loaded gun on our children was so scary, I can't describe the feeling. The smug look they give you, the disrespect, the no regard for life...itmakes you bitter and hateful. Thank you, Allah, for blessing me with some understanding of right and wrong, wherever it lies.

Chapter 40: For The Last Hooray

Saud and I decided we would take a road trip. We needed to get away and we wanted to see our families.

"Saud," I said, "I always wanted to drive cross country, but who will help you drive?"

"Good question," he answered.

After much thought, we thought we'd ask my brother, Shawn, if he would like to make the trip with us.

"Yea Sis, that sounds like fun."

"Ok Shawn, we will get you a roundtrip airline ticket from New Orleans to Los Angeles."

We couldn't fit in all of the kids, so we flipped a coin and decided on Hassan, Niani, and Niemah. Of course, Autumn and Nunu were upset but we promised they could go next time. We all crammed into the new white minivan and started our adventure. The trip wasn't what I had envisioned. I wanted to stop and see the sights. I wanted to go to a Native American reservation.

"I don't know why, but I am really excited. I love road trips." My face was pressed up against the window. I was taking in every leaf that blew, every raindrop, all of the farm animals, all while singing my favorite oldies. We would listen to an Islamic lecture in between, and stopped for salat (prescribed prayer) when the times came in.

Saud was driving at a normal pace, but speedy Shawn must have broken every speeding violation that each state had.

"Gosh darn it brother, if one mo' cop stops us. How many tickets do you have?" I laughed. I must admit, most of the highway patrol that stopped us were friendly enough. Still, getting stopped so often was no fun! We pulled into Cleveland three days later and went straight to our dad's house. Shawn went on his way, visiting his friends and family. Saud left me and the kids after a day and went on to New York and stayed there a short time. He didn't like the vibe in New York post 9/11. He said the cold city of his birth got a little colder. He made it back to Cleveland, and we began the trip back home. After all, we still had a business to run. Saud had hoped to visit his friends in Detroit but couldn't connect. He tried to meet up with several friends including Imam Luqman.

Imam Luqman, killed by Detroit policemen

I remember meeting him at the coffee shop one day when he and Saud had a meeting. The imam had a large family. But I was acquainted with three of his sons . One of his sons, Shuaib, married a young girl that I raised.

At the coffee shop we would have a ball eating Al Madinah dogs, which was our take on the famous Polish Boys' recipe from Cleveland. Instead of pork sausage, we made them with halal beef sausages, French fries, coleslaw, and my famous sauce. They were super messy, super fattening, and super good. We were still giving the coffee away free, and a good time was had by all. But, Saud was not feeling it. He didn't get to see his family and friends in Detroit and soon after we returned, he flew right back out.

"Why can't I go?" I whined.

"Because you can't," he said.

"Well, we just got back. Why didn't you just go while we were there?"

"Because we didn't Khadijah and quit asking me all these questions. You not going."

I sulked away angrily, but I got over it. Saud was gone for about a week, maybe a little more. It wasn't that I minded him going, it was the fact that we had been apart for so long, and I didn't want any more separation.

Chapter 41: When New Life Begins

Salina and her second husband, Jason, were expecting a child. Saud was leaving around her due date, so I really didn't want to go and leave her. It was too close to Salina's time. Also, our niece, Madinah, was expecting too and the due dates were close.

"Salina is in labor," I said.

"For real?" Saud asked.

"Yes, you wanna go to the hospital?

"Yes," Saud said, "let's go." He was so excited. Saud had returned from his Detroit trip just in time. We stayed at the hospital until Salina gave birth. Sakinah and I were tending to Salina, while Saud and Jason waited on the other side of the partition, cheering the situation on. Saud was in tears as he looked at his red grandbaby and said, "she's a little ladybug."

At the same time, my g-daughter, Golda, Niemah's sister, had a little man. She was struggling to keep him, and I was asked to intervene.

"I'll think about it," I said to her. Her mom, Austria, who is like a sister to me, was sick and couldn't help at the time, but she loved that little baby boy with all her heart

"I'll call her Ladybug," Saud said after calling the adhan and iqama in his new grandbaby's ear. Salina and Jason named their daughter Laila. She is still Ladybug to us.

Exactly a month later, Madinah, Sakinah's daughter gave birth to her daughter, Amaya. Saud was late to the hospital for Amaya's birth. He was due there to give the baby the blessing. We could not find him for over an hour. He was lost somewhere in the hospital, and for some reason he couldn't follow the directions we gave him over the cell phone. He finally got there to give this child the adhan and iqama in her ears.

Later that evening I found Saud sitting in the dark in our kitchen.

"Why are you sitting in the dark? Dang you scared me, why are you sitting here by yourself in the dark?"

"I don't remember," he said.

"What do you mean you don't remember?

"I can't remember why I'm sitting here, Khadijah," he said, with a look on his face that broke my heart. *Oh my God.* Sometimes I forget his age. *I hope it's not Alzheimer's.* He had been acting strangely, sleeping at the shop, not waking up on time for salat, and forgetting that he had made it.

"Saud, we are going to see Dr. Sheikh tomorrow and that's that," I said.

"Ok."

"Ok? Are you agreeing with me?"

"Yes," he said.

"Now I know something is wrong."

We got to the doctor on time, but Saud was hesitant about going in.

"Come on," I tried to coach him to hurry up before we missed the appointment altogether, "you said you wanted to come, now let's just get this over with."

Dr. Sheikh, who was also Muslim, was giving Saud a clean bill of health until I chimed in.

"Look, doctor. My husband misses salat, which is something that he does not do. He cannot remember when or if he's made it." Being a Muslim, the doctor could relate to what I was saying to him.

"He changes his personality often, and he is shuffling his feet instead of picking them up. He wandered around the hospital for an hour because he could not remember anyone's phone number. And he drove through a red light after sitting and staring at it."

"She is exaggerating, doctor," Saud said, laughing at me, "you know how they do." 'They', meaning women.

Dr. Sheikh made Saud get up and walk across the floor.

"Humm," he said, "well he's really not showing any signs of dementia right now."

"See, I told you," Saud said to the doctor, "she is always putting too much on something." They both laughed.

"Let me finish up by asking you some questions, Saud," the doctor said. "OK, who is the President of the United States?"

"Bush," he said.

"What year is this?"

"2006," he said.

"Do you want to harm yourself?" he asked with a chuckle.

"Nope," Saud responded.

"Do you want to harm somebody?" Dr. Sheikh asked.

"Yes," Saud said. The doctor and I laughed at that response until we both looked into Saud's face. There was that blank stare again that I had seen often lately.

"You want to hurt someone?" the doctor asked.

"Yeah, I'm gonna kill somebody," Saud said. The doctor and I were no longer laughing. We looked at each and asked him at the same time, "Who?"

"Don't worry about it," he said, "I got to kill someone and y'all don't need to know who."

"It ain't me is it?" I asked playfully, because now I'm scared – not scared that it was me – but scared to know that he wasn't playing.

Dr. Sheikh handed me a card and said, "I would like more tests on Saud. I've made you an appointment for tomorrow for blood work, x-rays, and a brain scan. Then when I get the report, I'll schedule him for another appointment."

"OK," I said, as we left the doctor's office.

After we got into the car, I asked Saud, "Dude, why did you tell Dr. Sheikh that you wanted to kill someone?"

"I don't know why I said that," he said, "it just came out."

"Who do you want to kill?" I asked him. He didn't respond and I stopped asking him.

Golda had reached out again and needed help with her son. Her biological mom, Austria, was not able to step in at the time to help with the baby, although she wanted to with all her heart.

"Khadijah, go help Golda with the baby."

"Saud, how am I going to help with a baby when you getting sick?"

"Girl, I ain't gonna be sick forever, go help that baby!"

Saud loved Austria. He always looked out for her and made me promise to help her with that baby. He would always have me call and check on her and didn't like her going home at night on the bus. When she came to visit us, he even got her a pocket knife to defend herself if it ever became necessary. They really hit it off almost immediately, which was strange for them both. He referred to her as his sister, and he wanted to me look out for her and the baby.

"OK," I said, "I will, but one thing at a time. Let's get you straight, first."

The appointment was for early the next day, which was Friday. Saud drove himself to the appointment because he wanted to go straight to Jummah prayer afterwards. I stayed behind and prepared the coffee shop for the after Jummah crowd. Along with the Al Madina Dogs on Fridays, I would make meals that we sold. Coffee was always free, the food was not. This Friday, I had oxtails with rice, cabbage, cornbread, and potato salad. We also had some fish and green salad.

I watched as Saud and his friend Muhammed Mubarak drove onto the lot at the same time. Muhammad is/was an original Panther. He is also a local artist, you can see his exceptional artwork all over LA. Muhammed has a granddaughter, Amirah, that was one of ours. She was always at my house doing what young girls do, giggling and holding secrets. Muhammed was such a friend to Saud, he would often drive him around. And more so when he found out that his friend was sick.

"Here they come," I said, as the cars began to pull up into the lot. The children from Al Hibah were about to go back to class which was right next door. Saud was sitting in the van just as my phone rang. I didn't answer it at first because I was so busy, but it kept ringing, so I looked at it and noticed that it was Doctor Sheikh.

"As salaamu alaikum, doctor."

"Wa alaikum salaam, Khadijah. Where is Saud?"

"He is pulling into the lot as we speak."

"You mean he's driving?" The doctor asked.

"Yes, he is just getting back from Jummah. What's the matter? He did keep his appointment, didn't he? He told me he was going to the appointment then Jummah."

"Khadijah, I need to speak to him and then you. But first take the car keys away from him and don't give them back."

Now everyone in the coffee shop was staring at me, including Saud.

"What is it?" he said.

"Dr. Sheikh wants you on the phone. Where are your car keys?"

"Right here," he said and handed them to me.

"As salaamu alaikum doc, what's up?" I watched Saud's face fall.

"What's the matter?"

He didn't speak, he just handed me the phone.

"Yes, doctor. What's the matter?"

Above the jazz playing quietly in the background, the voices of our customers laughing and enjoying themselves, the children, Kaliyah and Skylor, were behind the counter stealing candy. Saud always left it for them to find just in case one of us said no to them.

I felt as if I was having an out of body experience.

"You mean right this minute, now? We can't go home and change? But I don't drive," I told the doctor.

"What's wrong?" Teacher asked me. I looked at Saud, who sat there with a blank face and his arms folded across his chest, leaning back on the two back legs of the chair.

"Tell her," he said.

Chapter 42: The Hospital

"Saud has a large tumor on his brain as large as my hand going across his forehead," the doctor told me, "We have to get him admitted right now."

He told me not to go home, and not to let him drive. He informed me that if we didn't get him there soon, he may not make it through the night.

Teacher jumped into action and handled the coffee shop. She even found us a ride and cut her leg in the process of making our driver move faster. I heard her say, "I'll lock up, just go."

"Thanks," I said.

I went by the house anyway to grab insurance cards and my overnight bag that I never unpacked, a habit I have from the old days. When we got to the hospital they were waiting on us. After the examination, the doctors came out to tell me that Saud had a glioblastoma, the deadliest of the brain tumors. In order to save his life, the doctors said that they had to remove it immediately, and even doing that we were only talking about a few months more. I said to the doctors, "Allah knows best."

Teacher, Sakinah, and Sister Yvonne were there with me every step of the way. We made it through the night and the next few weeks. I never left the hospital. I slept in his room and in the hallway in the visiting room, but I didn't leave the entire time. When he finally was well enough to leave the hospital, Saud appeared to return to his normal self. I had to work but that meant leaving him in the care of others and I wasn't having that.

I sold my house in order to have funds to live on and to spend quality time with my husband and family. That decision would turn out to be a bad one. It caused problems for me and a beloved family member, but we were able to move past it. Nonetheless, it was done. Since we didn't have a Muslim blood family, Saud decided to make a video of his final wishes, telling his family how the Islamic process works; that we are buried in three days with no frills, no embalming, no casket, no whooping and wailing. He explained about the Islamic cemetery here in California. He felt that he had to because it's in the middle of the desert and that's where he wanted to go, and that no one should interfere with me. He told them that I intended to keep my stepson, Hassan, in my care, although Hassan is grown, he is still mentally challenged.

"Saud, that's why you went to Detroit isn't it?" I questioned.

"What do you mean?" he asked me.

"You knew something was not right, I could tell. That's why you wanted to go back home and see your dad and loved ones. That's why you went to Detroit, the place where Islam came to you, back to that family and your first real true love.

I felt the tears on my face as the reality hit me, my husband was dying, the one who taught me 90% of my Islam, the one who showed me another life, the one who helped me find my voice, my friend. I watched how Allah was cleansing him. Everywhere I looked, I saw someone who had been affected by his knowledge or wisdom, either from the street or straight from the book (Quran). With as much vigor as Saud put into the street life, he doubled and tripled what he did for us, his family and community practicing our Islamic beliefs straight up with no chasers.

Saud had become a viable part of the Muslim community. He was known to several masjids, and taught Hadith classes at Ibadillah on Jefferson on Sundays. He'd counsel brothers returning home from prison and had begun to speak at different venues about his relationship with Malcolm. He'd also attend Jummah at Mumin on St. Andrews and Abu Bakr on Crenshaw. People would ask him which masjid he attended, and his answer would be, "All of them."

"Khadijah," Saud said, "let's plan something big!"

"OK, what did you have in mind?"

"I don't know, something that involves the kids."

"All the kids?"

"All the kids that we claim," he said.

We planned a three-day trip to San Diego's Sea World. We had been there before and wanted to take our Muslim family. So, we took everyone, all expenses paid. By this time, Saud had to use a wheelchair. Here at home, he would get his pal José to help him around the house. José was my little brother; I was still collecting them. Saud could no longer stand or walk for long periods of time, but the children had a ball at Sea World!

We returned home happy, only to be greeted by a parole officer.

"You didn't report Mr. Walker."

"I am off parole," he told the officer.

"Well according to the state of Pennsylvania, you are not."

"They are a cold piece of work," I said. "They can come pick you up at any time for not reporting?"

The PO said, "Yes."

"But California says I'm done," Saud said.

"That's in California, Pennsylvania says differently."

"You don't see that he's sick for real?"

"You want to see some paperwork?"

"Yes, I wanna see the paperwork, and yes I can see he's sick, but you still have to report to Pennsylvania. They are mad at us for letting you off."

The Fall

After not being able to stand on his own for over a week, Saud managed to make his way to the bathroom just as the call to morning prayer was going off. This is what woke me up, along with the thud of him falling.

"Saud, are you okay?" I yelled out, "did you fall down?"

"Yes," I heard him say. I jumped up and went to the bathroom door. He had fallen behind the door, so we couldn't open it. Día, who had been staying with me, ran into the room to help me, along with Ranel. I looked into Saud's eyes and instantly calmed down. I cannot explain the calmness I felt.

I called Sheikh Shuaib and told him that my husband was dying. I then called 911. Día started to recite the dua over Saud and the Shahadah. I quickly got dressed and waited for the ambulance to arrive.

"They may be able to revive him," someone said.

"No y'all," I said, "if Allah has sent His Angels for him, then it's time to say goodbye."

When I think I am too tired to get up for prayer, or if I think that I am too tired to help out a friend, or if I think that if I spend my last...that Allah won't provide more for me, I remember the blessings and the miracles that were sent to me from Allah through him.

Saud had gotten Salina and all of his nieces a piece of jewelry to remember him by. His janaza funeral was huge. Muslims came from everywhere. All of the masjids in LA had someone there for Saud. I didn't realize he knew so many: Muslims came from Ibadillah, from Salaam, from ibn Rabah, from Mumin, from Omar ibn al-Khattâb, from the Islamic Center of Los Angeles, from the Bilal Center, from King Fahad, and Abu Baker. The Muslims kept coming. And the out of town guests kept coming. What made it phenomenal was that people stopped what they were doing and made it to LA in less than three days.

Saud had instructed me not to wait any longer than three days, and that included waiting for family, before putting him in the ground. The imam of the cemetery asked if Saud was a dignitary because there were so many people.

"It depends on who you ask," was my reply. The masala (prayer area) could no longer hold us all, so out into the rain we went giving my Beloved his final rights.

I can still hear his voice in my head from time to time and can see those flashing hazel eyes when something ain't quite right. I get strength to this day when I remember his last wishes to me. He said, "Khadijah, promise me that you will keep me clean and in wudu (purifying yourself for prayer) make sure that I am facing east in my bed if I am unable to do it myself."

"OK," I said, "I promise

Saud read everything that he could get his hands on about death, and I read the Islamic books on death with him, which did make it easier for me.

Saud returned to Allah on a Friday morning, Jummah, in the last 10 days of Ramadan.

For three months after Saud passed away, Feds hounded me about him. I finally sent them the address to the Islamic cemetery in Rosemead California where he could be found. After that, they left me alone.

I think I disappeared emotionally, because I can't remember a lot of what happened around that time. I remember that those little faces depended on me for real this time, and I had no one to go to, so I had to take it straight to Allah.

Saud.

May Allah make your grave spacious and may His rewards continue to come as a relief for you and a blessing for all of us that were chosen to come to Islam from your example, Ameen.

وَأَنفِقُوا مِن مَّا رَزَقْنَٰكُم مِّن قَبْلِ أَن يَأْتِىَ أَحَدَكُمُ ٱلْمَوْتُ فَيَقُولَ رَبِّ لَوْلَا أَخَّرْتَنِىٓ إِلَىٰ أَجَلٍ قَرِيبٍ فَأَصَّدَّقَ وَأَكُن مِّنَ ٱلصَّٰلِحِينَ ١٠

وَلَن يُؤَخِّرَ ٱللَّهُ نَفْسًا إِذَا جَاءَ أَجَلُهَا ۚ وَٱللَّهُ خَبِيرٌ بِمَا تَعْمَلُونَ ١١

And spend (in the way of Allah) from what We have provided you before death approaches, one of you he says. My Lord if only You would delay me for a brief term so I would give charity and be among the righteous, but never will Allah delay a soul when its time has come, And Allah is acquainted with what you do. Al Quran 63:10-11

Wow, yall.

This part took me a minute to get out,
yall still hanging with me?

To get through this process of grief
was something that I had never experienced.

Chapter 43: Where Did Y'all Come From?

I was about to lose my home. Teacher and I were still holding onto the school and coffee shop. I was relying on both the school and coffee shop to make money and make sense. Brothers were coming out of the woodwork.

"Girl, you got it going on," Teacher would say to me.

"No, I don't. These brothers don't like me like that. They think I got some money. They are trying to get a hold of the coffee shop."

Malik was always upset that he could not be with the family during this time; he was also upset that the imam of the prison wouldn't let him call home. We all thought that he should have let Malik call us during this time. He had to get his sympathy call through to us from the Catholic priest. Yes, just to be able to call me, he went through the Priest.

It was a long time before I let that grudge go, especially since we knew the Imam that had prevented him from calling. Even though Saud and Malik only had phone conversations, he was always calling to ask for advice from him.

Since Saud's death, I had to put on another game face, because for the first time in a long time, I had no big brothers around to deal with situations that were uncomfortable for me. I didn't and still don't like having to make deals and arrangements with brothers. It usually ends up with me having to prove that I am not a pushover and that I am someone who can think for herself. It would take a strong-willed person to deal with me. I was taught to be direct and to the point and I was just that.

Abdul Latif

My old buddy, Abdul Latif, would call and check on me from time to time. He had moved out of state and had gotten hurt while working a job at a motel he managed in Mississippi. Someone had tried to rob the place and Latif was seriously hurt. He was in a coma for weeks, but recovered.

"As salaamu alaikum, Sis. How's business? How are you and the kids?

"I'm fine Bro. and you?"

"Well, I ain't dead," he said, and we both laughed.

"My niece, Día, and her family have moved to Vegas, and I think I'm going to go visit her for a while. I like that community. I will have a few days of peace, In sha'Allah." I said. "I really need a vacation."

"How you gonna get there, Sis?" he asked.

"I think I am gonna fly. You know I still don't drive."

"Really, after all these years?" he asked in astonishment.

"For real, after all these years. And you really don't want me on the road trying to learn now either," I said. We both just laughed.

"I am a back and front seat driver and I have road rage!" We laughed again and said we would check on each other at a later date.

What's next?

It was harder for me to grasp what my life would be like. I even thought about going home to Cleveland at this point, but there was nothing at home for me. Saud had left me some money, and the money I had managed to get out of selling the house was running out. I had little desire to stay at the school. My intention was only to remain until my kids had all graduated.

But now, the coffee shop was another issue. It was no longer supported by the community enough for me to make a living, and it didn't seem like any of my children wanted it. Malik would be home soon, maybe that would keep him out of trouble if he had something to do. Everything was beginning to fall apart. It was a constant struggle to keep the place. All of the buildings were in disrepair. Bro. Mace, my tax lawyer and advisor, told me to drop the place and move on. But when you don't listen to your advisors, sometimes you pay the price for being stubborn. I paid the price.

A very learned student of knowledge had been working with the kids, but he had a shady past. He was accused of being a

Muslim spy and being involved in a police shooting. The story was in a book titled, *The Cell*. Well, one thing I know for sure is that if a Black man or woman in this country is accused of being involved in a police shooting, and everybody went to prison but you... hmmmm is all I have to say. But being myself, I went on to ask him personally.

"Hey, Brother can I holla at you?"

"As salaamu alaikum Sis, what's up?"

The brother was accused of setting up a beloved Sheikh and having him arrested; he was also involved in a shooting where some law enforcement officers got hurt and killed. "You were involved in a cop killing, and you on the street, and your comrades are locked up. hmm," I said.

After our conversation, we concluded that it would be best for everyone's safety that the brother move on. The last thing the brother said to me was, "At least you asked me. Not one brother came up and asked me anything." I often wondered if he was Saud's target. Someone hurting a Muslim, a child, or a woman, Saud would not have blinked. But I guess we will never know. What I do know is that I found a loaded .45 in Saud's things when I started to pack up his belongings a few months after his death.

I was getting so tired of doing everything on my own. Saud's comrades started hinting around about possible husbands; Shafiq and Mikal were relentless, and so was Bilal.

"I ain't trying to get married, and if I was, I ain't like y'all," I'd say, joking, not joking.

Most people think that Muslim women are oppressed; however, we are the most liberated women on the planet. What you see as oppression is maybe one's culture, but we have always had the right to education, to own and run businesses, to have our own money, and not have to share any of it with our husbands, if we don't want to. However, it is the husband's obligation to provide and protect with the provisions given to him from Allah (SWT). Muslim women who do share get major blessings for their generosity.

As for how we dress; we dress like Prophet Jesus's mother, Mary, may peace be upon them both, and so if anyone has a problem with that, then that's on you. It's our badge of honor to be modest. If showing your rear end brings you joy, just know that covering ours brings us an unimaginable joy for those who do it for themselves and the love of our Rabb (Lord).

I really did not want a husband. I really wanted a manager for the coffee shop, someone I could trust around kids and my money. (I didn't have a whole lot.) Plus, I didn't like always having to be in a brother's face because sooner or later I was going to have to prove that I was no pushover. The arrogance in this community was deep. I was always in the background where I wanted to be. If I wanted some attention, I would just pick up a mic. I was OK being in the shadows.

***

"Hey Sis."

"Who is this?" I asked, half asleep.

"Latif."

"Oh hey, As salaamu alaikum"

"Wa alaikum salaam."

"What's up Latif? How are you feeling?" Latif was still recovering from being attacked in Mississippi.

"I am better, but I gotta get out of Mississippi."

"Yeah, well it ain't nothing here in Los Angeles. If it wasn't for my kids, I would be gone myself. Ohio ain't the business either, though," I said. Latif was from Ohio too, but from Cincinnati.

"Well, I'm coming to Los Angeles, and Imma need you to find me a wife."

"Find you a wife?" I laughed. "And just how the hell am I supposed to find you a wife with a straight face? Remember, I know you're tore up ass. What am I 'pose to say?" I was cracking up. "When you getting here?" I asked.

"In about a month," he said.

"Man, y'all come up with the hardest stuff for a Sista, let me see who don't know you."

"I ain't that bad Khadijah, dang."

"Naw, you not, you better than most, but can you stay out of trouble? That's what I wanna know."

Abdul Latif showed up at my house about a month later with his eldest daughter, Tamar. When he got out of the car, it was all I could do to stand up straight. He stepped out of the car looking like one of The Jackson Five or a hippie from the 70s. He had a big afro and a dashiki top, jeans, and brown sandals.

"Don't be laughing at me," he said.

"How can I not?" I answered. "Y'all coming in?"

"No, I just wanted you to meet my daughter, Tamar. Tamar, this is Khadijah, one of my best friends and her husband was one of my closest friends." After a few minutes more, they left. Tamar told me that she was taking him to the barber shop.

"Good, 'cause you gonna scare these sisters off," I laughed again.

"I got my list of potential brides, but know this, I ain't lying on you or for you!" I shouted as they pulled off.

Latif yelled out to me from inside the house. It had been a few days since the visit with Tamar, and Latif was in the backyard trying to clean it up from the activities of the school day.

"Tell him I am back here, and give him some water, or juice, or something. It's hot out here," I yelled back into the house. Latif appeared in the back of the house, haircut, thobe on, and looking like a human compared to the other time. I started to laugh at him and said, "Ain't no sisters back here. I do have a few sisters in mind though. But, I am not gonna ambush nobody, so when do you want to set up a meeting? I can find out who you need to talk to, then you on your own. And why are you all dressed up? You going somewhere when you leave here?" I said all in one breath.

I was still going through the adoption process with my grandson, Ali, and he came rolling out the back door, plopped down right in front of Latif, and began eyeballing him as if he was from outer space or something.

Latif loved kids and that was always something I looked at when dealing with people; small kids, and pets. All of the kids loved Uncle Latif. He was funny, and he didn't realize he was so funny. The two began to play together as I continued to work on his lawsuit paperwork.

"You know Khadijah," Latif said, "when are you going to start looking for a mate?"

"A what?" I said, as I handed him the papers to look over. He was bouncing Ali on one leg and holding the papers trying to balance everything.

"You know, a husband. When are you going to start looking for a husband?"

"I never thought about it and frankly, I probably never will. I have all these girls, all these kids that I am responsible for, and you hear such horror stories from these families." I was in children's court a lot as a foster parent, and the things I'd heard and saw gave me chills.

"I don't want to have to hurt somebody and spend the rest of my life in jail because someone messed with one of these kids. Naw, I'm good," I said.

"Well, that's why you should marry me," Latif said under his breath, looking at his feet and playing with Ali.

"Negro, please," I responded and laughed at his suggestion, "remember I know you."

"Yes and that's why you should, you my best friend."

"I am not your best friend. I'm like your sister. Plus..." I said, looking at his face. "You are serious," I said, not laughing anymore. I got up from my seat and went into the house, leaving Latif and Ali outside.

"What's wrong with you?" Salina asked me.

"Uncle Latif just asked me to marry him, and I think he is serious. I am not going back out there. I left him and the baby outside."

***

I decided to say yes after thinking it through during the month of Ramadan, plus Shafiq and Mikal were relentless. They meant well though. After talking with one of my friends, who had been married to him before, I found out a few things. One was; you have to separate your Islam from the street, and that nothing improper had taken place. I also learned later that Saud had asked Latif to watch out for us. He had also asked his close friend, Little John, who had also been one of Saud's closest Muslim friends. I trusted them and I knew that if Little John didn't have anything to say, then I was probably safe. But Saud had asked Latif, specifically. He told Latif he was dying, something that I did not know at the time.

"Saud told you that?" I asked Latif, and the more he talked, the more things fell into place for me. "So, what am I, a pass-around pack or something?" I was kinda irritated at the whole thing. And a little insulted.

"I don't need you to marry me, as you see I can take care of myself really good. Y'all negros got some nerve, trying to control a situation from the grave, and you, got the nerve to insult me like this. You a cold piece of work." I turned back into my house.

This was playing out in my front yard. And now I had an audience of nosy neighbors.

I don't know what cuss words I used. I think I may have made up a few more. I went inside and called my Sheikh (advisor). He told me that was not an uncommon practice when a fallen comrade died. His friends would step in to look after the family and because we were not blood related, the only halal way to do so was through marriage. That we could not refer to ourselves as 'best friends'. Also, as Muslims, marriage is ordained for us, it is half of our deen (lifestyle). After all, Latif was someone that I could trust with my kids, my business, and my life.

I began working on my marriage contract. (Muslims have a marriage contract, in fact, we are commanded to reduce all agreements into writing.) I love this practice. My contract was about four pages long of dos and don'ts and I ain'ts.

"Dang Khadijah, what is this? A book?" Latif was referring to what I had written up as part of my marriage contract.

"You know I ain't doin' all this," he said. "

"Well, then I'm not doin' all this either," I said.

"OK, OK, OK, just let me get my imam from Ohio," Latif said. "That is all I want. He is very dear to my heart, and I will fly him out here to marry us."

"Really Latif? Well, if you love and respect him that much, then I don't have a problem with it," I told him.

"Also, Khadijah," he went on to say, "you have to cook for me. I don't eat anybody's food except for who I am married to."

"That's a lie, you have been eating my food for years."

"That didn't count," he said laughing.

"You do know that I know when you are not telling the truth, don't you, Latif? I'm sure every time I think of you as my husband, I start giggling. This is going to be an adjustment. I don't cuss or say bad words to my husband, and I don't expect my husband to say bad words to me. I don't have to worry about violence towards me. I know you don't hit women, and yes I have to say all this because I don't want any problems."

I really was scared to death. It had been almost 30 years that Saud and I were together. What was I supposed to do with Latif?

"Look," he said, "I have agreed to all your concerns. I am not gonna hurt you or the children. My fear of Allah is greater." I took a deep breath and jumped in!

Khadijah and Abdul Latif

I love weddings, they remind me of new life, new beginnings. After nearly 30 years of marriage with Saud, I was hesitant, but my friend was beginning to grow on me. Latif had given me a budget on how much I could spend on the wedding, then taken me to pick out my ring. A ring was not necessary, but he wanted me to have one. Not to compare husbands, because I was spoiled and blessed by both, but Saud spoiled me with what he wanted me to have, and Latif spoiled me with what I wanted. I didn't ask for much monetarily, I didn't require much. Latif was kind-hearted and nice to me and my kids, and I felt safe and protected. He loved his children. He would sit for hours telling me about his kids; Tamar, Omar, Desmond, and the twins, Rashid and Rasheeda. His telling me about them made me feel as if I belonged in the family.

Sometimes when fathers are incarcerated, they lose the ability to think and act like a parent. Latif had been incarcerated several times during his children's lifetimes. I can't speak about him and his kids' relationships. I only know that he loved them, and that he asked me to help out with them if anything ever happened to him. I have tried. I love them all.

Latif kept his word to me for the most part. He was stern when he needed to be, but he was one of the kindest men I have ever known. All the kids loved him. He and I had only one major argument during our whole time together.

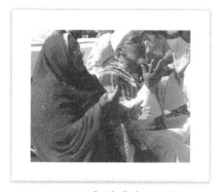

Me and Abdul Latif

"What are you up to Abdul?" He became Abdul when I knew he was up to something. It was usually something nice that he was doing for me, but this time I couldn't put my finger on it.

"Why you ask that?" he said.

"Because you keep acting strangely and your comings and goings are not adding up. What are you doing?" I replied.

Of course, he didn't answer me. I was right. Latif was caught up in something that eventually landed him in prison. I couldn't believe what was happening again.

"Bank fraud!"

Not again, after all these years, another husband in prison. I went to every one of his court hearings. Since there were banks involved, this made the crime federal and the court dates were all held out of state. I was feeling let down and ashamed. There was no way I could let any of my family back home know about this.

We all want to cry that we are the victims, and point fingers at everyone else. We will sing sad songs of woe when we feel that life has messed over us once again. Oh God, why me? How do I keep getting myself into these situations?

Welp, the truth is, we are given signs and we ignore them. We are given choices as well. It doesn't make us good or bad most of the time, but it does mean that those are the lessons that we fail to learn or flat out ignore and they will be repeated until we understand or 'til we get it right. I never used that word, 'victim', to describe myself. Whether it was true or not, I never wanted to give anyone that much power over me.

Prayer was my constant companion. My problem was that I didn't listen when He answered my prayer.

Chapter 44: Victim

I was losing my house and my business. My husband made a bad decision, trying to help me hold on to them both. We didn't trust that Allah would have gotten us through. I knew that something wasn't right and turned my head. I did not want to know what was going on with Latif, and that made me equally as guilty,

"Your Honor," Latif said at his court hearing, "I am ashamed and disappointed in myself. I let my family down. I acted by myself, there is no story to tell. As a Muslim, let me just say this is not our way, and I have to deal with the circumstances of my actions." I gained a higher level of respect for my husband. In other words, he did not snitch on anybody nor tell what anyone did, he took his punishment, and I took mine.

I ended up losing the house after all of that. That was my punishment for turning a blind eye. I was in shock. Nobody in my family had ever been in this situation that I knew of. I could not believe that I was being evicted from a home that I had worked so hard for. Even though during this time in the 90s, plenty of other families were going through the same thing, I was in such denial that I waited 'til the sheriff was at the door telling me I had to get out of my home.

My family was homeless, but I still had a business. In fact, I had two. We gathered up what we could of our personal belongings and went to the coffee shop, but before we left, I fixed the window, so that we could get back in. We were able to go in and out of the house, getting our things, some here and there. Our neighbor ended up telling on us.

"Reba, how are you going to sleep at night? Why can't you just mind your business?" I asked the nosy neighbor. We lived out of the coffee shop for a few weeks. Friends were helping me find a place for all of us, which wasn't easy because there were so many of us. I was not aware of all of the haters I had accumulated, the smiling faces that were happy about my situation. People that

I would have taken a bullet for, people I loved as sisters, didn't love me back. The lies that were told on me, shattered me. Social Services was told that I was keeping some of the kids from graduating on purpose, that I wouldn't help them. Some of the lies were so painful, even today I am triggered by them, because they hurt one of the children that I kept and scarred her 'til this day.

They said that I was homeless, and that I had the children in an unfit, unsafe place. I think what really hurt me was the fact that nobody knew me and my situation, and they were supposed to be my friends. They didn't even ask me. Nobody! By Allah's Grace and Mercy after all these years, still no one came to see if these stories were factual, and no one reached out to help.

I was promised a Hajj, but because of the lies that were told on me, that trip was rescinded. That hurt the worst of all. However, I did get over that because I know that we are invited to Hajj by Allah alone, and for me not to get to go was because I wasn't invited. That softens that blow a bit.

I can hear Saud in my head saying to me every time I think of the betrayal, *Khadijah, just because you are a friend to them doesn't make them a friend to you.* It was always a hard lesson for me to learn.

Imani and Cherno

You never know who Allah will send your way. We got help from friends, but some unexpected help came from a family who I will always hold dear in my heart, Imani and Cherno. They had just moved into a brand new condo with a brand new baby girl. I really didn't have a relationship with this family, but my husband, Latif, did. Latif's extended family and friends came to our rescue. Cherno and Imani offered us the entire downstairs of the condo that they themselves had just moved into. We had full use of the downstairs bathroom and of the kitchen. They had not furnished it, so it was just a wide open space, with a bedroom. I am not used to people doing things for me, so this test was great. I had to allow someone to be nice to me. I accepted because of my children. I never told my family in California or Ohio that we were homeless. My blessings were still great. I still had a business with an income coming in, that was more than most. This beautiful family was amazing. May Allah always increase their blessings.

I had planned to go get my things out of my repossessed house, but the new property manager gave me three hours to remove my things. I had already secured a new place, I just couldn't move in for a month. The bank that had taken over the house wasn't giving me an inch on my date or timeline to leave.

My Muslim brothers heard about how I was being dogged out by the bank and the bank's representative (who was a nasty piece of work). The brothers showed up to assist me. Rashad, Danny, Wali, Makail, and more who I don't remember. They told the bank manager that under no circumstance would I have only three hours to move my stuff. They said, "Our sister has until she is done – however long it takes."

They posted up in the front of my yard to safeguard me and to handle anyone saying anything different. The bank representative said, "I love the community support she's getting. Look at how many turned out to help you," he said to me with his phony concern. *Keep that same energy that you had to dog me out.* But, I could see that he was impressed by my show of support.

"Look," I said back to him, "I know that you are doing your job; however, I think it wise if you just stop talking to me altogether. When you thought it was just me, you talked to me as if I had a tale, now that you see my support group, you changed your tone. Keep disrespecting me like you were doing an hour ago." I rethought what I had said after a while, and I apologized. I was getting what I needed, and I could be a bigger person. The bank flunky simply accepted my apology and apologized to me as well.

I said goodbye to 2342 West 31st Street, goodbye to all the memories of the kids who had come through that door, goodbye to memories of Saud taking his last breath in that house, goodbye from being a stone's throw away from the masjid that my kids grew up in, out into the unknown.

I went away with a husband locked up, kids turning into young women, and a son, and a grandson entrusted to me to raise. I'd never had to raise a boy, this was going to be different.

North Hollywood

Over on 7560 Vantage Street, life was a whole lot different. We were now in North Hollywood, in the San Fernando Valley, if you will. This was also a house that was never finished, but it was so much better than where we had just come from. The house was in a small subdivision off of Laurel Canyon. Laurel Canyon reminded me a little of Crenshaw. Crenshaw would take us through various neighborhoods and so would Laurel Canyon. Laurel Canyon would take you through the beautiful Hollywood Hills, to the 'oh my goodness where the heck are we?'

There is even a movie named Laurel Canyon. Our new community was a much quieter neighborhood than the one in Jefferson Park, the Crenshaw area that we just left. We could probably get to LA in about 30 to 45 minutes.

I was struggling to pay the rent on the coffee shop, so I asked the landlady for an extension. Anyone that knows me knows how quiet and polite I am. I am not quick to anger. I am usually very cautious with my words, I don't call people names unless I'm very angry. But now this woman, who I paid rent to for almost 10 years, cussed me out and told me to get the f off her property. She talked about back rent and all the things she thought me and the Teacher owed her.

"Jannie," I said, "I have your money for the school, it's the coffee shop."

I tried to hold on to the coffee shop after Saud died, but I couldn't keep up the payments. I paid rent on five buildings on the lot, and we were paying for fixing up things on our own, managing her property for her for free, trying to be good tenants. She kept cussin' and fussin'.

"I'll be out of your place by the end of the month," I said and hung up the phone. My feelings were hurt and I was beyond mad.

"Jannie is on the line," my daughter Nunu said. "Hang up the phone Nunu." The phone rang again. It was her again.

"Yes," I answered.

"So Khadijah, when are you going to pay me the money that you owe??"

"I'm not," I answered, "I am paid up in full. We paid a water bill for the parking lot that was not ours but yours, we fixed your raggedy a** place – every time something broke down, we fixed it."

Jannie had never heard me cuss, so this shocked her. "After 10 years or more of doing business with me, I am short of cash, and you talk to me like that. Nobody talks to me like that. You are an old Jewish woman and I'm a Black Muslim woman, a grandmother, and I am telling you as nicely as I can that when you cussed me out, any debt that I thought you had with me is settled. I ain't paying you shit. Get off my phone and don't call me again. Am I clear?"

I felt her clutching her pearls and imagined her mouth swinging open. Whatever she thought after that, I guess she said to Teacher because the school kept going after my exit.

Getting used to living in NoHo (as North Hollywood was nicknamed) was easier than I thought it would be. When I got an opportunity to return to Los Angeles, I passed. The only problem was I was no longer close to a masjid. But Allah provided, I found a few of them. North Hollywood seemed to calm down my situation a lot. Our challenges changed but all alone with no community, it was almost like being outta sight out of mind, something that I had gotten used to. Now don't get it twisted, if I really needed something in a pinch there were a few who would come to our aid.

I continued my prison visits with Latif and Malik, and I would see Big Hassan on occasion. Latif and Malik were due to come home soon. I still had not told my family in Ohio that Latif was in prison, and since no one came to see me, I didn't have to explain why he was always in the bathroom when they called!

Malik had suffered so many health issues while locked up, a bad heart and seizures. He would not be able to come home and get a job doing too much because of his ailments and his incarceration. It was terrible that he didn't try to get better educated while locked up. All those years and the worst shame is that more options for rehabilitation are not offered that can be used when released from bondage. So much talent and expertise is wasted there. The skills that they do learn can be used outside the prison, but who will hire them?

Abdul Latif was a plumber, he'd learned his trade from his father who owned his own plumbing business. Latif's father was well-known in the LA community as a businessman and property owner.

I have always encouraged our youth to find something they could make an honest living at. I would tell them, whatever paper you received from the colleges, use it to help your community. You can have more degrees than a thermometer, it won't mean anything if you do not use it wisely. I tell them that Allah will hold them to account if they do not use what they know to help their community.

I was hoping that Malik would return home and marry the young lady who had become my daughter-in-law, Shalonda Burns. It didn't work out the way I would have liked but, I still got another bonus daughter.

Malik had done about 20 years total and we all stuck by him as a family. While Malik had a relationship with his birth mom, he had referred to me as his mom on some of his prison information. When anything went down, they would call me. His cellie had my name and number and that is how I was contacted every time he went to the hole or the hospital. But he could be a royal pain in the butt.

"Ma, how you gonna be on her side?" Malik would yell on the phone after having an argument with Shalonda.

"For one thing, because she is right, and for the second thing, you might wanna bring that tone down a notch."

"I'm sorry Ma, but why do you say she right?"

I said to him, "Because whatever she mad at you for, you probably did it." I have never been one to stand up for my kids and anyone else if they were wrong. Now I may defend you in a group, but you will surely hear about yourself later when we get home, and sometimes you hear about it on the spot depending on the circumstances.

Malik would come by the house and do odd jobs for me and show up on the holidays, but whenever he came by he kept his word. While locked up he said, "Ma, when I get out of here, every time I see you I'm gonna bring you some flowers." Malik knew that I love fresh flowers, but sometimes the flowers he bought me were questionable.

"Boy, where did you get these flowers?"

"Huh?" he'd say.

"You heard me. Whose yard did you get these flowers from?"

"Aw ma, I was in a hurry, so I just grabbed these along the way."

I would just shake my head, and we would crack up laughing.

Latif was home soon after Malik returned and had to make the adjustment that we had left the hood.

"I like the hood," Latif would say, "I can't deal with North Hollywood."

"You act like we in Beverly Hills," I said.

"We may as well be," Latif said to me.

"Latif, you didn't see all of them raggedy streets leading up to here."

"I just want to be around our people," he said.

"Our people, meaning who? Muslim, or Black, or both? Our neighborhood was now mostly Asian and Hispanic.

"You and Ali will fit right in here, until y'all say something, won't nobody know what nationality you are," I laughed.

"Yeah, well, I hope nobody says nothing to me," he said.

"They won't, this is a nice quiet street."

Latif was once in the Black Panther Party and MILITANT was an understatement. He was once FOI in the Nation of Islam. I was still learning about the old Nation and the civil rights fights that happened in California, how drugs were planted in the community, and the raids on Black Muslim homes in 1965.

"Just calm down, we good," I said to him.

Chapter 45: He Tried to Adjust

Latif was able to get a few jobs, and he continued to work as a plumber when he could. He would also join a lot of mentoring groups to try to give back to the community. The programs that provided jobs for the formerly incarcerated were a joke. The salary was not enough to pay for anything except a cell phone and maybe the carfare back to work. Thank God for those who had a legal side hustle or knew a trade.

I was Auntie Khadijah, and he was Uncle Latif to more than one group of people. We had spoiled each other terribly. He very rarely told me no in response to anything I asked for, and I fixed him whatever he wanted to eat, whenever he wanted it. Even if I went out of town, I would fix his food for however many days I would be gone, and if I didn't he wouldn't eat. I believe he snuck out to get a bean burrito every now and then.

Latif had met my mom before he went to prison on a rare visit she made to Los Angeles with her sorority sisters. She was planning a trip back and I wanted to check dates with Latif.

"How many days did you say they were gonna be here?" he asked.

"Not many and they are not staying here," I said. It was very rare that Mom came to see me. I could count it on one hand. My dad had just left here. He too was visiting relatives that I only saw me when my dad was in town. My cousin Jonae and cousin Wanda and I had gotten close, but my other family never showed up unless it was for show.

The visits were short and sweet. We had a good time, but everything immediately went back to normal. Latif never liked our new surroundings, and often returned to his beloved

Crenshaw area, where the masjid that helped build Abu Bakr was, and all of his lifelong friends were located. He really enjoyed the masjid. He had gotten a job and was working for Goodwill Industries, and he was in a pilot program, where he talked about recovery and accountability. Still, he began to act very strangely.

Ali, my grandson (Golda's son), had been living with me ever since Saud passed away. Ali was homeschooled, but I took him to a day program in order for him to interact with other kids his age.

"Get ready, Ali, we are going to be late."

"OK Nana, we can leave, I'm ready."

I had called for my Lyft to take us to Burbank where Ali's classmates were. Ali loved going there. He also loved acting and modeling. A friend, Gea Muhammad, had mentioned that Ali was talented and could make a few dollars modeling kid clothes or being an extra kid in a TV show or movie.

She was right. Ali loved it, he appeared in the show Parenthood and a few other movies. He would also go over to the Nickelodeon Studios in Burbank and watch a kid movie and give his feedback. But this morning, Ali was in a school production that was cut short because something at home was happening.

We had only been there an hour when I got a call from Latif saying that he wasn't feeling well and he was going to the emergency room.

"You going where?" I asked.

"I'll be ok. I just wanted you to know that I was heading out."

"Abdul, I will be home soon. Let me get an Uber or a Lyft. I'll go with you."

"No, that's ok. I can go by myself."

"What's wrong?" I kept asking. Like most men, if they want to see a doctor, then they are really sick!

"I have a boil that needs lancing."

"A boil, really?" I didn't believe a word he said, so I quickly returned home to drop off Ali and called another Lyft to take me to the hospital – it wasn't far.

Sister Yvonne Ali, the elder who'd caught me smoking at the masjid a while back, had been staying with us for a few years. The sheriff had called me one day telling me that she was being evicted from her home and my number was the only number she remembered. We tried to locate some relatives, but no one came forward, so Mom Ali (as we called her) has been here with us ever since. She was very self-sufficient, but an elder with memory struggles, so I needed to find someone to stay with her, Hassan, and Ali just in case of an emergency. All of the kids were grown and gone except for a few who were working and in school and living on campus. I finally got Día to come stay with the trio. Día once again came to my rescue. She actually lived in Vegas, but she was in town shooting her session on L.A. Hair. Día played the part of receptionist for a time on the show.

When I reached the hospital, I was taken to Latif who was fussing with the nurse.

"What's going on?" I asked.

"They are trying to send me to another hospital."

"Why?" I asked.

"Because we are not equipped to run certain tests," she said.

"On a boil? You need a certain test on a boil?" I asked. The nurse got quiet.

"I am not going to another hospital," Latif said.

"Maybe you should honey, I can see that the boil has busted and it's seeping through the gauze. If they can't do no better than this, maybe we need to go somewhere else."

"The ambulance is ready, Mr. Tawfiq," another nurse said as he peeped his head into the dividing curtains.

"Ambulance? Why does he need an ambulance? Didn't you drive here?"

"No," he said, "I came in an ambulance, I was in too much pain to drive."

"Yeah you must have been, but Día is here at the house, she can take us."

"He should go with the ambulance," the nurse said, "he is on an IV antibiotic drip, and we don't want to take him off of it."

"Oh, I see. OK then, I will meet you there. Don't let anything happen to my baby," I said to the nurse.

"We will take good care of him," she said back to me. Now I am getting worried. I am thinking to myself, *something is not right, they are not telling me the whole thing.*

They ended up keeping Latif overnight and I hated it. I didn't want to leave him there. I cried so hard my whole face hurt. He wasn't in a private room, he was in a dorm-like room with four other people. The insurance we had wasn't the best and from the negligence on our part, it hadn't been updated when he got home from prison.

"We will have to lance it and it will take a surgical procedure to do it," the doctor said.

"What you mean, a surgical procedure? It's just a boil."

"He has already been sedated, Ms. Tawfiq, but you can wait in here with him until we come to get him."

They had moved him into a waiting room area.

"Call my daughter," he said.

"Which one?" I asked.

"Tamar. Call her." I dialed the number and gave him the phone. The effects of the anesthesia were coming down on him and he sounded like a sloppy drunk. He was very comical.

I stepped out of the room and let them talk, plus I needed some air. When I went back in, he was asleep, and my phone was on the floor. I picked it up and put it in my purse just as they came to get him. We stayed overnight and went home in the morning.

"All this medicine for a boil and an ulcer," I said. Latif had stomach cramps as well, he told me , while we were there in the emergency room. He told me he had a stomach ulcer.

"They found a spot on my liver."

"What does that mean? You don't drink." He drifted off to sleep without answering me.

The next few weeks were back and forth to doctor appointments and everywhere we went I had something negative to say. They were not answering questions the way I felt they should have. But Abdul seemed OK with it. He went back to work after a week or two, but he always seemed wiped out when he returned. He would go straight to bed with very little appetite, as always I made too much food.

His friends and family were concerned for him and started calling to check up on him.

"He is OK," I would say.

There were always so many people in the house making all kinds of noise, and it didn't seem to bother him. Abdul loved children, the girls would have him eating out of their hands. All they had to do was cry, and they would get their way. Heck, that's all I had to do. But today was different, his baby girl Sheeda was home from school and coming to visit him. She was graduating from Clark University in Atlanta, and he was so proud of her. He kept asking me if she had arrived.

"No Latif, if she was here she would be up here with you. As soon as she gets here I'll send her up."

I had noticed that Latif's legs were swelling and asked him to elevate them.

"Why are you so sad? You have been in this bed all day. Don't you want to get up and move around?"

"No," he said , rather short.

"What's wrong with you?" I asked again.

"Them kids are making too much noise."

"They are? Well, why didn't you say something?"

"Say something like what? You hear them, don't you?" he snapped at me.

"I'm so sorry. I didn't realize that you didn't feel well. I'll go make them be quiet. Besides Sheeda is here. Do you want me to send her up?" He shook his head yes and told me to put his head back on the pillow.

Sheeda visited for a while and left in tears.

"What happened? Why is she leaving here crying?"

Latif just stared into space.

"Why is she crying?" He still would not answer me. A few hours later, Cheryle, Sheeda's mom, called me.

"Hey Khadijah."

"Hi Cheryle, what's up?"

"What's wrong with Latif? He acted like he was dying when Sheeda was there."

"Dying?" I said, "Naw he ain't dying, dang, he taking this too far. Let me go upstairs and talk to him."

I went upstairs and Latif was sitting up on the bed.

"Latif, why did you get Sheeda so upset? Don't do that, the girl thinks you are dying. It is not funny," I said.

Later that day, we had a nurse come out to the house and check his wound because it looked infected to me. The nurse was a nice-looking young woman who I thought was fresh out of school. She was so cute and very efficient

"He needs to go to the hospital," the cute nurse said.

"Why?" I asked her.

"He has no pulse." I made a face. "Really, honey?" I said to her sarcastically, but nicely because she looked about 16 years old, and I did not want to hurt her feelings.

"If he didn't have a pulse, he'd be dead," I said.

"Well, I am a hospice nurse," she shot back at me, "and your husband needs to be in a hospital."

"Look lady," I said, "OK, thank you see you soon." I escorted her out of the door, then went to deal with Mr. Latif.

"Man, you are playing way too much, and now your doctor is sending a hospice nurse over here. We needed a wound care nurse. You had Sheeda crying, this is too much. A hospice nurse is for someone that is dying. I'm calling your doctor and telling them that they need to send a wound nurse over here. Shshhh."

I went downstairs to finish cooking dinner. I went over to Latif and kissed him on his forehead, then walked out the bedroom door and down the steps.

I finished making dinner, in spite of his antics. I decided to make him one of his favorite meals. I made my homemade burrito and black beans. I knew this was a heavy meal. *God willing, he would be able to get some of it down.* I took his plate upstairs to him, but he wasn't in the bed. "See, he is not that sick, he went outside," I said to anyone that was close. Latif had managed to get downstairs and outside. I didn't see him go out, nor did I know how long he was out there. I also noticed that he seemed to be in great pain, trying to get back up the stairs.

Latif needed help getting back into bed. He slept for the longest time and woke me up asking me to take him to the doctor.

"Khadijah, I need to go to the doctor because my legs are so swollen I cannot stand up."

"Really?" I asked, as I climbed around him to get to his side. He was sitting on the side of the bed, his feet were on the floor, and you could see the swelling.

"OK," I said, "but I'm going to need some help. Let me call your nephew, Muhammad." Muhammad Touré was Muhammad Abdullah's son, who was Latif's best friend.

"That's OK Khadijah, I think I'll just soak them, it will be OK," he said. But I called Muhammad anyway and he hurried right over. By the time Muhammad got there Latif still could not stand up. I left the two of them alone and went to sleep in Ali's room, only to be awakened by Muhammad's knock on the door.

"Aunty," he said, "we need to take Unc to the emergency room. We have to call for an ambulance." I jumped up and ran past Muhammad to find Latif sitting again at the end of the bed trying to put his clothes on.

"You want to go to the hospital, honey?"

"Yea, I need to go," he said. I dialed 911 and it took them no time to show up. After about five minutes of working on his vitals, they had him strapped to a gurney and down the steps.

"Where are you taking him?" I asked. They shouted out the name of some hospital I had never heard of.

"We can follow them in my car," Muhammad said.

"Come on Aunty, I got you." I was kinda nervous. Latif was too cooperative.

"He will be OK, Insha'Allah," (God Willing) Muhammad said.

Muhammad and I got turned around trying to find the hospital, and by the time we made it to the emergency room, Latif was already in a room and had seen the doctor.

"Dang, I like this service," I said, smiling as I came in the door. Latif smiled back at me, and asked me for a hug.

"I ain't hugging you, you may be contagious." We both laughed, but I went over to my husband and gave him the biggest hug.

"What did they say about the boil on your butt," I giggled, "no for real, is it infected ?" Just then the doctor came in and looked at me.

"This is my wife," Latif said.

"Oh, hello Ms. Tawfiq, so Mr. Tawfiq here it is. They say you want to go home."

"You mean you examined that quickly? We were only 15 minutes behind the ambulance. I like this service," I said again.

"You want to go home," the doctor said again, "well, if you go home, you may have a week, if you stay here maybe two weeks to a month."

"A week? For what?" I asked because I still was not catching on or processing the entire ordeal. The doctor looked at Latif and said, "She doesn't know? I'm sorry, you told me to go on," the doctor said to Latif.

"Wait a minute," I said, "are you telling me that my husband has a week to live? What are you saying?"

"The spots on my liver is cancer, Khadijah, and it's too far gone."

"You said cancer before, but you said you were OK. What about the herbs and the treatments? You said they were going well? Abdul, this doctor is saying a week."

Latif burst into tears. "Khadijah, I couldn't tell you, after everything that you went through with Saud and me, I just couldn't tell you that it was that bad."

The doctor said quietly to the both of us, "We can set you up at home in about three hours if you want to go home, or we can put you in a room here."

Latif grabbed my hand and said, "I know what you have been through, and I couldn't tell you." Seeing him break down like that broke my heart. "But please don't leave me here to die."

"Man, ain't nobody about to leave your butt in here." *Straighten up Khadijah. Stop all this crying and pull yourself together.* I had gone outside his room for a second in order to get myself together.

"Man, you trippin'," I said with a little laugh when I went back in, "I wouldn't leave your ass in here for nothin'. Just tell me what you want me to do."

The doctor said we had to wait here for three hours while they set the house up. I had given them instructions on where to put everything and called home to prepare everyone there.

"Call my kids," Latif instructed me. "Call Tamar first, then call my ex-wife Cheryle, she needs to tell the other kids. Tell them I want to see them."

I went into the hallway with Latif's phone to start making the calls, but first I went into the bathroom and screamed into my hands.

"Ya Allah, I am in this bathroom crying out to you. You want me to do this again."

I got to get myself together. This is no place to be having a meltdown, in this hospital bathroom.

"They are saying to me that in two weeks, I'll be a widow again. Allah, what do You say? What is Your verdict? I don't want to do this again, alone again. Please send me some relief, please protect my heart, so that I can do what is needed." Almost immediately a calm came over me. I washed my face and came out of that bathroom. I peeked in on Latif and I saw that he was sleeping. I went back into the hallway and began making the calls.

We got Latif home and got him settled in, and then came the barrage of loved ones to say goodbye. Cheryle stayed with us the entire time. She felt more comfortable being with Sheeda, their baby girl. She was also a calming blessing to me. Latif had a special bond with his daughters, like most daddies do. He was finding his way back into his sons' lives due to their incarcerations and his, but he loved all five of them. He would sit up at night telling me about how he wished he had made better choices when it came to his kids, and he'd say that Cheryle was a good person and that he couldn't ask for a better mom for his kids. Cheryle was the mother to three of his children, Tamar and Desmond had different mothers.

I had fallen asleep. I didn't even remember lying down. I was awakened by Cheryle calling me, "Khadijah, I think you had better come in here." I went into the other room and looked at Latif. He was lying there with his eyes fixed, staring into space, taking deep shallow breaths. "It's OK Latif," I said, "Are the angels here for you? It's OK, Allah got you. You were a good husband to me. May Allah bless you with the highest of Jannah, Ashadu La ilaha illallah. Wa ashhadou an Muhammadur rasulullah (I bare witness that there is no God, but Allah, and I bear witness that Muhammad is His slave servant).

I watched his eyes as they followed his soul leaving his body. I witnessed this beautiful miracle. It was as if I was all alone with him, because I didn't hear the sounds of others weepin'. Everything was going on around me, but all I could think of was the blessing that Allah had just shown me. The color had returned to his handsome face, and the longer he lay there, the more his expression changed. By the time the Islamic Mortuary picked him up, he had the biggest smile on his face. He had so many friends and family to see him off.

Alhamdulillah. Ya Allah don't leave me to myself not even for a blink of an eye.

That day I had to return a gift on loan to me, as I have had to do before. But this time it was different, this time I had no one to confide in, brother or sister, but I did gain a family. Cheryle and his children became my family that day. She was there and never left me or her children the entire time, and I thank God for her.

We buried Latif out in the desert where Saud and so many of our community are. I don't know to this day how long Latif knew he was so ill.

Losing Latif hit me harder than any loss I had experienced, mainly because after our Lord, Latif put me first. He made sure I was OK. He would check on me constantly, he was fun but could get serious. He rarely said no to me, but when he did, he meant no and don't ask me again. For the first time in my life, I felt as if I had no one. Well, I still had my daddy, who I also relied on.

Latif was one of the greatest gifts. To my surprise, my silly Abdul Latif left me enough money to live on for the next few years, and that was wonderful because I was shutting down in my own way, trying to find my way back to myself. But first, I would have to figure out who I was, and so it began...

Reflection

إِنَّ ٱللَّهَ عِندَهُ عِلْمُ ٱلسَّاعَةِ وَيُنَزِّلُ ٱلْغَيْثَ وَيَعْلَمُ مَا فِى ٱلْأَرْحَامِ ۖ وَمَا تَدْرِى نَفْسٌ مَّاذَا تَكْسِبُ غَدًا ۖ وَمَا تَدْرِى نَفْسٌ بِأَىِّ أَرْضٍ تَمُوتُ ۚ إِنَّ ٱللَّهَ عَلِيمٌ خَبِيرٌ

Indeed Allah (alone) has knowledge of the Hour and sends down the rain and knows what is in the wombs. And no soul perceives what it will earn tomorrow, and no soul perceives in what land it will die. Indeed, Allah is all Knowing and Acquainted. Al Quran 31:34

Chapter 46: Khadijah Time

The years just seemed to mesh together, one into the next. My health wasn't the best, and I had lost interest in anything that ever meant anything to me. The kids were grown or almost grown and were finding their way in life. I had to sort my life out and show some sort of feelings. I was numb. I was drifting on my memories.

I still couldn't stand to hear about or see anyone being mistreated by law enforcement, these mass shootings and all around craziness, children that couldn't speak up for themselves, and Black men and some women all around me getting locked up. I had opinions about how I felt about the harm of locking up folks for the simplest of things, but mostly kept my opinions to myself.

I would reach out to help who I could but on a quiet note. I had a friend named Jewell Willis. She was a gymnastics teacher, and my girls would attend her classes. Gymnastics LA was the name of her business. Jewell and I partnered together and started to have food and school supply giveaways. We would use the coffee shop as a place to distribute what we had collected. It was a good feeling. I learned a lot about giving back from Jewell and her two daughters, Trudessa and Miss B (the B stood for busy body).

I didn't want to bring too much attention to myself. I enjoyed helping people. It was the love of doing that kept me going. Giving gave me a purpose, but it seemed like I was always defending why I did what I did.

Someone always had something to say about who I chose to help. Mainly, I guess because most people found me, not the other way around.

"She is taking advantage of you, Khadijah," Marian would say.

"Well, whose sin is that?" I would ask. "I don't do anything that I don't want to do and so if their intention is not good that's between them and Allah."

"How much do you charge for people to stay with you?" she asked.

"Why?" I asked her. "Are you gonna pay me for her being here? Stop worrying about how I do what I do."

My mom wanted to come and visit me, which was a strange request, but of course, Mommy would come, and we would have a ball. On one visit, we took her to Miss Effie's Tea Parlor on East Adams. It was a historical house owned and operated by a Black family. It was once a privately owned home that still had the original furniture and layout from the era.

My sister, Yvetta, had accompanied Mommy on one visit, and we were able to go see the Universal Soul Circus. This circus was predominantly Black. It was also nice to see so many talented people of color. We had so much fun, it was nice to be able to share that with her and the kids because it wasn't long after that Mommy wanted to come back again. It seemed like it was right after she left.

I had planned a big surprise party for her, a tea party at my house this time, with a live band and all of her favorite foods. Nicole, Yvetta's daughter, brought Mommy out to California this time. Mom was going through early signs of dementia. I think Mom knew that her memory of us was fading and that she wanted to see us while she still had some recollection of us. It was too hard to watch.

Mom got a chance to play with her very first great grandchildren. She seemed to have a ball. They went on an outing together to Color Me Mine, a pottery arts-n-crafts store, where they all made ashtrays and plates and mugs. Mommy made a coffee mug that I still have today. I will always cherish it. When Mom left California, I knew in my heart that it was for the last time that she would be able to visit, and the last time that I would see her and she knew who I was. That year was 2017, Mommy would be with us until 2022.

Alzheimer's is a nasty disease that robs us of our loved ones twice. To watch year after year the deterioration of your loved ones' mind, to wonder where they are mentally while we watch the face that once loved you, smiled at you, cried for you, now stare blankly back at you with no recognition. All the lost conversations, all the 'what I should have dones', begging Allah to please protect you from the same fate. My Aunt Anita,

Mommy's middle sister died of this dreadful condition. My cousin Michael, her son, wrote a detailed book of my Aunt Anita's journey through Alzheimer's entitled *Rusty's War*.

I cannot imagine not knowing my children or that I am Muslim. My heart breaks even now. I would lose Mommy all together in March of 2022, while writing this book. As I continue telling you about my journey, I'm sitting here and staring at her photo. I want to tell her about all the silent lessons learned from her that we never talked about.

I talk to my Mommy's photo, all about the unspoken forgiveness that was never acknowledged by either of us. The strength that she showed us with her silence. The pain she endured that took me a lifetime to understand, and all the lessons and the reason for this book.

Was I able to pass on every lesson good or bad? Was I able to embrace each mistake and to thank Allah for every last one of them?

I am thankful to Allah for allowing me to come into existence through her, to learn more about how amazing she was. Yes, we may have lost Mommy twice, but in losing her, I would find more of myself and my reason, *my* why.

Chapter 47: Let's Bring It Home

Atra had been trying to get me more involved in the community. She knew of my involvement with law enforcement and dealings with us as Black folks, which was difficult at best. I had not cared too much about anything since the death of Latif. I also didn't realize that I was depressed. I needed something to do. Since leaving the Bond Court Hotel over 30 years ago, I had never worked for anyone except myself... oh, and Roscoe's. I had created my own sources of income, but what was I going to do now?

I couldn't remember what it was like to have a boss. I tried to rekindle the old daycare. At least I would be my own boss, only this time I had no clientele. I was so isolated from the community in my self-imposed isolation, it had taken over my life once again.

This time the isolation was self-imposed from my being widowed once again, and it was self-imposed from always trying to hide the incarceration of those I loved; self-imposed so that I did not have to deal with the outcome of my choices and Allah's decree. I also didn't want to be found out. I thought it was a weakness, not knowing what to do next. I was being too full of myself.

What I did learn was this: When it was all said and done only a handful really cared anyway.

Some of the younger sisters in the community were there for me, Patrice, Rasheeda R, Amirah, Um José, Haqiqah, Gea, and of course my kids. Only they didn't know how to help me. Some didn't realize that I was drowning. Haqiqah saw it all, and understood it.

Sister Sabreen, a good friend of mine and my sister, would call to check on me from time to time. She had just returned from a cruise and was telling me about all the fun she'd had.

"Khadijah, you should come on the next one, it's so much fun."

"Sabreen, I ain't got no money for a cruise," I said.

"Khadijah girl, it's not that much, plus you can make payments. There are so many people on the ship, you get to share a room and see all these countries." Well, the whole thing was beginning to sound better, except for the part where I would have to share a room. Just as she said that, I panicked and backed off a little. I agreed to go but then changed my mind when I thought of having to be around people.

Wow, how am I going to get out of this? I know, I will take Ali and Ladybug with me. Nobody wants to travel with kids.

Truth is, Ali and Lady would never leave my side. They would sit by my bed. They saw all my tears and could feel my sadness. They waited on me hand and foot and were everything a grieving grandma would want in a grandchild.

It was selfish of me, but I didn't realize it at the time. *This was ideal for them.* The cruise director whose name was Felicia Farr, made a comment on how cruising could open doors to the youth to get to see countries they would not normally get to see. It also drew me in because Felicia had the same name as my little sister, and although she lives in Atlanta, she was from my parents' hometown of Atlantic City.

The cruise was taking place when school was in. Since I was no longer homeschooling, I couldn't just take the kids out of school, or could I? *First let me see if any major testing is going on. Then let me see how the grades and behavior of these two are.*

"Lady, Ali, come here," I yelled down the stairs where they were playing Uno.

"OK, Nana, here we come."

"Y'all want to go to Puerto Rico and to Mexico with me?"

"Yeah," they shouted.

"OK," I said. "Ali, you know your Papa told you to look out for me and not to let me travel alone, remember?"

"Yes, Nana, when are we going?"

"Well," I said, "it's on a ship, it's a cruise, but you are still in school. You both can go if you keep your grades, A or B. Cs can't go with me!"

"I don't have any Cs," Lady said to me.

"Me neither," Ali chimed in. The two cousins were like a set of twins, they were so close in age, and they watched out for each other and still do.

After all this contemplation, I called Sabreen back and told her I would go, but that I was bringing kids with me. Ali and Lady loved their Auntie Sabreen and so did I. I just wasn't ready to be around people, even after all these years of losing Latif. The cruise was a major hit. I still go every year that I can.

Chapter 48: Essie

Now Atra kept hitting me up to come with her to some meeting.

"What is it all about Atra?" I asked.

"Khadijah, Essie is a group of women who have had somebody locked up."

"Well, the only ones I still have locked up are my stepsons and Malik, who should be home soon."

"Well, come on anyway and get out of the house. This group of women treat you right. They feed you good and they even have some sort of class where if you finish you can go on a retreat."

"A retreat! Really, I can go for that. Where do they go and how much?"

"It's free, everything is free. They will even help you get there, since you don't drive, but the first meeting is in Palmdale at a sister named Karen McDaniel's' home."

"Aw, here we go, more people and women too. Are they Muslim?"

"Not all, maybe some, but it's not a religious gathering. We are a group of women who held down someone locked up."

"Okay," I said to her, but my heart wasn't in it. I just went because she was my friend, and she was beginning to bug me in a loving manner. I had known Atra for years, but we were not really close. I knew that her son was incarcerated somewhere, but I had never asked her about her son, and she never asked me anything, either. Even on the ride to Palmdale, we didn't discuss much about ourselves, just chit chatted and made small talk on the drive to Karen's.

I love car rides, probably because I'm never driving. Car trips have always been a way for me to relax; that's if I was in the car with the right people, listening to oldies or the Quran, and not talking too much. I really learned how to zone people out on car rides in order for me to enjoy the ride. Some sisters would pick me up just to get me out of the house, but in my mind, I could see myself choking out the driver for their constant, non-stop chatter. I would quickly forget those thoughts because, who was going to drive me back?! *That was a joke ya'll, for those of you who have been paying attention to my story*! Atra and I got along well enough, so this wasn't a problem.

Once we arrived at Karen's house, I met Esi, Anita, and Mercedes. They began to talk about their experiences with an incarcerated loved one. I just sat and listened for the most part. Soon after, Karen joined us, she had been out getting food when Atra and I had first arrived. All I can remember was this amazing salad she'd made. I would ask her to make it for the next two meetings that I attended! The women seemed pleasant enough, very open and inviting. I had to admit that I enjoyed myself, but I was feeling so uneasy, in a good way.

When Atra dropped me off, she asked me if I wanted to attend the next meeting. I said that I would, and I was hoping to see the same ladies again. I also liked the ride out there. We met a few more times and I was invited to join a cohort of Essie's Healing to Advocacy program. Now I had no idea what a cohort was, so I just played it off and tried to sit there and look semi-intelligent.

The next meeting was held at Chuco's in Los Angeles. Chuco's was a community center and school in the Hyde Park area of Los Angeles. They had a turnout of about 25 to 30 women, but this time the room was very diverse. I thought this was going to be a gathering of Black Women. I really couldn't tell what Karen's nationality was, and frankly, I didn't care. She was so sweet, yet forceful and straightforward. Unbeknownst to me, she had her own organization. Karen's organization focused on helping incarcerated fathers stay connected to their kids through a book program and a camp where children actually got to spend a few days with their dad. A Place for Grace is the name of her wonderful organization.

I was surrounded by so many amazing women. Esi was a minister and life coach, and I took to her right away. She was a voice of reason and Lord knows I could use that. Anita was wise and she helped facilitate the cohort group along with Gina Clayton.

Soon to join our group were Dianna, Diane, Mercedes, Hawan, Desire, Arvene, Liz, Lizz Teresa, and of course, Atra.

Karen didn't join us for whatever reason, but I would follow her amazing journey, nonetheless.

After the nine-week cohort, as we began our healing from trauma, from life, I was ready for that promised retreat. For the most part, I just sat silent, listening to the others tell stories that I could relate to, but kept my mouth closed with very little participation. This was on purpose; I wasn't about to spill my guts.

The retreat wasn't what I thought it would be at all. Essie sisters came from all over the state. We met in some beautiful mountain resort where cell phones didn't work. We saw signs along the way that referred to mountain lions and bears!

"Where are we going? I don't think I signed up for this."

"Just show me my cabin," I'd said when we arrived. As with the cruise, I couldn't imagine myself sharing a space with anyone, not even Atra. Alone at night was when I was overwhelmed by the feeling of being alone. People didn't make me feel secure but made me feel more alone because of the trust that I lacked from everyone except my kids. So, I had dragged Ali with me. There would be other children for him to relate to, plus I really did depend on him to help me. I had developed osteoporosis and sometimes the pain was really bad, especially at night.

"You will have fun, Ali. We are staying in cabins and everything," I said, trying to convince him. The very next morning we were given an agenda. We were being introduced to everyone and all gathered in the main cabin. That's when it hit me.

I had been tricked into thinking that this was a no work retreat! But there was no spa, no maid service. We worked from sunup to sundown, but it was one of the most rewarding situations I had ever been in. All my life, I had fought against injustice on my own, just trying to figure out how to help, doing things one on one, and supporting friends and family when they needed help. Essie was showing me how to fight on a larger scale. I always had a big mouth, but I didn't know how to use it.

Chapter 49: The Sisterhood of Essie

My thoughts and daydreams have taken me back and forth as they do for most of us. Sometimes they run together as they did that day at my Essie graduation. Over the next few years from 2017-2021, I became an active Essie sister. I took an active role with the sisterhood, becoming a facilitator and a facilitating coach. I was appointed as part of the first Statewide Strategy Team (SST), the Black Momma Bailout, and a few other committees.

After the retreat, I also joined Initiate Justice, an organization led by a brilliant young woman named Taina Vargas. Taina educated us on how to fight the system through politics and relationships with our elected officials. I enjoyed this because it showed us how low down and dirty this system is, but it also showed us how to fight and win! Most of the members were formerly incarcerated or still incarcerated. It was real support. We were offering help from people who could relate to the situation. We went straight into the offices of our senators, congressmen, or state reps. They would be amazed that the person who was addressing them was a person who had been formerly incarcerated. I loved it. Once again, I could go straight to the source.

You never knew who you were sitting next to in Essie. From homemakers to lawyers, we all had one thing in common, a locked up loved one and a f***** up system that needs to be torn down and rebuilt. We all knew that the laws were not meant for us, and that most of them were there to keep us enslaved. We knew that with this current system, you couldn't do much of anything, except fail. There is no real prevention or rehabilitation.

Initiate Justice was able to put a bill together and got it passed, giving the formerly incarcerated their voting rights back. That was a big win!

Essie would later become a more powerful group of sisters through their work in 2018 with *Because She's Powerful*. *Because She's Powerful* is a national report written by Gina Clayton and Lily Madlin, along with a few other Essie sisters. It's beautifully written which focuses on the plight of all women, Black and brown women in particular, who support or have supported an incarcerated loved one. If you read it, you will probably find yours truly smiling at you on a couple of its pages. Then, there was the Breathe Act 2020. You can read up on this incredible piece of work by going to the website, breatheact.org. These were a couple of projects I am proud of and was blessed to be a part of. Essie also led the way, offering free mental health support to its members.

Our fight continues.

Chapter 50: Bringing in The New

I was able to give back to Essie by being a voice to new sisters, by becoming a facilitator for new cohorts, and by being on the Black Momma Bailout Committee. The Black Momma Bailout was a coalition of different organizations that used private donations to pay the bail of a Black Momma on or around Mother's Day.

We don't use a bail bondsman. We use the hard-earned cash that comes from donations from everyday people like you and me. Regardless of how much the bail was set for, we go in there with all the money, not needing the modern-day slave catcher, better known as the bail bondsman.

So we go walking into the jail with a couple hundred thousand dollars to get a deserving Black Momma. However, not using a bail bondsman would put a spotlight on us, walking into the jail with every dime of the bail. The first two times they gave us a hard time and they really did not want to accept the money.

"You can use a bail bondsman," the clerk said, rather nastily.

"We'd rather not."

"Who is Essie? If she signed this check, we need to see her ID or one of y'all name has to be on this check."

We knew that wasn't true. They jerked us around for hours. They kept coming from the back to the window, where we were standing trying to get the bail paid. We knew what they were thinking. *Where in the hell did these Black and brown bitches get this money, that they can afford not to use a bail bondsman?* It got easier the next few years, but that first year was downright ugly.

One judge got so mad at us, he went back on a $300,000 bond and found more charges to impose on the sister. He raised the bail another $200,000. Well, Essie got those funds in about an hour and went and got our sister.

Who was chosen to get bailed out comes as a surprise to us and the Momma. We only get that information when we are on our way to get her. Who's bailed out comes from someone else's decision. From the time we post bail, and the bail is accepted, we wait until she is released, and meet her with flowers, gifts, and whatever else we can think of. We make sure she can make her court dates and help her in any way we can. We have witnessed great life-changing stories. This is what success looks like! I love the feeling of liberating a sister and watching her successfully put her life back together.

Los Angeles has the highest bail in the world. Being arrested does not make you guilty, but waiting to prove your innocence can affect you for the rest of your life, especially if one of the reasons for your arrest is mental illness, which is true in more cases than we care to count.

Mothers sent to jail lose the most. Most of the time they are the breadwinners, and they lose their children to the system. How many children have gone through my daycare and foster care because of a mentally ill parent? How many have been brutalized and traumatized as a result of being locked up, because they couldn't find any tangible help on the street?

Being locked in jail in Los Angeles, you are deprived of the simplest of things, like sunshine. You lose all track of time when you can't tell night from day. When you are deprived of food in jail you then have to watch how it gets thrown into the trash. Some didn't have access to clean water during Covid, while others were only given one mask for their entire confinement. These are jails in LA, yet it sounds like a third world country. Again, jail is not prison. Not that prisons should deprive anyone of their human rights, but this inhumane treatment was something that I couldn't sit still for.

UNTIL BLACK WOMEN ARE FREE, AIN'T NOBODY FREE!

We once sat in that filthy Lynwood jail from 12 noon until almost 3 AM before they would release this 75-year-old Black great-grandma who had been there for months because she had no money. Her crime was chasing some squatters off her land with a knife. Because she went off her property, she was arrested. The squatters now had free range of her home. She was afraid and confused when she appeared in the foyer of the facility.

"Who are y'all? she asked. We explained to her who we were and because of the lateness of the hour, we put her in a nice hotel near the airport, and when I say nice, heck, I wanted to stay! We provided her with all the necessities she needed that night and came back in the morning to take her home, but first what about the squatters?

"Bro. Rashad, there is a sister here in a situation. This elder needs to feel safe and secure. You feel me?"

"Got you, Sis," was the response back to me. By the time we were ready to take our bailed-out grandma home, the squatters were gone and she had all new locks put on her doors. Freeing that elder out of bondage was one of the greatest feelings in my lifetime. A modern-day Harriett Tubman is what I felt like. Ha, I wish.

Going from Essie Justice Group to Initiate Justice seemed like the right next step. Initiate Justice was mostly operated by the formerly incarcerated, and they were able to get a lot of bills passed in California. One in particular was getting their right to vote back.

Essie Justice was part of a study group entitled, *She is Powerful!* I am very proud to have been a part of both these groups, making changes and changing history. This is where I found myself again. I found my purpose and a way to fight. I just needed to make sure that I did not compromise my faith and beliefs and what I knew to be true. Thank you everyone that never gave up on me finding me.

Chapter 51: Niani Again

"As salaamu alaikum Ma, is she pretty?" Malik asked, all excited, "Is Niani OK?"

"Boy, quit calling me every 5 minutes. Wa alaikum salaam. Yes Malik, they are fine."

Because of Covid we could not go see the new baby or Niani. Niani was Malik and Salina's daughter, my granddaughter. She had just given birth to my first great-grandchild, and Malik, her dad, was ecstatic.

"Can you send me a picture to my phone please? Can you tell her that I love her?" Malik said with so much pride and love in his voice.

"Yeah," I said, "but promise me that you will give Harley her phone back." Harley was his other granddaughter from his oldest daughter, Tajanique.

"OK Ma, you know I'm just stubborn." Malik was always fussing with his daughters, but he loved his kids, and the girls loved him.

"I know you are stubborn, but knock it off. Life is too short for all that."

Little did we know that in a matter of hours, our lives would change for ever.

***

My grandbaby thinks I don't know, but Niani always calls me when she is hurt or in trouble, and when she doesn't call me first, it is because she thinks I'll disapprove of her choices. I can feel her. Niani and I have a different kind of relationship than my other grandchildren. Salina had her when she was young, so she was raised by me mostly, along with Nunu, Autumn, Robin, and Niemah.

Salina was always there and was a good mom, but I was always Nana Momma to Niani, and Auntie to most of the community. Niani has always called me when she was in trouble as far as I know, and I was always there to help my child. My radar was up.

"Nana!" my grandbaby, Niani, wailed into the phone. "The police just killed my daddy!"

"What, slow down. Where are you?" I questioned, not believing my ears.

I was sitting in the examining room of my heart specialist's office and was receiving a clean bill of health after losing 120 pounds. Most people who had never seen me small, thought I was sick, when in reality I only went back to my original weight. I was feeling better and better although we were in the middle of a pandemic and on lockdown for most of the year.

The doctor had just given me a clean bill of health, but it felt as if I had been stabbed in the heart.

"Wait, what are you saying? Baby calm down," I said.

"They killed him, Nana."

"Where are you Niani?"

"I'm still in the hospital with the baby. I can't leave because the baby is still sick. Nana, they are saying that the police killed my daddy!"

Niani had just given birth to my great-grandchild, and she and the baby had developed serious health issues. During the Covid crisis of 2021, you couldn't have any visitors in Los Angeles hospitals. She was alone, sick, and had a sick baby.

It took me back to her own birth with her daddy, Dana Malik, and Salina. How scared they were and worried about Niani.

Niani went from a scared mother with a sick child and being sick herself–she almost died with the birth–to crying for her dad.

"Ya Allah, don't let this be so," I shouted.

"I got you, baby, let me see what's going on and I'll call you back."

"Where's Tajanique?" I asked.

"I don't know, Nana, they are saying they killed my daddy! Nana do something," Niani cried into the phone, "they said the police killed him!"

Waves of anxiety reached my stomach. I jumped into an Uber and blanked out. On my way home, I let my tears just roll down my face. I cried for us all in the back of that cab, but I think most of the tears were for myself. I was tired. I am tired, but my tiredness turned into rage and put me into fight mode.

Did she just say they killed my boy? He was just here at my house, the flowers that he had gotten for me were still there dying on my desk. He had just finished moving me in and painting Nunu's room. After years, after a lifetime of incarceration, they all returned home to die.

The day and time of death are a part of the unseen. And no man knows when it will come. It is upon each one of us to love each other and live our lives as believers and to worship Allah alone.

***

Bro. Rashad, a close family friend, had given Malik a job with his company, *Ultimate Paints*. Being formerly incarcerated himself, Rashad was always willing to help out a brother in need of work. But it wasn't a handout, you had to prove that you could handle the job.

My dear sister, Rashida R had also given Malik a job cleaning the masjid and working on the masjid grounds. Everyone was happy with his work. Malik had just given Ali a tool belt with tools as a gift and had begun showing Ali how to use some of them. Malik had also just confided in me that he thought he was a new father. He had just asked me to help him find an apt. near my place, so that he could help me out more. Life seemed to have turned a positive corner for the young brother.

"Momma?"

"Yes, Malik," I'd said into the phone.

"My girls are mad at me, but Momma I am trying so hard."

"Well try harder," I said to him, "they will come around."

"You want to go into business with me?" he'd asked. Malik had just asked me to be his partner, selling food.

"Heck naw, you not about to work me to death," I teased him. He had just asked me to help him tell his Aunty Debra (the same Debra who has been all of my kids' Aunty Debra since my days at Roscoe's) that he was going to move out of the room that he had been renting from her but still help her out financially when he could.

I can still hear his voice while taking the Shahadah. It's funny how you can still remember your loved one's voices in your head.

They killed my boy. Omg, what was he doing to make them kill him? How many more of these encounters are we going to have to deal with? Why does it always end up with the killing of our men?

Yeah, I can hear all your voices, including my own. What was he doing, out there? Why did they kill him? (Well, for one thing he was Black). I can hear y'all loud and clear.

"Oh, so you are one of those moms who want to blame the police when your people are out there committing crimes but now you want to be upset when your kids get killed?" You ask?

No, that's not who I am. Right is right and wrong is wrong, no matter if it is against your own self or your family.

But in Los Angeles, we have the highest number, as of writing this, of people in jail (or being captured for the purpose of jail) to end up killed there, or in the process of being arrested. You rarely get to see a fair trial and making it to court is a luxury some don't even get.

Malik didn't get that luxury.

***

"Niani," I said into the phone, "I just got off the phone with an attorney. They want you–."

"No, Nana, I can't do it. Please do it for me," she interrupted.

"You can't do what baby?"

"I can't talk to nobody. Can you please do it for me?"

"OK," I said, "I got you. I can't let them get away with murdering my son like that. Tajanique is the oldest, though, so I have to ask her if it's OK with her, me making these calls and speaking for y'all."

Lies and More Lies

We found out later on, the coroner had withheld information about Malik. He was shot in the back and at the back of the head. The sheriff murdered him, mistook a Black Covid mask for a gun. But the sheriff didn't tell us. Malik's barber did, the day of his funeral.

We almost didn't get this information. Because of Covid; nobody was allowed into the funeral home, but the funeral director at the last minute, allowed Malik's barber in to cut his hair. While cutting his hair for his funeral, the barber found a gunshot wound in the back of his head. The barber made a call to Taj, and she called me. Taj being the oldest and the legal next of kin, gave me permission to dig into the situation more. I took this information to every organization that could help.

I was already on board trying to stop these murderous cops and sheriffs, but now it hit home, again; Teddy, Tracy, and Saud to name a few. Dignity and Power Now and BLMLA were all ready to help me. The Coalition to Check the Sheriff and of course, Essie, were all on board to help as well. Had Allah not sent the barber, we would have buried Malik without ever knowing he was executed like that.

They had left Malik's lifeless body lying in that alley for 14 freaking hours, enough time to fly from LA to NY and back twice, enough time to work a double shift, enough time to set up a false version of what had happened.

We found out that the Deputy Sheriff, Kevin Walker, had previously been in litigation involving a man coming home from work. This man had been beaten blind and was so afraid of the sheriff gangs that plague the streets of Los Angeles, that he moved and left town, letting his attorney speak for him.

It is extremely hard to control the gang activities on the street among our people, but when the biggest gang on the block belongs to the LASD, the ones who have sworn to protect and serve its citizens, it's no wonder that we can't get our citizens to trust or respect law enforcement.

***

It's now been a year since Malik was murdered and we are still fighting for justice to be served. My Essie sisters have been supportive of me, including reminding me of the anniversary of it all.

Gina had assigned a young woman named Titilayo to be my support, to help me when I was too emotionally drained to continue. I would speak to the Los Angeles Board of Supervisors. I would speak at rallies and to the media about Malik, and also about the conditions of the broken jail system here in Los Angeles. I would run my talking points past her.

Titilayo helped me to get my thoughts out and made them make sense. Taj, Niani, and I relied on Titilayo's input when dealing with the attorneys and media coverage. Titilayo is brilliant, beautiful, Black, and had a law background. She became a trusted, loyal, loving, and caring part of my team.

One morning, I was awakened by Titilayo's call.

"Ms. Khadijah."

"Good morning, Titi, what's up?"

"Well, we were wondering if you wanted to do something special for the anniversary of Malik's death?"

"Something like what?" I asked.

"Humm, you know, like a vigil," she said.

"A candlelight vigil? Titi, I don't know what they actually do. I see people on TV standing around holding candles and talking about their loved one after that. Then what? No, Titi I don't think I would want to do that. If I do anything it would have to be big and meaningful."

"Well, what do you have in mind, Ms. Khadijah?" Titi asked.

"Well, for one thing, I did find out that superintendent Holly Mitchell was able to get the board to agree to look into Malik and two other Black men's deaths at the hands of the sheriff, and they have agreed to a sheriff inquest."

A sheriff inquest had not been done since the 70s. Finally someone is doing something that is making a difference.

"Yes, I think I would like to thank them, and I would also like all the other organizations that have helped me to be recognized for the work that they do. I was fortunate to have an Essie Justice Group to help me, as well as Dignity and Power Now, Initiate Justice, and BLMLA. But, what about all those other people who have lost the lives of loved ones, the ones whose lives were just stolen from them? I want their families represented. There are almost 1000 of us in this club."

Chapter 52: The Rally of Stolen Lives, 2021

"It's getting chilly out there," I said to no one in particular. For October, to me it was cold. I didn't know what to wear, but I did know that it had to make a statement. I had a few outfits like the ones the Black Panthers wore back in the day. They stuck out in my closet. If there was one color that I have a lot of, it's black. Everything that I do now for this cause has to make a powerful statement, including how I dress.

My grandbabies depend on me. Their father was killed, murdered by the Los Angeles Sheriff's Department, and we were all hurting. I was going to be speaking on their behalf at the rally and so it had to be good. I had arrived on time to the rally in my Uber. As soon as we pulled up, I could see everyone scurrying around, trying to set up.

"As salaamu alaikum Sr. Khadijah," one of the organizers said.

"Wa alaikum salaam," I returned the greeting.

"The people from the Spectrum Cable Media Company have agreed to show up and interview you and some of the other family members at your rally," Bro Mustafa said.

We had planned out the rally and I was able to get the new Chuco's as a venue. This Chuco's location was on Central Ave. deep in the hood. This place, that was once a Juvenile Hall and a jail for kids, was now used as a school and community center.

How ironic, that a place that used to try, convict, and lock up former gang members, was now being run by former gang members.

Unity Two, a gang intervention organization from the 90s, were instrumental in stopping a lot of gang violence in the 90s. Kevin Fletcher (Br. Mustafa) ran the organization and was a good friend of my family. He donated the outside area of Chuco's to me for Malik's rally and the area was perfect.

We named it Rally for Stolen Lives.

We dedicated it to the lives that had been taken from families by law enforcement, the Sheriff's department in Los Angeles in particular.

Muslim United, BLMLA, MuslimARC, The ILM Foundation, INKERIJ, Initiate Justice, Dignity and Power Now, CAIR LA, local politicians, Spectrum TV channel, and other organizations to name a few, came out to support us. Helen Jones, whose son was murdered inside Men's Central jail was there, along with other families that had lost loved ones to police in a questionable manner.

I had Michele Infamy and Mr. Terrance Keel, a professor from UCLA, who had done a study on the coroner's office and its practices. We were fortunate enough to be chosen as a part of this study with Dana Malik's case. It was here we learned that the sheriff had lied and the coroner had covered up the fact that Malik was shot entirely from the back, unarmed!

This report was made public. This report proved how over 200 Black and brown people had been murdered in LA jails, with 59 conclusive findings over the course of several years.

I, along with other families who have had loved ones killed by law enforcement, all joined together to fight the abuse of power they used on our Black and brown people. With America leading the world in crime, gun violence, and incarceration, we wanted to find alternatives and preventative methods to use.

There are a lot of people who can't see the vision of intervention and using alternative prevention methods. When a crime is committed, most people want the perpetrator to feel the same punishment that was inflicted on them, and I get it. Most people are afraid of change but let me ask you this: If America's way of dealing with crime, mental illness, and homelessness worked, then why are we leading the entire world with these social ills?

Why are we so arrogant that we cannot model other places and cultures that seem to have this figured out? I was a part of DNP (Dignity and Power Now, BLM-LA, Initiate Justice, and, of course, Essie Justice Group. I had begun attending meetings of some of the Muslim justice organizations, like CAIR and MuslimARC. Some of these groups I was a part of before Dana Malik's murder.

I just couldn't wrap my head around the fact that it had been a whole year since my adopted son's death.

Malik was my ex-son-in-law and the father of some of my grandchildren!

Oh, Malik, You never got a good running start in life, son. But I am going to fight for your legacy 'till the end. They are going to try to drag your name through the mud to make us all believe that you deserved to die on the street.

We can't even say he died like a dog in the street because animals get better treatment, respect, and protection in this country than a Black life. I never said Malik was an angel, and I do not uphold wrong, whoever the wrongdoer is, even if it's against my family or myself.

When we have communities that don't hold their community members accountable, it's a problem. Leaders in the community have to hold their members accountable. It is also a problem that the ones who are supposed to serve and protect us cannot be trusted. Two wrongs don't make a right.

We will never get to the bottom of Malik's case because before he could have his day in court, the law blew his brains out, from the back of his head to his lower extremities. He was killed execution style.

My granddaughters' attorney was even beginning to back peddle on the case after a year and a half but they hung in there. I am learning that this happens a lot in these cases. Very few are interested in the truth in the end, it's about all mighty dollar and political power that holds the interest of our so-called judicial system. That's nothing new. The law team decided to take some action on Niani's part but I have not had any information on the events. I would not be surprised, though, if they had to sign a secrecy agreement on the outcome.

Chapter 53: It's time to speak.

Everyone wanted to hear from Taj and Niani, but neither one of them were able to speak, so that was left up to me, and I was glad to do it. How many people have I been friends or family with that have suffered this pain? If there had only been some sort of help, that could have steered minds away from a bad decision.

As I was preparing what I was going to say, I could hear Malik and Saud in my ear, voices that offer warnings and some comfort. I had to compose myself because this day held more meaning for me than anyone could have imagined. Not only was this day about Malik, it was also about those other families and their fallen loved ones.

The ones who never got to stand trial, the ones who were beaten to death in their cells while awaiting trial, the ones who had a mental health issue and could never get the proper care. It was for the ones who just needed a little bail money and lost their lives while waiting for it. It was for every family that didn't have an Essie Justice Group or Dignity and Power Now, CAIR LA, or a loved one with the courage to stand up. For all of the unkind things that were done to us for supporting our loved ones which made us fall silent into the background.

I could feel them pushing me, telling me that I could make a difference just by showing up, and being a part of the force that was fighting back.

And let's be clear, I was never a victim back then, and I am not a victim now. My struggle led me on a path that I am grateful for. Sometimes I do think about what would have happened if I had gone to that appointment at Showtime at the Apollo. I sometimes still grab a mic to see if I've still got it. I remember back in the day, when Thai and I had to chase drug dealers and junkies out of the courts where we lived. I remember chasing the

Hebrew Israelites out of Leimert Park after they called us Hoes for Muhammad. I think about breaking into that apartment with Deb to rescue little Jorge.

Now I am hearing these voices from my past, telling me that I ain't done. In fact, I may just be getting started.

I sat there waiting on my turn to speak, trying to hold back the tears as I watch Atra, Alice, Janet, Melinda, Cheryle, Wanda, Desire, my Sheeda and Shalonda, Parker, Titilayo, and my Essie Sisters who've shown up for me. My Muslim community, Suaad and Keesha, Haqiqah, Sabrine Gea, Hakeem, and Mustafa (who returned to Allah before I could finish this book), and Umar, Marguri, Nairobi, and Madinah, and Hakeem who all flew in from the East Coast to support their Auntie and cousin. They showed up for justice.

I flashed back to St. Elmo, where I first remembered Teddy. How far I had come with no end in sight of me stopping. I took a deep breath and began.

Chapter 54: My Speech

Bismillah, As salaamu alaikum, my name is Khadijah Shabazz.

Dana was the father to my granddaughters. Besides my grandchildren, Dana was a father, a brother, a son, a cousin, a friend. I have always been involved in some sort of activism. Some of the groups I have mentioned, I was a member of long before Dana was murdered. But that gave me a starting point that some families' victims of police violence do not have.

My advocacy work mainly was directed around children, and later around women whose lives were impacted by some sort of incarceration; either themselves or a loved one. That's what Essie Justice Group does. But for me, this rally is all about standing up to, and for, people that have been bullied and mistreated. In this case, standing up to the law enforcement responsible for taking the lives of our loved ones. If you have ever felt separated or felt isolated or felt that you had no voice, we are here to fight for you today. We fight for us.

Some of us have remained silent, keeping our stories to ourselves about what happened to our loved ones. Those stories can be so painful and scary, especially if you have to constantly see the ones who have murdered them on a daily basis, in our communities, on the street dressed in their uniforms that we all recognize as their gang attire.

We don't speak up out of fear of retaliation, which draws us further into isolation. Most of us here are women, head of our households, and most of us Black – one in two Black households have a family member incarcerated. And Latino families, are not far behind.

There are over 1000 families statewide who share stories like mine and yours, who have had a loved one murdered by LASD or some law enforcement here in California. Today I will be the voice of my granddaughters, along with other families who have had a loved one murdered. I am not here alone, there are other families here, we will support each other.

There is another rally going on in Torrance right now addressing this very real problem. At this time, I would like to thank Supervisor Holly Mitchell and Hilda Solis, who co-authored the motion on behalf of my son, Dana Malik Young, Dijon Kizzie, and Samuel Herrea, all killed within days of each other. The motion passed unanimously.

This policy will help others to get the information they need when a loved one is hurt or killed by LASD under the California public records act. Information must be made public in any police-involved killings, unless they can justify a reason not to.

More than two years after SB 1421 (the right to know act) went into effect, the sheriff had failed to produce records on any deputy misconduct and serious use of force. But, because of families fighting this, alongside Supervisor Mitchell, Solis, and Ocean, we pushed back, and we won!

Some of us have gathered here today to tell our stories of pain, grief, and trauma. When we told our stories as single families, we were unseen and unheard. When there were no civilian cameras, we had only the sheriff's version of what happened. We come here today as families, backed by these organizations that you see here today.

Before I get into my story I need to ask you a question: What can you do in 14 hours?

The 13th amendment to the United States of America reads as follows, "neither slavery nor involuntary servitude except as a punishment for a crime where of the party shall have been duly convicted shall exist within the United States or any place subject to their jurisdiction," which means to me that we are still looked upon as less than, and it means to me that they intend to keep us with a slave mentality.

The frightening part is that we accept it! They get away with killing us because we won't stop them from killing us! In fact, in some cases they can just sit back and enjoy us killing each other. Oops, y'all wasn't ready for that one.

Some of us are here fighting back and using everything that we have, but it will take all of us. It's not enough and it will never be enough until it's done!

They left Malik lying dead on the ground for 14 hours. In 14 hours you can take a plane from LA to New York, have dinner, and come back!

In 14 hours, you can work almost two eight-hour shifts, drive to Arizona from here and back. They murdered him and shot him dead in a dead-end alley, unarmed.

All gunshots entered his body from the back, including the one that blew his brains out! For weeks you could see the blood-stained ground. You could see the outline of his body where he fell dead. Dead animals are picked up quicker than that.

It took 14 hours to make up a story, I guess; the story they went with was the one where they mistook a black Covid mask for a gun.

The difference between us killing us, and law enforcement killing us, is law enforcement are paid to uphold the law and protect us.

So, who do we call when we need help? We will never know of Malik's innocence or guilt, because the LASD decides who goes home and who doesn't, if you live in Los Angeles. When our loved ones are out of control due to mental breakdown, who do we call knowing that calling for help can find you, and a loved one, dead?

How can we better control our youth and teach them self-worth, and pride for themselves and their community, when the biggest bully on the block is the LASD?

Who can we call, when it is the LASD that harasses, arrests, locks up, and beats up citizens who speak up? They jail us and then terrorize our families for speaking out. People are dying and being murdered inside Men's Central Jail. Los Angeles has the worst jail in the country and the most incarcerated in the world. I said the world, in case you didn't hear me.

You have stolen the lives of many. And until Los Angeles, the City of Angels – should be called "the City of Shame" – until LA fixes this problem, there is blood on your hands.

For everyone who has a voice to help change this, I am talking to you. I am talking to clergy and community leaders, I am talking to you, I am talking to the parents who may not feel that they can stand up. You have just as much blood on your hands as any gang member or domestic terrorist. LASD and LAPD, your job is to arrest and detain, not maim and kill, you cannot be our judge, jury, and executioner.

When you live in a city that is so dysfunctional that the sheriff, police, politicians, coroner, and some citizens are unwilling to take hold of the problem, that's a problem. We know the reason is because the target are its Black and brown citizens.

When will we accept the wrong that is being done here and across this country? I can only imagine where this will all lead. I came here today to shake you up! For those of you that are sleeping, nap time is over.

Those who are in need of a voice or a hug, we got you. We are well over 900 families strong with that number growing daily. If you feel as if you cannot help us make this city feel our pain, our agony, our anger, from those who have stolen our loved ones' lives, then you may need to get the hell out of our way.

For all of the families that had no voice, we can speak for you. For those who were bullied and shamed into silence, for those whose hearts hurt down to your soul, we got you today.

Until we change the laws and policies that allow law enforcement to get away with murdering us. Until we stop fighting each other and pushing ourselves backwards, we will continue to arm them against us.

We are over 900 families strong and I pray that we don't get any bigger. As I quote my sister Assata Shakoor, she said: "NOBODY IN THE WORLD! NOBODY IN HISTORY, HAS EVER GOTTEN THEIR FREEDOM BY APPEALING TO THE MORALE OF THE PEOPLE OPPRESSING THEM.

But right now, this minute, you all are looking too comfortable. Get up out of them chairs, stand up for your lost loved one, get up, y'all know the drill.

I want them to hear us all up and down South Central. Let them hear us from the highest heaven down to the pit of hell, get up out of those seats!

How dare we sit comfortably while the blood of the dead cries out for us to do something! (I screamed this out while my whole body shook!)

Make a circle, you all know the drill. Get in formation. Where are my Essie sisters? Where is DNP Now? MuslimARC? BLMLA? Muslim United? INKERIJ? Get Up!

Our sister, Assata Shakoor, wrote this for all of us, and we are going to repeat it here in this space as you say their names, scream them out.

I HAVE NOT FORGOTTEN YOU, MALIK.
I HAVE NOT FORGOTTEN YOU TEDDY, OR TRACY.

LOUDLY REPEAT AFTER ME:

IT IS OUR DUTY TO FIGHT FOR OUR FREEDOM!
It is our duty to fight for our freedom

IT IS OUR DUTY TO WIN!
It is our duty to win.

WE MUST LOVE, RESPECT, AND HONOR EACH OTHER!
We must love, respect, and honor each other.

WE HAVE NOTHING TO LOSE BUT OUR CHAINS!
We have nothing to lose but our chains.

WE HAVE NOTHING TO LOSE BUT OUR CHAINSSSSSS!

Allahu Akbar. As salaamu alaikum...

THE END, I THINK........

About the Author

www.kshabazz.com

Khadijah Shabazz, a former foster mother trained to care for infants prenatally exposed to harsh substances and small children with behavioral difficulties, a public speaker and advocate for community change, was born and raised in Cleveland, Ohio. She received all of her formal education in Cleveland, and after that she picked up the most valuable lessons in the University of Life.

She is the mother of two biological children, five adopted children, and twenty-five foster children. She is a wonderful mom, sister, aunt, mother-in-law, loyal friend, grandmother, and great-grandmother.

Although she never signed up for all of this, her hard-learned lessons acquired in the neighborhoods of Cleveland, Pittsburgh, and Los Angeles, equipped her with a unique skill set that made her perfect for advocating for prison change and children caught up in the foster care system.

She is also a speaker who brings awareness to the broken criminal system and offers solutions for communities.

Her message: Start with yourself it.

She also knows the importance of telling our own stories and how important it is for self-healing and growth.

Currently, she lives in Sylmar, California, 30 minutes outside of Los Angeles and is dedicated to helping women find their voices in whatever form that looks like.

Above all, she is a devoted Muslim. Her faith gives her the strength to advocate and support the members of her family and community.

Khadijah is a member of the following organizations:

- Essie Justice Group: A nonprofit organization of women with incarcerated loved ones taking on the rampant injustices created by mass incarceration.
- The Place for Grace: Helps incarcerated parents and their children develop strong bonds through various programs like Family2Child, which is a literacy program that records incarcerated parents reading a book to their children.
- Muslim ARC: Provided faith-based racial justice education and training
- Dignity and Power Now: Their mission is to build a Black and Brown led abolitionist movement rooted in community power towards the goal of achieving transformative justice and healing justice for all incarcerated people, their families, and communities.
- Black Lives Matter LA: A political and social movement that seeks to highlight focuses on racism, discrimination, and racial inequality experienced by black people, especially police brutality.
- Initiate Justice: Their mission is to end incarceration by activating the power of the people it directly impacts.
- Inkerij: INKERIJ's blueprint for leadership advises individuals and organizations in identifying empowering social opportunities vitally important to their role. They help leaders remain relevant in a constantly changing world – including preparing for a post-COVID era.
- Muslim Power Building Project: This project harnesses the strengths and resources of multiple organizations to

facilitate a comprehensive community-organizing, leadership development program for Muslims nationwide.

Acknowledgements

Bismillah

There are so many of you that guided, or should I say pushed, me into finishing this work. There is not enough room to express my gratitude or acknowledgements.

First, let me thank Almighty Allah for allowing me to complete this work.

Thai Harvell, my sister who said I could, so I did. Debra Milton, my sister, who was always with me. Denise Kavanaugh, my Cleveland sounding board. My cousins, Michael Bennett and Jonae Watts, for always having my back.

My sister Sakinah, you know what they will never know. My children, all of y'all, and my siblings, who allowed me to put them on blast! My son-in-law, Lavelle Aqueel, thank you for holding on to the family. And love you Layne!

My nieces that grew up in my house, Día Autumn, Madina Madinah Amirah, and Little Khadijah.

AUNTY O, I love you oceans full.

And to my Barbie Doll, I burst into tears when I think of your courage and unselfishness. When Allah sent the angels for you on the same day He brought you into existence, I felt my soul shake, baby sister. I loved you so much and I miss you. But we lost Mommy first and I sat here trying to close the writing of this book when Allah (God) decided that Daddy had put in enough work here on earth and told him to return to Him as well.

My daddy, my knight in shining armor. Now I really know how it feels to go numb, I lost all three of you in less than six months.

Throughout my journey, I have found so many reasons to smile and love the life that I was blessed with, and to be grateful for each lesson learned. I thought I was done writing, but I realized that I had left out so much. Like the time I was kidnapped, did I tell y'all about that? Okay, I'll include that in part two, In sha'Allah. Stay whole and prayed up!

Smooches.

APPENDIX

The following are family pictures and memorabilia that are important to me. Even through all of my many moves, I kept these images close.

ATRA AND ME

**MALIK, SALINA, AND NIANI.
(IN THE SMALL DRAWING SOMEONE'S
IMAGINATION CAPTURING MALIK AND ANI J.)**

SALINA AT AGE 6, HASSAN, AND RANEL

ESSIE COHORT

ESSIE COHORT GRADUATES

DAVID RANEL

SON-IN-LAW AQEEL AND GRANDKIDS

MOMMY AND AUNTIE

DAUGHTER NIECE AUTUMN AND GREAT NEPHEW QUADIR

MY BROTHER, SHAWN

MY SISTER, BARBARA

GRANDSON AND GRANDNEPHEW

ME, MY GRANDSONS, AND SON-IN-LAW

SALINA

NIANI AND ANI

SON-IN-LAW AND FAMILY

ME AND MY DAUGHTER, NIEMAH

SISTER YVONNE

LADY BUG AND LAILA

ME, LAILA, AND ALI

MY DAUGHTER NAJALAH SHABAZZ

MY SISTER, FELICIA

MY MOM, SISTER YVETTA, AND MY DADDY

ALI PROTECTING HIS LAND

DADDY AND MY SISTERS

LITTLE HASSAN

ESSIE COHORT AND MY KIDS

GEA MUHAMMAD
2022 ESSIE COHORT GRADUATE

I DIDN'T SIGN UP FOR THIS!!!!
www.kshabazz.com